Open Innovation in the Financial Services

Daniel Fasnacht

# Open Innovation in the Financial Services

## Growing Through Openness, Flexibility, and Customer Integration

Springer

Dr. Daniel Fasnacht
Berghaldenstrasse 56
8053 Zürich
Switzerland
open.innovation@gmx.ch

ISBN 978-3-540-88230-5 e-ISBN 978-3-540-88231-2

Library of Congress Control Number: 2008936473



*Cover design*: WMXDesign GmbH, Heidelberg, Germany

Printed on acid-free paper

9 8 7 6 5 4 3 2 1

springer.com

# Foreword

Money is the ultimate commodity, with virtually no differentiation between different pots of it. Globally integrated financial systems have eroded differences in currencies, and even the almighty Dollar's status as the world's reserve currency is under pressure. So one form of innovation is simply facilitating the ever more efficient movement of capital from the sources of savings to the applications of greatest value. But that is not what this book is about.

Daniel Fasnacht's book explores the role of innovation in financial services to do much more than simply move money faster at lower cost. His book demonstrates how innovation can enable capital to do new things for customers, things that previously were infeasible or were done on an ad hoc basis (and often done rather poorly at that). The ability of innovation to offer new capabilities, new services, and new solutions for customers makes this book one of enduring interest.

There is much discussion in the United States, Europe, and Asia about the role of intellectual property and innovation. While the overall discussion is complex and subtle, the pole positions are diametrically opposed. At one extreme, where strong intellectual property protection is deemed essential to join "the fuel of interest to the fire of genius" (in Abraham Lincoln's words), innovators can innovate only when they can be assured a temporary legal monopoly to enable them to capture the value generated by their activities. At the other extreme, typified by open source software development, intellectual property is anathema to the ability to harness the creative abilities of communities of users to share enhancements and ideas with one another. "Innovation wants to be free" is the mantra of this extreme.

The financial services industry is a fascinating one to observe the interplay of these arguments at work. On the contrary, as Fasnacht notes, financial services firms typically enjoy little or no intellectual property protection for their innovative activities. One advancement in, say, using financial derivatives to hedge against currency movements can be quickly reverse engineered by other firms, and then copied. A rather dated but powerful example of this was Merrill Lynch's introduction of the Cash Management Account, whereby Merrill Lynch "swept" each customer's account each day and put all the residual funds from sales and trades into a money market account. This was a significant innovation in its day, and one that was rapidly copied. Further complicating the ability to appropriate value from innovative activities in the financial services industry is the fact that people move frequently between financial services firms. When they move, they take their knowledge and experience with them, further diffusing advanced practices and processes from one firm to others. Under these circumstances, who can afford to invest the money and take the risks of innovation?

As this book demonstrates, though, the absence of strong intellectual property rights has in no way eliminated the incentive or ability of financial services firms to pursue new innovations. What has happened is that the processes through which innovation occurs have shifted. There is much less emphasis on PhDs in white lab coats housed inside a corporate research laboratory far removed from the daily concerns of the world, struggling to master fundamental natural and physical properties to create breakthrough products. Instead, the PhDs (and there are many, though now in disciplines like finance, economics, computer science, complex adaptive systems, etc.) develop highly sophisticated computer models, validate those models on real historical data, and then deploy those models on live data. Firms must come to know their customers' needs quite deeply to match the promising new discoveries with the emerging unmet needs of their customers. Specialization becomes the order of the day on the supply side. The historical and live data are areas where companies can maintain some degree of differentiation, as each firm has a unique record of trading experiences, and each firm's customers may also have unique requirements.

Meanwhile, on the customer side, solutions integration is the order of the day, whereby a financial services provider brings a complete solution to the needs of its customer. Each customer differs on his/her objectives, current position, risk preferences, life circumstances, and so forth. There can be no "one size fits all" solution to the needs of customers. And typically, as customers' wealth increases, their financial needs become even more diverse. These wealthy clients insist upon (and will pay for) integrated financial solutions that tie all the many pieces of their portfolio and estate together.

At first blush, deep specialization seems completely inconsistent with one-stop shopping. Depth of expertise necessarily comes at the expense of breadth of application. This is where the book makes its fundamental contribution. No firm, however large, however experienced, can afford to meet all of its customers' needs through offerings that are exclusively created and managed internally. To meet their customers' needs, *firms must open up their innovation processes and, as we shall see, business models*, to incorporate both internally managed services and externally accessed services. Only a hybrid combination of internal and external services can hope to span the range of offerings required for a complete solution to be delivered.

Thus, through this book, we come to learn that open innovation is an essential prerequisite for the ability of modern financial firms to achieve differentiation, expertise, and specialization on the supply side, while providing superior service to highly satisfied customers on the demand side. Because customers do not care where a particular financial product originated, they care deeply about how it connects to the rest of their portfolio and how their portfolio comports with the other aspects of their lives and estates. As we shall see below, however, there are some important business model issues that must be worked through to balance both internal and external offerings.

What I find enormously encouraging is that my own research into open innovation came from in-depth study of so-called "high-technology" firms, largely operating in the Silicon Valley of California. In my book *Open Innovation*, I examined how Xerox struggled to capture some of the value it had created in its Palo Alto Research Center (PARC). I then compared that experience to those of IBM, Intel, Lucent, and two life science companies, Genzyme and Millennium. At no time in that book did I consider whether or how open innovation might relate to financial services industries.

One test of the value of an idea is whether it has utility in explaining the actions and behaviors of actors in the setting in which it is observed. This is termed *internal validity*. Open innovation has come to be accepted by many in the high-tech industry as a valid description of how innovation is evolving in that world. To more precisely define the term,

> Open innovation is a paradigm that assumes that firms can and should use external ideas as well as internal ideas, and internal and external paths to market, as they look to advance their technology. Open innovation processes combine internal and external ideas into architectures and systems. They utilize business models to define the requirements for these architectures and systems.[1]

A second, and perhaps more demanding, test of an idea is whether that idea can inform an understanding of the actions and behaviors of actors in different settings, far more where the original idea was developed. This is termed *external validity*. Prior to the publication of this book, it was an open question as to whether open innovation offered any explanatory power for the many innovative developments that have occurred in financial services. Now, with the arrival of *Open Innovation in the Financial Services*, it may be said that the concept enjoys substantial external validity as well.

*Open Innovation in the Financial Services* convincingly demonstrates that financial services providers have embraced both the "outside–in" component of the open innovation model (where external ideas are accessed and offered to customers through the company's own business model) and the "inside–out" component of the model (where internal ideas are allowed to go outside to other companies for use in their business models). The outside–in aspect is clearly demonstrated in the growing percentage of mutual fund offerings by global institutes, in which the mutual funds were originated and are managed by an external party. Incorporating these third-party products into the firm's offerings allows it to provide a much richer set of fund possibilities to its clients. More subtly, it reduces the risks of having to create a new kind of fund, only to learn that the market for that fund is less than anticipated or that the fund's managers are less capable than hoped for.

---

[1] Chesbrough, H., Vanhaverbeke, W. and West, J. (2006) *Open Innovation: Researching a New Paradigm*. Oxford University Press, p. 1

But this outside–in approach has its costs as well, as Fasnacht is quick to note. For one, the gross margins on funds that are managed internally are much higher as the margins on third-party-managed funds. So helping your clients broaden their portfolios with additional third-party products risks cutting the profitability of each client's portfolio to the firm. This is essentially a function of the new business model of most global banks. In that model, the provider takes a commission on the sale of financial products (here, mutual funds) to its clients. That business model, which was very common among most financial services providers until 15 years ago, actively discourages the incorporation of third-party funds, precisely because there is another party who needs a cut of the commissions.

Thus, open innovation in financial services also requires business model innovation to make externally sourced ideas and services financially attractive to the provider, as well as the customer. In this case, the fundamental business model innovation was to shift how profits were earned from customers. Instead of receiving a commission on trades, innovative firms moved to an asset management model. In this model, the provider takes a small percentage of the total value of assets under management, in return for comprehensive advice and management of the portfolio.

This shift completely changes the attractiveness of third-party mutual funds for the financial provider. Before, such funds drastically reduced the commissions to the provider. After, the provider now wishes to grow the value of assets under its management and is relatively indifferent to whether those assets are internally or externally managed. In addition, this innovation is arguably beneficial for most clients. The earlier model implicitly motivated higher trading activity since that was the source of the commissions. The later model can easily accommodate passive index fund investing as well as active trading activity. And, the incentives of the provider are more closely aligned with those of the client in the later model as well.

Fasnacht also shows the benefits of the "inside–out" aspect of the open innovation model for financial services firms. This dimension involves the marketing of a successful internally managed fund to other firms for them to offer to their clients as well. This enables strong funds to attract more clients – and more capital – sooner. It rewards excellent performance by fund managers more rapidly and more strongly. This further motivates the development of even more expertise and specialization. At the limit, fund managers need not care about whether their funds are held by clients of internal or external financial service providers. They need only care about the performance of their fund.

As the above definition of open innovation points out, companies need to create architectures and systems to connect internal and external sources of innovation with internal and external paths to markets. Fasnacht's book finds explicit support for this approach in the financial services industry. He argues that successful financial services firms must create open architectures and comprehensive advisory processes to best serve their clients. These open architectures seek out the best-of-breed financial products and complement to advisory services for their clients, and enable clients to enjoy superior financial performance and satisfaction.

This journey from closed to open innovation in the financial services is not an easy one. There will be shifts in business models required for which resources and capabilities have to be redeployed or newly developed. Cultural changes will need to take place as well. New reward systems will be needed. New relationships with a growing network of participants must now be developed and managed. These strategic initiatives involve significant time, money, and risk. Yet the alternative, as this book shows, is much more risky. For a continued reliance on a closed model condemns customers to accepting less than the best financial products and incomplete advice and service. As customers gain increased visibility into financial market performance, they have many options and many other financial service providers to turn to. Financial markets are too sophisticated, too liquid, and too competitive to allow underperforming firms to thrive for very long. That is the real risk to avoid. *Open Innovation in the Financial Services* charts a course to manage this very real, very dangerous risk.

Henry Chesbrough

Adjunct Professor and Executive Director
Center for Open Innovation, Institute of Management,
Innovation and Organization
Haas School of Business, University of California, Berkeley

# Chapter Overview

# Contents

# Introduction

## Aim of the Book

This book investigates the financial service industry, which is currently in radical transformation triggered through a number of developments in markets, economics, demographics, customers, technology and policy, and regulations. In particular, regulators have placed added pressure on banks to manage the various categories of risk as a consequence of the global financial crisis. Banks around the globe have become subject of stringent monitoring with respect to capital adequacy, corporate governance, and transparency. What began in summer 2007 in the United States with the subprime mortgage market has impacted the global economy severely and revealed how interwoven-free financial markets are. Although many financial service firms have unveiled a staggering swath of losses, this book does not focus on the recent turbulences. In fact, we extrapolated a number of long-term trends into the future and found what strategies, structures, and capabilities firms may exhibit in response to developments in the business environment. Traditional approaches to strategy are proving to be inadequate to deal with these changes. Those firms that want to survive and succeed in a hypercompetitive global environment need business leaders with more dynamic, innovative, and interdisciplinary and systemic approaches to strategic management.

We identified the shift from a closed to an open innovation paradigm as one major consequence of the analyzed trends. In a closed innovation paradigm, traditional company policies prevented them to review, accept, fund, or distribute any innovation from outside the organization. Where such isolated firms focus on own resources, open and flexible organizations focus on collaborative innovation to grow. During the last years, many firms have recognized the need for open innovation not only to increase competitiveness but also to survive. Open innovation is not merely a new business model to acquire intellectual property, it is a mindset characterized by openness, flexibility, and customer integration. The open model of innovation is the best way of creating value and required for operational excellence and profitable growth. However, it has wide-ranging implications for management. A number of actual case studies and examples of global financial institutes illustrate how senior executives approach the transition to open innovation. In particular, we discuss how banks adapt open innovation concepts from manufacturing as these strategic

D. Fasnacht, *Open Innovation in the Financial Services*,

approaches and tools for innovation capabilities are advanced. Implementation can only be done upon the development of a set of new dynamic management practices. To gain a better understanding of the phenomenon, we suggest a framework based on interrelated capabilities, namely ambidextrous thinking, intrapreneurial attitude, and a systemic and holistic view on the firm. We would like to emphasize that the transition to new ways of organizing in the open innovation paradigm is based upon an open innovation culture that cultivates social capital as a set of resources embedded into relationships into which other resources can be invested. This is crucial, as delivering innovation successfully to the market calls for trusted relationships with diverse sets of people and institutions.

We have attempted to capture what managers know and integrated it with the latest social science research findings based on the doctoral research of the author. One aim was to generate a set of managerial practices in the context of the financial services that the reader can use to set the stage for the transition to open innovation. We are confident that the integrative aspects of the book contribute to the production of knowledge for both academics and banking executives. In a few words, this book is to show how a firm – if open, flexible, and customer-centered – can create value from the open model of innovation and leverage it for profitable growth.

## Remain Open and Flexible and Succeed in Business

The global financial service industry is in a process of secular transformation with growing emerging and frontier markets (those economies not yet evolved enough to be called *emerging markets*), reshaping the economic landscape, and creating a new paradigm characterized by liberalized open markets but also by the many disorders. Gaining a comprehensive understanding about growth and innovation is vital for businesses to survive. As history has shown, innovation alone is not enough and growth alone is not enough either. Apple, Inc., considered as one of the most innovative companies, for example, has reinvented itself three times since the 1980s. Firms need to focus on continuous innovation and efficiency, and simultaneously they must expand their global reach or exploit local advantages to deliver superior customer value propositions. However, there is no universal strategy for success. Pioneering ideas develop differently and what is more, they cannot be adapted easily as they have sometimes a long history as the example of Wells Fargo demonstrates.

Wells Fargo's 155 years history included great events in America's history. It is rich in detail and will be forever linked with the image of a six-horse stagecoach thundering across the American West, loaded with gold and anything else valuable. Rapid delivery by the fastest means possible – stagecoach, railroad, steamship, pony rider, telegraph, or recently airplanes and computers – and always satisfying their local customer's demands and the reputation of the name made Wells Fargo a successful and truly innovative firm. What Henry Wells and William Fargo started in 1852 – providing freight service between New York and San Francisco – quickly expanded to a number of supportive services such as buying and selling of gold dust, bullion, and specie. Soon, they offered basic financial services like money orders, traveler's checks, and transfer of funds by telegraph. They were selling paper bank drafts as good as gold. A network of express and banking services were established in key communities and mining camps bordering the gold fields throughout California. The management of the firm early realized that collaboration with partners by subcontracting express services to established companies rather than by duplicating own services yields into success. With this revolutionary strategy at that time, the number of banking and express offices grew from 436 in 1871 to 3,500 at the turn of the nineteenth century.

By 1918, Wells Fargo was part of 10,000 communities across the country. That year, however, the federal government took over the nation's express network as part of its effort in the First World War. Wells Fargo was left with just one bank in San Francisco. In the 1910s and 1920s, Wells Fargo served as a commercial bank in San Francisco, supporting the West's growing business and agriculture, including fledgling auto, aerospace, and film industries. At least, the Wells Fargo stagecoach became a regular actor in Hollywood westerns. Through the twentieth century, Wells Fargo rebuilt from just one office in San Francisco. From a premier downtown San Francisco institution, it expanded in 1923 to two marbled banking halls. Wells Fargo became a "banker's bank" that served the entire west in the United States. The bank helped to meet new consumer banking needs in the prosperous post-World War II era. After many unsuccessful expansions to Asia, the United Kingdom, and parts of Continental Europe, Wells Fargo returned to its historic territory throughout the Western of the United States where it has unbeatable cultural advantages. Recently, new banking concepts changed not only *where* people banked, but also *how* they banked. As in the stagecoach days, Wells Fargo has been a pioneer in bringing banking convenience to its customers. They have always been at the forefront of high-tech banking, emphasizing drive-up tellers, banking by phone, credit cards, automatic teller machines (ATMs), online banking, as well as the small-staffed supermarket branches. Because of its innovation capabilities and capacity to adapt to change, Wells Fargo has become one of the ten largest banks in the United States, providing diversified financial services. In autumn 2008, Wells Fargo even bought Wachovia as the financial crisis took on a new urgency and Wachovia's shares plunged. With this acquisition, Wells Fargo significantly increased its coast-to-coast branch network and raised to a retail banking powerhouse.

Innovation, collaboration, and organizational transformation illustrated with the example of Wells Fargo challenges us to explore not just what changed in certain industries but what firms require to remain successful. We must understand innovation as a dynamic form of change that has the power to transform not only companies but also industries and economies. This form of innovation, referred to disruptive innovation can be seen as the engine of "creative destruction," to borrow the term from Josef A. Schumpeter, one of the most influential economists and political scientist of the twentieth century.[1] The theory, however, allows firms with the right strategy to prosper and let firms with the wrong strategies or relatively inefficient operations to die. Destruction, and the following reallocation of resources, enables the cycle of construction and destruction to begin anew. That is what has recently happenend in the financial services industry. We should therefore refresh our knowledge in terms of Schumpeterian theories and read this book as it provides understanding of such dramatic and complex changes in the economy. We attempt to show the reader how to manage strategic change and simultaneously increase efficiency and flexibility by aligning various initiatives and strategies. To do so we sought for examples that explains the process, rather than just the outcomes of social actions. Through this approach, it became apparent that the successful transition to open innovation and doing business in the new paradigm rely heavily on the firm's leadership and their ability to provide the organization with conditions that facilitate innovation and learning. We believe that a firm can only be brought to new levels of performance and leadership if we understand all the interacting components and if we have the ability to put them all in place.

## Why the Financial Services Industry?

### *We Live in a Service Economy*

The Industrialization began in England sometime after the middle of the eighteenth century, triggered through the invention of the steam engine, and related technological innovation such as locomotives, steam ships, pumping stations, and other engines that drove machinery in factories and mills. This radical process of social and economic change with the steam engine as central part of modernization transformed a huge human group from the primary sector to a fully developed industrial economy (secondary sector). Where in 1700, 80% of the population of England earned its income from the land around the year 1800 that figure had dropped to 40% in favor of the secondary sector. Recently, we have seen the shift from industry to services triggered through a number of innovations. Today, the service (tertiary) sector accounts for more than 70% of the OECD (Organization for Economic Cooperation and Development) gross domestic product, where the secondary sector accounts for about 18%. The recent paradigm change to services can be exemplarily evidenced with the growth in gross value added.[2] No doubt, services have become the largest sector in most industrialized economies, and they offer an important contribution to economic growth and employment. In particular, knowledge-based business services play important roles in facilitating innovation across developed economies.

Based on the latest report of the Office for National Statistics, finance and business services continue to form the largest single sector of the United Kingdom economy since 1991, and today contribute to roughly one-third of the gross value added.[3] The manufacturing industries contributed more than 20% of gross value added from 1992 until 1998, when it stood at 20%, but has fallen every year since then, to 14% in 2004. It is striking though that the service sector has grown about 160% between 1992 and 2004, compared with total gross value-added growth of 91%. Over this period, most of these business services have grown at a higher rate than the economy as a whole. The rationale for the steadily growing service sector in favor of the manufacturing sector in developed economies is linked to globalization effects where toll processing and trade liberalization provide manufacturers with increased competition from imports of cheaper goods produced in much lower wage economies. In addition, the enhanced use of information and communication technology (ICT) and the increasing spending in research and development (R&D) in the service sector have been other stimulating factors.

Longitudinal research by the OECD found that the continuous increasing labor productivity over the last two decades has attributed to knowledge-intensive activities and notably to the use of technology.[4] Accordingly, the most productive sectors are high technology, computer, software, and financial services. The performance of knowledge-intensive industries has been especially affected by the adoption of information and communications technology. For example, banks and insurance companies depend heavily on information processing, and banks in particular consider information about money equally important as money itself. Therefore, transforming information into knowledge-based advantages is vital. We argue that innovation results from the application of knowledge and technology, and if employed ingeniously increases competitiveness.

That the discussion of innovation and its management are still dominated by manufacturing studies is in contradiction to the fact that the service sector is the main contributor to developed economies. In particular, in European countries, services have not been studied much, hence understanding is poor. One may say that service firms have been traditionally less innovative compared with manufacturing firms. One reason for that may be the relatively specific nature of innovation in services, which means that they are often incremental solutions to specific problems. Innovation processes are in some respects similar to those in manufacturing, while in other respects different from it. Innovation in services has been underestimated for a long time, though some firms have recently improved their service innovation activities. In fact, almost all understanding of innovation derives from studies of manufacturing. We believe that innovation awareness can be further increased in many service fields. But there is diversity in the innovation traits of different industries within services that have to be analyzed carefully. This means that some technology- and knowledge-based industries within the service sector are similar to manufacturing industries in relation to their high research and development effort or technological intensity. On the other hand, traditional manufacturing firms have shifted to services. Look for instances at IBM, Siemens, or Volvo that have had a long tradition in manufacturing and hence an advantage for adapting their approved procedures to services. Some of these companies changed their business models so radically that they are generating today more revenues with services than with their original products.

The recent developments in services increased the significance of the various interrelations between technology, knowledge, and innovation in economic activity. Described as the cornerstone for competitive advantage, this view has received growing attention in recent years. It has further led to information-based, knowledge-intensive, and service-driven businesses and radically changed the traditional ways in which firms did their business. Relatively, few studies seek to unveil and theorize the fundamental renewal of many firms in the service sector, as previous studies tended to focus upon manufacturing and not services. Yet, we observed that since the middle of the 1990s increasing academic and management attention has been paid to the general importance of services. The literature has grown substantially regarding the development of concepts for services[5] but also for the management of innovations in services.[6] What is missing is a transdisciplinary view that includes open innovation and the corresponding management practices. Employees and customers are two additional undervalued assets to banking and not covered in management books. We aimed to combine these areas, in particular the concept of open innovation and the transformation in the financial services with constant focus to create knowledge about knowing *what* and knowing *how*. We claim that this book explains these interrelations as a system with focus on banking, as this industry is a significant contributor to the economy and affected like no other service industry due to global trends and a number of recent specific developments.

## *Financial Service Firms Are Raising in the Global Market*

The financial service industry encompasses a broad range of businesses – banks, consumer finance, stock brokerage, asset management, credit cards, insurances, and so forth – that deal with the management of money. The financial service industry is one of the central pillars of a national economy, in particular for countries in which it makes an important contribution to the gross domestic product. Major part of this industry makes up banking. Since the first modern bank, Banco di San Giorgio, was founded in Genoa in Italy in 1406 with the purpose to provide traders or *bankers* with a desk to make transactions, banking has expanded to a number of services. Banks, as they used during the Renaissance, no longer simply provide funds to allow businesses to purchase inventory; they today service companies as well as individuals. They significantly influenced economies and politics for centuries. Within the last 25 years, firms belonging to the financial services have raised to top global companies. Forbes publishes yearly a comprehensive list of the world's 2,000 largest, and most powerful, public companies. The institute assesses global companies based on factors such as sales, profits, assets, and market value. As of March 2008, measured by number of firms, 315, the banking industry has the biggest presence out of the global 2,000 largest companies. Although oil and gas operations lead all industries in terms of revenues, banking dominates in assets and profits. Regardless whether we look at the top 10, top 20, or top 100 rankings, banking, insurance, and diversified financial firms make up roughly 50% of the companies listed. This picture looked completely different some decades ago. Although the banking industry has constantly improved its market performance, their figures dropped.

In 2007 and especially at the beginning of 2008, the financial services industry has been facing huge losses because of the meltdown in the US housing market. It is an unpleasant – but fact – that modern financial markets have the power to distress economies more strongly than it used to. Clearly, the recent crisis can be attributed to the globalization of financial markets. Financial services are interconnected to real economies (the parts of the economy that produce goods and services, rather than the parts involving buying and selling on the financial markets). We learned that a collapse of financial service firms poses threats for the real economy, but we also know that every economic downturn calls for solutions and measures to prevent future crises. Corrections inevitably follow peaks and do not worry those who have a memory of past economic downturns. Unlike in the past, for instance in the era of the Great Depression of the 1930s, where economic downturns were called "panics," today there are political leaders, central banks, and market regulators that have the capacity to provide the financial system with liquidity. Panicking due to short-term market volatility is unscientific, although it sometimes happens as the case of Indymac – one of the biggest savings and loans mortgage banks in the United States – recently showed. The bank saw panicking savers withdraw more than US $1.3 billion in deposits on July 15, 2008 as the bank was facing on the brink of bankruptcy under the weight of mortgage defaults. With respect, such events are exceptional, however, frightening as they demonstrate that things can slip out of social, political, and economic control. The current environment should not distract us from the developments that have shaped the structure of the financial services industry for the last 20 years. The crisis brought home the necessity of a better governance and transparency of financial institutes. Notably, we must negotiate effective regulation for financial markets, on our economic policy makers' reliance and on asset inflation to power profitable and sustainable growth.

Aside the current turbulences, long-term trends in the financial service industry such as demographic changes and wealth accumulation patterns will ensure that the industry is set to significantly increase its revenues and profits within the next 10 years.[8] Although this sounds rather optimistic at the moment, we believe that global wealth continues to rise; thus, the financial services industry will most likely benefit. There is still untapped market potential. Just look at the emerging and frontier markets with their increasing contribution to economic growth. Their is a high degree of uncertainty about the length and depth of the recent turmoil in financial markets, but we expect the industry to recover and regaining strength. Certainly, we need new rules and regulations but then banks will likely return to raising funds and to lending and making money. This expectation is backed by the shift of wealth pools from mature and developed markets to new markets in Asia, Latin America, and the Middle East. It is the deep penetration of financial services into the global economy – everybody and in particular every company needs a bank – that corroborates our assumption. With key stakeholders from employees, customers, business partners, suppliers, media, civil society, government, regulators, auditors, rating agencies, and shareholders, succeeding with growth and sustaining their success in creating value is a challenging task. Achieving profitable growth becomes more difficult as profitability in banking has already reached a high level. However, there is still potential to further increase efficiency through the appropriate utilization of technology, especially by renewing proprietary system architectures. We state the strategic value of the future for financial service firms to be in the combination of innovation, knowledge, and technology. Likewise, we must watch profitability that is driven by strategic decisions about geographic focus, client segmentation, products, services and solutions, organizational setup, and platforms. In any case, we must take client-centered strategic decisions. We will approach this notion further and discuss why strategy should be concerned with doing things better for clients, doing more business with existing clients, and acquiring new clients, while at the same time exceeding the expectations of shareholders.

Although many financial service firms have been in transformation for the last years, it is only recently that innovation within this industry has been studied in its own right. One reason for this is that technological innovations over the last two decades accelerated the pressure for strategic change in many firms. As banks are very much impacted by the developments in technology, they are among the heaviest investors in information technology. This, at the same time, acts as a lever to increase operational efficiency. The necessity for transaction processing, market-intelligence, analysis, or risk and opportunity assessment in conjunction with other banking activities relies on technology, tools, and systems that map to business models. In that case, the business model becomes a cognitive device to convert technical aspects of products and services into business and customer value. The recent advances in information and communication technology allowed them to provide their customers with better and faster information and services across the globe.

We see additional reasons for the increased attention paid to service innovation as due to the progressive adoption of marketing in banks. Many firms regard services as the antidote of commoditization. Offering differentiated products and services geared to specific customer needs is probably the best way to overcome commodity perception among customers in financial services. Services are a strategically important business activity and a key differentiator and therefore have become the source of sustainable and competitive advantage in a global financial market. Financial service institutes have the pressure to innovate. Currently, they do not tend to be as innovative as firms in other industries. But one must not ignore the increasing number of structured investment products and sophisticated advisory processes. Consequently, traditional business models have changed. We suggest a service-oriented business model since this is of paramount importance to differentiate from competition and to create valuable and long-term customer relationships. Many firms have opened up and intensified collaboration to grow with a clear focus on processes that add more value to the customer.

## Heading into a New Business Paradigm

We all know that banking has traditionally been a conservative industry, resistant to change. It used to be a moderate dynamic market for decades. The stable industry structure, defined boundaries, clear business models, and identifiable players made change linear and predictable in the past. But this has all changed significantly in the last 20 years. Our observation showed that progressive developments have led to an industry with ambiguous structure, blurred boundaries, open business models, and new market entrants and intermediaries, where speed, flexibility, reliance, and efficiency have all become equally important factors for success. This strategic transition is challenging firms to make extensive adaptations to the changing environment, with innovation as a source for profitable growth.

Selling financial products, services, and advising customers has not changed significantly during the last two decades. What has changed radically is the process by which ideas are identified, required knowledge is incorporated and utilized, innovations developed and distributed. The reasons for this change are the volatile, uncertain geopolitical climate driven by increasing competition, economic pressure, regulatory changes, technological innovations, and the changing nature of demand. The demise of the dotcoms, the terror act on September 11, 2001, rapid growth of developing economies like Brazil, Russia, India, and China, as well as the boom in the equity markets has resulted in rapid and substantial wealth creation in the mass-affluent segment (commonly individuals with US $100,000 to 1 million of liquid financial assets). This has led to a wealth management shift and changed many management agendas considerably since the turn of the millennium. The wealth creation activity is no longer restricted to mature markets as emerging markets are being tightly integrated into the global economy. Not to forget frontier markets, where new wealthy investors, in large numbers, are arriving on the scene in an unprecedented manner. They expect professional guidance from their financial service provider to grow, protect, and transfer their wealth freely across borders, to enable them to maximize their wealth as well as diversify their interests.

The above-mentioned specific developments indicate that it is time for change to realize future success in a new competitive landscape. Managers are forced to rethink their firm's business models. We argue that the blend of openness, flexibility, and focus on the core business with the customer in the center of the organization captures the innovation *zeitgeist*. The overall phenomenon that will drive change, beneath the surface of banking in years to come, is anticipated to be the shift from a closed to an open innovation paradigm. The adaptation to the new business rules calls for organizational transformation. In recent years, most banks have transformed their value chain and embraced *open architecture* as a model that offers clients a full range of products, regardless of suppliers. Some banks have gone even further, put the client into the center of their organization, and restructured their client advisory processes as a complementary service to their product portfolio. These strategies to increase customer value can all be associated with the concept of open innovation. One may say that some initiatives look like a drop in the ocean of innovation with hard accounting facts, showing that banks do less innovation by value as they insist they do. The consistent implementation of open innovation strategies is, especially in unfavorable market environments, more important than ever.

The recent meltdown in the US subprime market and the ensuing global financial crisis is a good example where we can evidence a radical shift in the business model of banks. Without going into details, we would just briefly note that providing easy money to finance homes has from a social viewpoint something positive because subprime mortgages make it possible for people with low or fluctuating incomes to acquire residential property. These borrowers usually do not qualify for market interest rates with their poor credit histories and weak documentation of income. They also lack the capacity to support the monthly payment on the loan if interest rates are rising. Twenty years ago, banks would have taken the full risk of such subprime loans because they financed their mortgage lending through the deposits they received from their clients. Within this traditional model, mortgages would have been concentrated on the origin of the loans – the homebuyer. The crises would have affected the United States only. But this model limited the amount of mortgage lending they could do. That is why recently many banks moved to a new model where they sell on the mortgages in the form of securitized assets to the bond markets. Through this innovation, they pooled subprime mortgage loans and repackaged them into saleable securities. This has made it much easier to fund additional borrowing. In most cases, banks no longer kept credit risks on their own balance sheets but pass them on in securitized form as credit derivatives to, for example, hedge funds managers or pension funds. The model changed from a closed system to an open collaboration between financial institutes to disperse risks on a broader basis across the financial markets. Therefore, the losses fell on a number of global final investors. This form of collaborative innovation also laid bare the growing global influence of private equity firms, hedge funds, and sovereign wealth funds if we loose control of collaboration with respect to the governance of some of the world's largest corporations. The real vulnerability is not the network of partnerships; it is the high complex and global financial system and the management of the risks coming with collaboration.

The change of business models as well as multiple product offerings, serving, and advising clients across the globe justifies an increasing focus on collaboration and innovation. But leaders are called to take regulations more seriously than they did in the past. They must expand their negotiation networks and increasingly interact with policy makers and governments. For those banks affected by nationalization efforts, the business model and process of work may radically change. Collaborative innovation is clearly leading to new ways of working and organization and has triggered investments in organizational and technological infrastructures. Many firms are in the process to renew their platform not only to provide the organization with the required flexibility, but also to increase operational efficiency. In the book, we elaborate how new approaches to collaboration are breaking down traditional organizational and business boundaries in the pursuit to innovate and grow and for some to survive. The capability for open, flexible, and aligned interactions has been proved in successes in the manufacturing industries where many executives are by now familiar with open innovation. Based on our research and confirmed by the cases discussed in the book, we are convinced that open innovation is as important in the financial services as it is in manufacturing. By looking outside the firm's own boundaries, we can evidently gain better access to knowledge and technology. In the current market environment, dominated by the global financial crisis and fear of recession, such perspectives are essential for all business practices. We must be open for a new mindset for business – not only for expansion strategies in general, but also during turbulent times.

## Outline and Structure

The assertions and conclusions made in the book are grounded in advanced management research and theory. They rely not on a large sample of observed facts, as it is believed that our body of knowledge does not increase from a number of (confirmatory) observations. Certainly, we can learn a lot from empirical data – but not as much as we needed to build general business rules. Approaches applied in the past cannot necessarily be used for the future due to different circumstances. For instance, there is no guarantee that Wells Fargo's strategy can be adapted by a Chinese bank. In general, social phenomena are hard to model and extrapolate because they exhibit abundant feedback loops. Therefore, testing hypothesis using observation and generalizing was not the intention of this research. Instead, we preferred to integrate high-quality strategic thoughts of senior executives, concepts, and extended cases to make the material as engaging, concrete, and useful as possible. With this approach, we attempted to encourage the reader to open his/her mind for new ideas rather than just impart information.

The language used is the first person plural although *I* wrote the book without additional help. With this writing style, I feel more comfortable as many findings derived from various information sources – some from secondary research and others from reputed leaders in academia and the business world. The process of writing this book is what eventually increased my knowledge. Likewise, I hope that reading the book will increase your knowledge.

The book consists of six main chapters, excluding *Foreword*, *Introduction* and *Conclusion*. Each chapter begins with some general theses that reflect the key viewpoints of the author. They are elaborated further within the chapter and shall stimulate the reader about a certain subject. Throughout all chapters, practices from many executives have been integrated and tied together with our strategic thoughts. Examples and cases derived from firms such as American Express, Axa, Bank of America, Citigroup, Credit Suisse, Deutsche Bank, HSBC, Merrill Lynch, Banco Santander, UBS, Wells Fargo, and Zurich Financial Services among other smaller firms like EFG International, Julius Baer, Nykredit, Pictet, PostFinance, or Greycourt. The global brands were not chosen because they perform better than small institutes but they offer a wider area of research ground. In addition, universal and global banks are more affected by the recent trends, and thus their executives are more likely to read books that provide new ideas and management advice. On the other hand, smaller firms are used to show niche innovations. We are aware of the fact that the banking landscape changed during the process of writing this book. However, the economic failures and nationalizations of some institutes are not commented. We rather decided to keep the examples as some strategies generated value by the time they were launched where others may be seen as lessons learned.

The *Introduction* includes the aims of the book and clarifies why we think that the open model of innovation in the service sector, in particular, for the financial services becomes increasingly important. We give you a brief synopsis of the challenges and opportunities arising out of open innovation. Further, we introduce the structure of the book, which is illustrated by the overall model that guides the reader through the book (see Fig. 1 at the end of the introduction).

*Chapter One* lays the foundation for the ensuing discussions by emphasizing the strategic importance of growth and innovation for companies and economies. Therefore, we examined the current literature about growth and innovation and linked it with current practices. Through the process of reviewing various interpretations and definitions, we attempt to increase the reader's understanding of profitable growth and demonstrate the strategic importance of innovation. We explain the various routes and types of innovation as well as the differences between innovation in manufacturing and services. Focus has been put on the innovation process in services including what determines its success. The chapter concludes by summarizing the drivers for profitable growth and gives an outlook on how growth can be achieved through innovation.

*Chapter Two* mainly explains the changing business environment. So do we initially explain what we understand under strategic change and what the causes are. Then, we briefly discuss issues regarding the philosophical stance of this management research and its justification as a means to understand the strategic thoughts made. Core of this chapter builds the various changes in the market. Thus, we elucidate the main trends in the financial service industry, namely globalization and competition, the changing nature of demand, technological innovations, regulatory, and policy changes. In respect to the turbulence in credit and money markets, triggered through the subprime mortgage market in the United States that spread to the global financial markets, we did not accentuate on that in particular. Instead, we show the implications and challenges of all the relevant developments for the financial services.

*Chapter Three* initially presents how the recent developments changed the financial service industry. We explain the challenges of most banks to effectively set their growth strategies with the recent economic environment. Further, we will elucidate the main obstacles to increasing profits, including new regulations. The trends force firms to the transition from an old – closed innovation – to a new open innovation paradigm, if they want to achieve profits and growth projections. Accordingly, we discuss the threats of closed innovation models and then make the link to collaborative models as they incorporate knowledge, resources, and experience into the firm from external sources. The discussion of the implications of collaboration sets the foundation for open innovation. We compare and contrast open and closed business models and give you based on a number of examples an idea what is meant by openness. Finally, we introduce the open model of innovation and declare it as the new business paradigm.

*Chapter Four* is considered as a major chapter, where we elaborate the practical use of the concept of open innovation. As the journey to open innovation requires the right transition strategies, they are explained with a number of examples. We emphasize the importance of open architecture models as this was evidenced as an early strategy of collaboration. Further, we stress client integration by discussing client segmentation and organization around clients. Consequently, we explain the client advisory process as integral part to enhance the client's experience. To deliver a premium client value proposition, we suggest the development of a flexible service-oriented architecture. We explain in detail what we understand under architecture, namely the combination of strategy, organization, and technology. At the end of this chapter, we discuss what can be learned from collaborative models and what must be considered for the strategic transition toward open innovation.

*Chapter Five* brings the structural and implementation requirements of open innovation into focus. We argue that open innovation can only be established upon the development of new resources and capabilities. Thus, we suggest three mutually dependent dynamic capabilities, namely ambidextrous thinking, intrapreneurial attitude, and a systemic and holistic view on the firm. Every organization must learn how to incorporate these capabilities so that they become a core set of management practices. To leverage this system of capabilities, we suggest enabling conditions such as a clear vision, strategic focus, and strong leadership qualities besides sufficient financial resources.

*Chapter Six* synthesizes the various thoughts made in the book. We assume that bringing together what we learned from the investigation in the financial services helps to build up comprehensive business model that is beneficial for the firm and increases customer satisfaction. The strategic transition to open innovation, however, is a transformative change, whose success relies on various factors. Social capital is considered as vital and that is why we suggest it to be part of the strategy. We reason that open innovation culture is fundamental for the strategic transition as well as for operating the open model of innovation. Further, we argue that it is a leadership responsibility to provide the organization with the appropriate culture.

In the *Conclusion*, we briefly recapitulate some key messages of the book. We further raised a number of questions that, if you are able to answer them with yes, corroborate that you learned a lot. The book concludes with the voices of our interview partners, namely Walter Berchtold, a top leader in banking, and Professor Henry Chesbrough, the "founder" of open innovation. We hope that their views create awareness for the importance of topical issues discussed in the book and thus encourage an exchange of thoughts between author and reader or practitioners and academics.

The *Notes* throughout the book are grouped at the end of each chapter, so that you can read the book without distraction. The notes are mostly not extensive. In some cases, they just identify reference information and citations. Others explain the basis for assertions made in the text. Figure 1 gives you a systematic overview about the combination of theory and practice that you are about to read. It offers a conceptual framework that is meant to serve as the guiding principle to action. The content of the chapters is grouped around these topics.

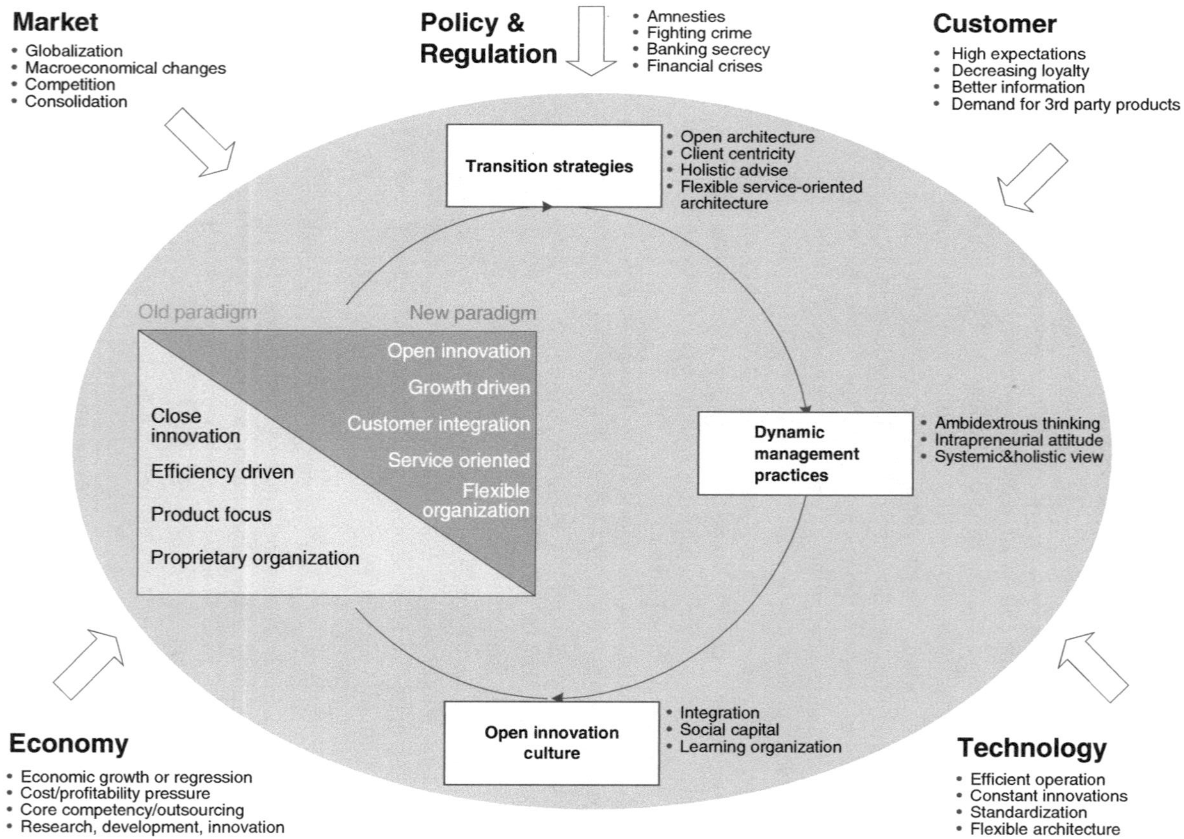


**Fig. 1** The open innovation model

## Notes

1. Schumpeter, J.A. (1942) *Capitalism, socialism and democracy*. Harper&Row, New York.
2. Where the Gross Domestic Product (GDP) is an integral part of a country's national accounts and provides a measure of the total economic activity, the Gross Value Added (GVA) measures the sum of the value added created through the production of goods and services within the economy. The GVA refers to the production or output of an economy and can be used to show how much different industries contribute within the economy.
3. Office for National Statistics (2006) *United Kingdom input–output analyses*. 2006 Edition, Consistent with the European System of Accounts (ESA 95) and published with the permission of the Controller of Her Majesty's Stationery Office (HMSO).
4. OECD (2003) *Science, technology and industry scoreboard 2003 – Towards a knowledge-based economy*. OECD, Paris.
5. For research on innovation in the service sector, see De Brentani, U. (1991) 'Success factors in developing new business services', *European Journal of Marketing*, 25(2), 33–59; De Brentani, U. (1993) 'The new product process in financial services: Strategy for success', *International Journal of Bank Marketing*, 11(3), 15–22; De Brentani, U. and Cooper, R.G. (1992) 'Developing successful new financial services for business', *Industrial Marketing Management*, 21, 231–241; De Brentani, U. and Ragot, E. (1996) 'Developing new business-to-business professional services: What factors impact performance?', Industrial *Marketing Management*, 25(6), 517–530; Edgett, S. (1996) 'The new product development process for commercial financial services', *Industrial Marketing Management*, 25(6), 338–361; Edvardsson, B. and Olsson, J. (1996) 'Key concepts for new service development', *The Service Industries Journal*, 16(2), 140–164; Vermeulen, P. (2004) 'Managing product innovation in financial service firms', *European Management Journal*, 22(1), 43–50.
6. Good introductions of the management of innovations in services give Miles, I. (1994) 'Innovation in services'. *In:* M. Dodgson and R. Rothwell (eds.) *Handbook of industrial innovations*. Edward Elgar, Aldershot, 243–256; Debackere, K., Loy, B. van and Papastathopoulou, P. (1998) 'Managing innovation in a service environment'. *In:* B. van Looy, R. van Dierdonck and P. Gemmel, (eds.) *Service management: An integrated approach*, Financial Times/Pitman, London, 387–405; Sundbo, J. (1997) 'Management of innovation in services', *The Service Industrial Journal*, 17(3), 432–455.
7. A scenario by McKinsey & Company indicates that global banking revenues will grow, on average, by 7.5% a year from 2006 to 2016. Consequently, it is expected that the banking industry will generate US $5.7 trillion in revenues and US $1.8 trillion in after-tax profits by 2016 – more than twice the levels at the end of 2006. The market capitalization of banks will likely be US $12 trillion higher *than it* is today. McKinsey (2008) 'What's in store for global banking', *McKinsey Quarterly*, January.

# The Strategic Value of Growth and Innovation

- Grow profitable and faster than investors expect to get further investments.
- Create an international strong brand value as this is instrumental for global expansion.
- Develop a profound knowledge about the characteristics and intricacies of service innovations to render a coherent solution to clients.
- Link innovation and growth and put it on the leadership's agenda.

## The Challenges of Growth

### *Understanding Growth*

In biology, growth is the increase in size and mass during the development of an organism over a period. Growth is often measured as an increase in biomass (mass of organic material) associated with the differentiation of cells to perform specific functions. All organisms grow although the rate of growth varies over a lifetime. Typically, growth in an organism follows an S-shaped curve, in which growth is at first slow, then fast, then, toward the end of life, nonexistent. Growth may even be negative during the period before death. *Do we understand growth now?* Of course not. In general, we cannot adapt definitions from nature for our purposes. However, if we look closer to economic growth, we can detect similarities. Under economic growth, we understand the increase in value of the goods and services produced by an economy. As it is conventionally measured as the percent rate of increase in real gross domestic product (GDP), one may say that strong growth reflects an increase of the average standard of living of individuals in a country. Over the last years, we have observed a steady increase of wealthy people in the world. These so-called high-net-worth individuals (HNWI) control more and more wealth. This is directly reflected in the GDP and market capitalization of a country. In particular, market capitalizations in Asia and Latin America have grown rapidly driven by foreign investments, strong corporate profits, or IPO (Initial Public Offering) activity and accelerated wealth creation in those particular economies.

D. Fasnacht, *Open Innovation in the Financial Services*,

By doing the math, we know that over long periods of time, even small rates of annual growth can have large effects on economies. Hence, a growth rate of just 2.5% per annum will lead to a doubling of GDP within 28 years, whilst a growth rate of 8% per annum (experienced by some emerging markets) will lead to a doubling of GDP within 9 years. Eight percent growth is also required, e.g., for India just to cover the annual requirement for millions of new jobs and to be able to keep poverty under control. Global economic growth so far has been the strongest upswing since the 1960s. Obviously, growth is the key pillar of economic activity – and for countries like India a must.

But let us look at the financial markets as they have grown very aggressively since the 1980s and became much bigger and more powerful than entire economies. In fact, the total global financial assets including equities, government and corporate debt securities, and bank deposits were about equal to global GDP in 1980 but by 2005, the global capital market had grown to about three times world GDP, or US $140 trillion and is expected to grow further to over US $210 trillion by decade's end.[1] This has an enormous impact, especially for firms in the financial service industries. Through their fees, they generate revenues from the management of these assets. Where most people in the financial service industry think better liquidity and access to capital for borrowers as well as more efficient prices are generally good things, after all, a global pool of capital implies also threats. Strong growing global capital markets paint a picture of the world with high stock prices, low interest rates, and increased debt levels. In case of an exogenous event – slower economic growth or a recession, rising inflation and interest rates, oil prices spiking higher, geopolitical shocks, or war – this is doomed to failure and can get ugly in a big rush. To present a bad example of uncontrolled growth, just take the recent mortgage crisis. In the United States, about two-thirds of retail banking revenues in 2006 came from mortgages and consumer finance, where in Germany this segment contributed only about 5%. During the summer of 2007, it became painfully apparent that the enormous swell in household borrowing in the United States was largely responsible for the strong balance sheet growth of many retail banks. The examples demonstrate that growth varies by product segment as well as by a country's sociodemographic patterns.

Coming back from macroeconomics, most of us tend to attach a particular value to the annual percentage change, perhaps since it tells us what happens to our wage check. Where employees feel growth with salary increase, for businesses to survive, growth is an imperative, not an option. There are several answers to the ultimate question, *why growing?* Regardless whether we take the perspective from an economy or company, growth is important to maintain competitiveness. It is required to retain and increase market share. Growth also compensates increasing cost through economies of scale. If we look at growth as an increase in wealth, we see that the growth in assets under management of a wealth manager consists of roughly half from net inflows, which means new money that clients brought into the bank, and half through improvements in investment performance of existing assets.[2] The inflow of money can be referred to as *organic growth.* Any type of growth of a firm meets the increasing demands of all stakeholders of that organization. Shareholders, in particular, are interested in strong growth rates as it gives them confidence to invest in the firm. This money is required for future investments such as innovations, increasing productivity, or business expansion. A firm that has been growing over years is more interesting for suppliers and customers either. Growth finally creates employment and contributes to an economy with prosperity.

The growth strategies of many banks during the last years have been striking. It was learned that growth is still vital, yet the patterns of growth changed. We should perceive sustainable growth via differentiation from competitors to superior product and service quality, customer satisfaction, and employee excellence. The key sources of competitive advantage are quality in products and services, customer service, sales branding, and marketing. In addition, growth strategy suggests that a business' attempts to grow depend on whether it markets new or existing products in new or existing markets. Thus, firms need to become more innovative when seeking ways to grow. This means applying new technology, product, service, process improvements, and human capital management. The message in a highly competitive global environment is simple – perform better than others. A good performance is reflected in the willingness of shareholders to invest in the company. But increasing total revenues alone is not enough. We simultaneously need to watch product and service profitability, customer profitability, and even employee profitability.

## *Profitability Drives Value Creation*

Never forget that the bottom-line goal of every company is to create superior returns to shareholders. In today's dynamic and competitive environment where markets rise and fall over time, companies need to change rapidly, radically, and measurably. Financial markets relentlessly pressure top executives to grow and keep growing faster and globally. To deliver a rate of return to shareholders in the future that exceeds the risk-adjusted market average firms must grow faster than their investors expect. Simplified, its stock price can only be prevented from falling if the rate of growth exceeds the forecast and if the growth is profitable. The price per share divided by the earnings per share, known as *P/E ratio* or *multiple,* is a good performance measure of success and reliable sign of whether a firm is winning or loosing. The P/E ratio serves as an indicator of business problems and opportunities. By relating price and earnings per share for a company, one can analyze the market's valuation of a company's shares relative to the wealth the company is actually creating. Therefore, it is important to understand why a premium P/E, one that is higher than the overall market's average, is imperative. For example, if one stock has a P/E twice that of another stock, it is probably a less attractive investment. But comparisons between industries, between countries, and between time periods are dangerous. To have faith in a comparison of P/E ratios, you should be comparing comparable stocks. Historically, the average P/E ratio in the private banking market has been around 15, compared with 10–12 for retail and universal banks. In the banking industry, the ratio has always been much lower than for the high-tech industry. The financial service institutes currently make up the bulk of P/E lists as a result of the financial crisis. We saw market valuations of far below ten for a number of giant banks. In a normal market environment this would mean that these stocks are inexpensive as compared to it's earnings and hence a good investment. The problem though is the uncertainty of the future of many institutes. There are few reasons a stock has a high P/E ratio. For example, Google exceeded a P/E ratio of 100 during the summer of 2005. This is typical for companies that have not made much money yet but expect to do so within the next quarters or years. Here, the market expects the earnings to rise rapidly in the future. In contrast, a high P/E ratio can also be explained with the fact that the company was previously making a lot of money, but in the last quarter or year, it had a special one-time expense. This so-called *charge* lowered the earnings significantly. However, stockholders usually understand that this was a one-time issue and will still buy stock at the same price as before, and only sell at least that same price. Also note that a specific stock may have a temporarily high price when, for whatever reason, there has been high demand for it. This demand may have nothing to do with the company itself, but may rather relate to, e.g., an institutional investor trying to diversify out risk. These are just a few reasons that affect P/E ratios.

To show that the earnings in P/E do not bias us, let us show that we are well aware of that issue. Finance experts explain the multiple with *nongrowth* and *growth* elements. The so-called nongrowth element indicates that much of the P/E comes from the firm's performance at present. This means the firm performs exactly as it did last years, every year in the future. In that case, the nongrowth element would constitute its entire P/E. In contrast, the growth element reflects the market's expectations for the firm's profitable future investment opportunities. It will give investors good reasons to expect significant performance in the future; hence, that is where nearly all the opportunity lies. In fact, just four factors determine whether the growth element of a firm's P/E is large, moderate, low, or even negative. It is crucial to understand that any action a manager takes to increase the share price and the P/E must come down to affecting one of those factors. Firstly, the *return on invested capital* together with the *capital cost* measures the true profitability of future investment opportunities. This financial measure simply quantifies how well an organization generates cash flow relative to the capital it has invested in its business. In particular, the difference between the above-mentioned variables, the *spread*, is a good indicator for investors to see the forecast of a firm. Secondly, the *investment*, the amount of money a firm invests back into its businesses in excess of depreciation and amortization each year, is another strong growth lever in pushing the P/E up or down. To achieve respectable growth, investments must be at least enough to maintain the business's assets, better it should be greater of what is required to cover depreciation. Lastly, there is the *duration,* the length of time a firm is able to maintain returns on new investments in excess of capital cost. Of course, a firm can arrive at any given P/E through different combinations of the four factors. One thing is for sure, firms with a P/E ratio above market average will be the winners in the competition to attract capital. They will not only best be able to satisfy shareholders by investing their capital for sustainable growth, but also to hire best people and serve customers.

Though this sounds logical, study after study confirms that roughly 90% of all publicly traded companies in developed economies have proved themselves unable to sustain for more than a decade a growth trajectory that creates above-average shareholder returns. Christensen and Raynor discussed in their book "The innovators solution" this growth paradox.[3] Based on their own research and a number of studies, they concluded that growth and innovation is interdependent. The failure to consistent, persistent growth is not due to lack of great ideas, unpredictable innovations, or capable managers, nor is it because of the changing nature of demand and erratic customer behavior. Sustainable growth fails because companies unwittingly strip the disruptive potential from innovations before they ever see the light of the day. Besides this, companies need to be profitable. The question though is, *what drives value creation?*

## *The Levers of Value Creation*

A study by the Boston Consulting Group in 2005 explains that although the top 20 global banks have focused on effectiveness by increasing their average return on equity (ROE) to about 17% over 2005, most are struggling to maintain its efficiency with cost–income ratios (CIR) below 45%.[4] Despite the fact that banks have reached high levels of profitability until 2005 compared to other industries, they have to be aware that pure efficiency gains have limits. One may say that increasing operational efficiency is less difficult to undertake than growth because growth exposes an organization to greater risk and an increased need for the innovation. Thus, growth not profitability drives size of market capitalizations. Accordingly, profitability seems to be a prerequisite for value creation and a strong driver for total shareholder return when starting at a low level. Profitability increases from high levels add only limited additional value with ROE converge at 15% for banks above the US $20 billion market capitalization level. In addition, if we look at empirical cost-income ratios, only banks with market capitalizations below US $20 billion achieved regularly ratios below 45%. The reason for that is that increasing complexity and variety of large firms account for efficiency constraints. Although the conclusion of the study sounds logical, we argue that growth alone is not always positive. By looking back to our biology example, not everything that strengthens is commendable as one can grow by gaining fat. The point we want to make is that growth must show muscles, because only through growing muscles one is gaining strength. Just translate this to economy and you understand what we mean by profitable (healthy) growth.

The third factor that we have to consider if we want growth and profitability to sustain is *risk*. The notion of risk is independent of the notion of growth and profitability. In financial markets, we measure credit risks, the risk of loss due to a debtor's insolvency. For financial investments, there are a large number of financial instruments to mitigate risks. *Hedging*, for instance, means that a specific financial instrument is purchased to reduce the risk in another financial product. Many financial risks can be hedged with sophisticated products. However, we cannot describe all the risk categories within the context of this book but there are many more such as consumer credit risk, interest rate risk, liquidity risk, volatility risk, currency risk, or equity, all with dedicated models and scenarios for monitoring. Risk in business is a reality and has to be considered, especially during strong growth periods, though some risks are difficult to manage. In particular, financial institutes that act as intermediator are confronted with various risk categories that are interdependent. The subprime mortgage collapse has intensified interest in risk management. The deregulation of the banking industry led to irresponsible homebuyers and predatory lending practices with increasing complexity of financial instruments. We are confident that our oversimplification exemplifies the importance of risk management. To improve growth and profitability while successfully managing risk, it is important to leverage synergy of people, processes, and strategy. Thus, appropriate organizational and technological architectures help to mobilize the workforce to pursue ambitious targets with their full commitment in line with risk management measures. This is born out of a culture that sees performance as a value and relies on outstanding leadership. As we discuss later on in this book, a trust-based open innovation culture is thus essential to unleash the forces of innovation and growth. Although we must never neglect consistent financial risk analyses, to assure profitable sustained growth the management has primarily to focus on innovation. And, the innovations that can satisfy stockholders demands for growth require taking risks. To succeed with this mandate, we need to understand the forces that shape innovation, in particular that act upon the individuals involved in creating innovation and new growth businesses. Mastering change, innovation, and growth, while keeping track of costs and risks, is challenging. The impact of profitability and growth on value creation, however, varies between big and small companies, industries, and countries. Therefore, we must better understand key growth strategies and actions that drive success inside the vast area of innovation. This confirms the theory that growth can be undertaken through mergers and acquisitions, alliances, joint ventures, outsourcing, corporate venturing but also organically.

## *In Pursuit of Profitable Growth*

For the assessment of profitable growth, we need to relate value and profitability. Ratios such as revenue and income as well as net margin and asset growth are indicators that show the real top performers. Often, top performers calculate the economic profitability of every one of its customers on a monthly basis. Such stringent performance management helps them to spot where to improve value propositions for existing clients and to identify clients that they should try to acquire. But it also maintains risk management. Essential here is to shift the mindset and understand that not every product per se must be profitable rather every client relationship or relationship with a group of clients.

Almost none of the top wealth managers represent high profitable growth. Certainly, many wealth managers steadily increase their assets under management but if we take a closer look, we see only few banks having the capacity to increase the asset under management net margin (profit over asset under management), while growing their asset base. One might say that growth can only be achieved if acquisitions are part of the strategy. On the other hand, organic growth is necessary likewise. Regardless the strategy, how to build on profitability should always be considered. Organic growth might be an option if there is no other company in the banking business to acquire or merge with. Growing organically in mature markets and making successful acquisitions in markets with strong growth rates might be thoughtful. If we look to Asia and Eastern Europe, the rise in business confidence during the last 5 years has increased the level of merger and acquisition activity. Deeper analyses demonstrate that this new wave of restructuring in financial services is different from the transactions of the 1980s and 1990s. It is likely to be characterized by alternatives in alliances, joint ventures, and outsourcing as well as innovation where straightforward mergers and acquisitions may not be the way ahead. However, growing through acquisitions has always been an option for increasing scale and geographic diversity. In June 2006, Axa, the French insurance and asset management group, unveiled the purchase of Winterthur, a European insurer, from Credit Suisse for CHF 12.3 billion. According to Henri de Castries, Group CEO of Axa, this transaction is merely a unique opportunity to reinforce their leading position in core European markets and increase their presence in emerging markets, notably in Eastern Europe and Asia. Winterthur, the Swiss-based company, serves 13 million clients in 17 countries with a mix of life, property and casualty, and pension products. This deal helps not only to quench Axa's thirst for growth, what is more it is part of the strategy to double sales and triple the profits by 2012.

Radical blockbuster mergers and acquisitions in the range over US $50 billion of huge institutions as we have seen at the merger of JP Morgan Chase and Bank One in July 2004 or Bank of America and Fleet Boston in 2003 may be of questionably value. The recent takeover proposal for ABN Amro by the Royal Bank of Scotland of about US $90 billion was even the largest in banking history and the third biggest over all industries. Although history evidenced that half of the deals failed to create their expected value – some even destroyed value, there still seems to be optimism that synergy opportunity exceeds integration costs. In particular, crossborder deals have been disappointing compared to domestic merger and acquisitions. So synergies are often not available if banks from different countries merge. The same applies to crossborder acquisitions. The explanation for many failures in crossborder transactions are the increasing complexity of regulatory issues, politically obstacles, compliance with government, cultural differences, in addition to stakeholder expectations that change faster today than 20 years ago. We saw firms where more resources went into consolidation and integration than into growth. Postmerger integration involves massive change in terms of restructuring. Therefore, the top management must consider crossborder acquisitions more carefully and should do it only if they have the capacity to run the business well.

## *Strengthening the Domestic Platform Before Going Global*

At a global level, during the 1980s and 1990s, the economic rationale for mergers and acquisitions was conclusively. Increased cost bases favored larger, consolidated players seeking synergies between the acquirer and acquired firm. But even today, we should not neglect the potential of having cost synergies beyond the traditional 10%. Although a primary type of deal puts economies of scale first, modern consolidated players are seeking to expand market share and increase their product and service capabilities. Certainly, there are still acquisitions driven by pure cost considerations as the acquisition of Abbey National, the English retail bank by Banco Santander, the biggest Spanish bank, in 2005 evidenced. The overall goal was to reduce Abbey's cost base by 20%. Consolidation has accelerated in recent years but the rational for acquisitions has changed. Thus, one reason is that most assets that private banks seek are not new assets, but are already being managed by competitors. Consequently, aggressive growth strategies to capture wealth creation worldwide require acquisitions. Regardless whether we consider costs, growth, or a combination of both, resources are always a crucial issue.

According to the resource-based view of the firm,[5] every company is a collection of unique resources and capabilities that provide the basis for its strategy and the primary source of its returns. To grow organically, a firm would have to acquire resources in the form of inputs such as capital, equipment, knowledge, and people, independently in the new market. In addition, the expanding firm would require new capabilities, conceptualized as the capacity for a set of resources to perform a task or action, which would not be available within the organization. Therefore, individual resources would not increase the firm's competitiveness. To form competitive advantage, synergistic combination, and integration of sets of resources is indispensable. It is ascertained that, e.g., global banks cannot rely on organic growth if they want to be leading wealth managers. On the other hand, established midtier private banks should strengthen its domestic position before expanding globally. There are some banks that credibly claim to be a top 20 wealth manager, but a closer look often reveals that this is the result of very profitable domestic businesses. Universal banks such as Bank of America, Citigroup, JP Morgan Chase, Wells Fargo, HSBC, Royal Bank of Scotland, ABN Amro, or BNP Paribas earn on average 70% of their revenues from their respective home retail markets. The large-scale domestic consolidation in European markets such as the United Kingdom, Italy, Germany, France, Spain, or Switzerland shows a similar picture than in the United States where a number of players have a global presence that is weaker than it is at home. Evidence suggests that leading players have established and grown their wealth management franchise by scaling up their international private banking operations from their home market.

The lack of organic growth forces these institutes for acquisitions. To take this assumption up, we suggest restructuring as a key investment theme for successful acquisitions. Over time there have become fewer and fewer true merger and acquisition stories within the banking industry. While many banks offer restructuring potential, we would like to elaborate the levers of a strong domestic position for profitable growth further with the acquisition and restructuring story of Julius Baer.

## *Acquisition and Restructuring Comes Down to Management*

Julius Baer that roots date back to the nineteenth century has become the third largest Swiss wealth manager (behind UBS and Credit Suisse) following the acquisition of the independent private banks Ferrier Lullin, Ehinger Armand von Ernst, Banca di Lugano, and the asset management business GAM (Global Asset Management) from UBS, for a total price of about CHF 6 billion in September 2005. Although, Julius Baer operates on the fields of private banking and asset management for private and institutional clients, similar patterns apply as for universal banks. A decisively client-centric approach as well as premium investment products combined with comprehensive investment expertise is the strengths of Julius Baer. With more than 4,200 employees in over 30 locations worldwide, the Group managed assets amounting to CHF 364 billion as of June 30, 2008.

Bankers have questioned the high price for purchasing the private banks as an unofficial rule, say that usually not more than 2.5% of the asset under management of the acquired institute should be paid. According to this practice, Julius Baer should not have paid more than CHF 5 billion. Raymond J. Baer, the president of the board, justified the high price with that they bought more than just assets under management. Accordingly, the deal includes intangible value. In particular, the acquisition of GAM provided the bank with access to superior investment products for its clients. Although the management believes that the new Julius Baer Group is more than the sum of its parts, we put the gains in relation to the net margin (income divided by the average assets under management) to show that the deal, at least at the time being, reduced the bank's profitability. Besides this calculation, the deal implied several other challenges. The two most important risks we need to understand are the bank's gearing to financial markets and the fact that no acquisition goes entirely smoothly. In addition to the mentioned risks, there are usually other elements of uncertainty occurring in acquisitions. This means you can never be sure whether the management team does get along or whether relationship managers of the private bank leave following the integration. From experience, we know that in private banking acquisitions, an average of 10% of a target's client base is lost in the first year following the transaction. Only if a deal has no client overlap, you can assume that there will be no lost assets under management. Another contentious issue is always the taking of client assets from a relationship manager. This typically happens when two relationship managers are servicing the same client. At Julius Baer, there was luckily no overlap among the client bases of the acquired firms and Julius Baer. Regarding the management team, we have seen within the banking industry that excellent management teams are able to overdeliver when it comes to restructuring. In particular, the relationship and collaboration of the key positions, in our case that of the CEO and the heads of private banking and asset management, can really boost a share price through a successful restructuring.

Overall, the upside potential outweighed the risks and has made Julius Baer a true restructuring story. The deal doubled the bank's assets under management and gained synergies including revenues from cross-selling GAM products. In addition, the private banking business increased its gross margin by selling in more hedge fund[6] products. What is striking though is that two years after the date of the acquisition announcement, Julius Baer has positioned its brand as a truly dedicated global wealth manager. Julius Baer's clear strategy and business model that focuses on managing wealth for HNWI can be seen as competitor advantage. Thus, there is no direct exposure to the subprime mortgage market. The bank's full dedication to view their clients at the center, rather than capital market debtors, is what wealthy clients actually expect from their private bank.

## *How to Become the Largest Wealth Manager in Just 10 Years*

The case of UBS evidences that organic growth and growth by mergers and acquisitions should be complementary strategies. Irrespective of the problems UBS is currently facing as an integrated bank, we decided to elaborate its growth strategy by emphasizing on the bank's wealth management division. All of the firms that make up today's UBS Group look back on a long and illustrious history. The two Swiss predecessor banks, Union Bank of Switzerland (UBS) and Swiss Bank Corporation (SBC), came into being in the nineteenth century. In the late 1980s, neither of UBS' Swiss antecedents were prominent outside its domestic market, nor did either rank among the top 20 global banks. In Switzerland though, both were well positioned. Measured by balance sheet size, their combined market share reached as high as 50%. In the early 1990s, the two Swiss banks were commercial banks operating mainly out of Switzerland. It is in the past decade that the current identity of UBS began to take concrete shape.

The two banks shared a similar vision, namely to become a world leader in wealth management and a global bulge-bracket investment bank with a strong position in global asset management, while remaining an important commercial and retail bank in Switzerland. Union Bank of Switzerland, the largest and best-capitalized Swiss bank, opted to pursue a strategy of organic growth, or expansion by internal means without any growth from takeovers, mergers, and acquisitions. In contrast, SBC, then the third-largest Swiss bank, decided to take another route by starting a joint venture with O'Connor & Associates, a leading US derivatives firm that was fully acquired by SBC in 1992. O'Connor was noted for its young, dynamic, and innovative culture, its meritocracy, and team orientation. It brought SBC state-of-the-art risk management and derivatives technology. In 1994, SBC acquired Brinson Partners – one of the leading US-based institutional asset management firms. Both the O'Connor and Brinson deal represented fundamental steps in the development of the firm's products and processes. The next major steps followed in 1995, when

SBC merged with SG Warburg, the British merchant bank, and the old-established investment bank Dillon Read, New York in 1997. The deals helped to fill SBC's strategic gaps in corporate finance, brokerage, research, and investment banking business in the United States. Most importantly, it brought with it an institutional client franchise, which is still at the core of today's equities business.

The merger of Swiss Bank Corporation and Union Bank of Switzerland in 1998 brought together these two leading Swiss financial institutions, creating the world leader in private banking and improving the new firm's chances of becoming a complete investment bank, not to mention providing it with greater capital strength. The Boards decided that the new leading global financial services group would operate under the name of UBS Group. The rationale for this merger was that ongoing globalization and deregulation of the international financial markets, tougher global competition, and the resulting worldwide wave of consolidation in the financial service industry have made size an increasingly critical factor for any financial service provider with ambitions to be amongst the most successful players worldwide. Nevertheless, there was still a major item left on the firm's broader strategic agenda. It needed to garner a significant presence in the key US market to be fully credible as a truly global player in investment banking and wealth management. That was achieved when PaineWebber became a part of the UBS Group in 2000. The advent of PaineWebber dramatically changed the demographic and cultural balance of UBS. Before the deal, UBS was still essentially Swiss, with two-third of its almost 50,000 staff based on its home country. At the end of 2007, we count just one-third Swiss employees out of its 84,000 employees. As a measure of its success in creating a truly global firm, UBS now earns the greater share of its operating income outside Switzerland. The bank's workforce is distributed globally, with a very sizeable presence of 32,000 people in one of the world's largest financial market, the United States.

Since the merger in 1998, UBS has made enormous progress in all its strategic markets. In doing so, it has reaped the rewards of the transformation that started in the late 1980s. Within its growth strategy, the bank has incorporated a number of wealth managers into a single integrated global firm with a common set of aspirations and values. Within its European wealth management initiative, the bank acquired since 2004 Lloyds (France), Merrill Lynch (Germany), Laing & Cruickshank and Scott Goodman Harris both in the United Kingdom, American Express Bank (Luxembourg), Sauerborn Trust (Germany), and Etra SIM (Italy). Further, overseas acquisitions included Dresdner Bank (Latin America), Julius Baer (North America), Piper Jaffray and McDonald Investments in the United States, Banco Pactual (Brazil), Caisse Centrale de Réescompte Group from Commerzbank (France), and VermogensGroep (Netherlands). These additions have helped UBS to expand its international wealth management presence significantly, added clients, and increased invested assets. Although UBS has flourished over the past 20 years due to beneficial conditions such as the combination of low interest rates, booming asset markets, and rising demand for credit, the results from the case suggest that strength can only be sustained if a firm continuously develops the ability to adapt to changing conditions and understands how to manage its risks.

Between the end of 2004 and the end of 2007, UBS' balance sheet increased by more than 40%, with UBS Global Wealth Management and Business Banking reporting invested assets under management of more than CHF 2.3 trillion. In little more than a decade, UBS became the world's largest wealth manager with a market share of invested assets of around 3.5%. However, in little more than 1 year, since summer 2007, the subprime crisis is giving way to disastrous value destruction for the brand. UBS has become the most mauled European financial player in the global credit crisis with about CHF 50 billions in subprime- and mortgage-related writedowns. The underestimation of risks not only clouds the investment banking's future, rather it could also hurt UBS' core wealth management business.

Regardless whether a company is merging or acquiring to achieve top line revenue growth, it needs stringent risk management and long-term strategies of enhancing shareholder value once the transition is completed, and initial and obvious savings have been made. Through the process of acquisitions, a firm must remain focused on building an integrated business and an open innovation culture that is shared by all business groups – both essential ingredients for a continued success of any firm. The example of UBS that bought over 30 institutes in the last 6 years or HSBC with over 60 smaller acquisitions shows that the consolidation process and merger endgame are not finished yet. The consolidation that has taken place in the banking industry since the beginning of the century is a strategic response to globalization and reflects a business background, demanding greater competitiveness and efficiency. Consolidation is an economic and cost imperative rather than an operational necessity. Most institutes have been engaged in a battle to establish and strengthen supremacy in an increasingly competitive market. The consolidation of their resources with their competitors plays an important role in coping with increasing growth and profitability expectations of their shareholders. The recent crisis may even amplify the process of consolidation as some institutes are hit so hard that they have to sell their profitable businesses to comply with the regulatory capital requirements.[7]

The strategic value of growth is based upon a complementary strategy that balances organic growth and growth by acquisition, and that depends on aligning everyone and everything around a single set of corporate goals. Not to forget the stringent risk management that banks must not neglect in the pursuit of growth. However, growth can be achieved by looking at business opportunities along several dimensions. It is suggested that companies develop their growth strategies based not only on core competencies but also on assets that are hard to replicate by competitors. In particular, for geographical expansion, as one of the most powerful options for growth, local expertise in the form of relationship capital is a crucial success factors.

## *Global Expansion Strategies*

Embracing opportunities in new markets is one promising strategy to grow. Firms compete aggressively to grow at above market average and capture a disproportionate share of net new asset growth. There are two ways of doing business, namely by accessing markets through local operations domestically (onshore) or internationally (offshore). Offshore means that the firm does business out of its jurisdiction and tax domicile. Where some simplify offshore banking with tax optimization, others justify it with that there are many places in the world where people are uncomfortable with the political, economical, and social context. In these countries, wealthy people wish to invest their money outside the country. There is no common sense whether offshore banking remains significant or whether it decreases in importance. However, emerging hubs in Singapore or Eastern Europe may replace traditional offshore hubs such as Switzerland in the near future. Even so, there is tendency that the onshore model is replacing the traditional offshore private banking model gradually as the regulatory environment is developing and getting more sophisticated.

One strategy of global banks is expanding their wealth management franchise to emerging markets, predominantly to markets such as Brazil, Russia, India, and China (BRIC), Eastern Europe, or the commodity-driven Middle East. This makes sense, as in particular, the BRIC markets have in common that there is almost unlimited workforce, massive potential of consumers, and high gross domestic product growth. In addition, the three billion people have an optimal age pyramid. If we look at emerging markets' economic performance, innovations, use in technology, or education, we have to acknowledge their progress and classify many of them as emerged. Even though, there are other factors such as human welfare and rights or political stability that setback their growth. However, the development, driven by globalization, open, and free trade over the past two decades, is now entering a new stage as the next wave of developing economies is welcomed into the fold. Visionary leaders should thus assess early-stage investment opportunities in so-called "frontier markets." These economies are not yet developed enough to be called "emerging markets" but will become the next emerging markets. This is part of a natural progression as today's emerging markets are considered as developed with already fierce competition. To name some of these economies, we would like to refer to the Morgan Stanley Capital International (MSCI) recently published index of 19 frontier markets: Bulgaria, Croatia, Estonia, Kazakhstan, Romania, Slovenia, Ukraine, Kenya, Mauritius, Nigeria, Tunisia, Bahrain, Kuwait, Oman, Qatar, United Arab Emirates, Lebanon, Sri Lanka, and Vietnam.[8] For all – emerging and in particular frontier markets – expanding domestic franchises comes with a high proportion of incalculable risk. It is a capital-intensive route and therefore pursued especially by larger firms that have the capacity to get over a loss-making investment.

The other route to grow is focusing on mature Continental European and US markets, which are effectively the world's largest wealth management markets. These markets require regional organization that is already provided by a number of established firms. Because clients in these markets increasingly want to be able to call on financial expertise close to home, many banks attempt to strengthen their international presence essentially with local footprints. The problem is that there are barriers to entry. For instance, building up a distribution network in international onshore countries with internal resources (organically) may be dissatisfying. A lack of deep and interpersonal relationships with local businesses and contacts to governments in these new markets entails increased management complexity and risks. Local rivals have developed strong ties to a number of stakeholders over years that yield trust in business partnerships and trust and recognition of customers in the bank. Relationships are a valuable resource and cannot be duplicated for historical and political reasons.

Let us briefly illustrate the current challenges with the failure of Citigroup in the German market. Citigroup just copied regional rivals in Germany like Deutsche Bank. Accordingly, Citi's onshore banks were weak and margins were squeezed by competing genuine national banks that have stronger social capital. As a result of the underestimation of culture together with increasing subprime losses, Citi sold its German banking operations in July 2008 to Crédit Mutuel of France for US $7.7 billion. The future will show whether Crédit Mutuel is able to integrate the 340 branches and satisfy the 3.3 million customers in Germany. Similar was experienced by Merrill Lynch, which illustrates that implementing an onshore strategy is not without difficulties. Relationship managers thought that they could be what they were in the United States to clients in Europe, but it quickly became apparent that it is not easy to go head to head against the heavily entrenched and powerful domestic banks. The increasing pressure on multinational firms to become *local* is clearly one of the major challenges of globalization. Certainly, there are also success stories. The unofficial best-in-class in geographic coverage is HSBC – "The global local bank." The trend of the onshore model has played to the group's strength of solid domestic franchises. The bank has been busy expanding in emerging markets – also with investments into local financial institutes. The bank that was born in China in 1865 by the Scotsman Thomas Sutherland and a group of international traders who founded the Hong Kong and Shanghai Banking Corporation to finance trade between China and Europe is returning there. It became the first foreign bank to open a rural branch in China with today more than 60 retail outlets. Similar to other global firms, HSBC is standardizing processes, technology, and management information systems to leverage global scale. At the same time, they accept private banking as a local business where they position themselves as a natural competitor to the Swiss alternative.

For this time, let us just analyze the wealth management businesses as most banks in Europe have had a rather conservative approach to investment banking, knowing that it is hard to beat the top Wall Street investment banks. Ironically, HSBC's penchant for being local is partly why it did not come out of the subprime meltdown untouched. We observed that wealth management firms have made a number of acquisitions in Europe to attract clients in the United Kingdom, Italy, Germany, France, and Spain. As previously indicated, these countries account for ~80% of potential wealth investments in Europe.

## *Why Size Matters*

We have to face that in a global business environment, size matters in the pursuit of growth. To focus on future challenges such as international growth, firms need to be able to invest abroad. Size gives them the identity, positioning, and power to invest in the expansion of international businesses. Critical size in growth markets ensuring local knowledge and proximity combined with traditional private banking culture and entrepreneurial spirit is vital. We believe that in the future of banking, size is bound to play an even bigger role. It is clear that only a big bank is going to have the money and power to operate globally. To be recognized as an active player in the ongoing consolidation process, wealth managers need to have a critical mass of at least US $70 billion client assets managed. Institutes with such volumes include much know-how and are able to develop more innovative products and services and distribute them globally on various channels. This gives them the capacity to provide a demanding and sophisticated clientele with local tailor-made solutions.

In a service industry, the advantages of economies of scale are unarguable. Banking is not like selling computer software, where you can distribute thousands of copies for quite the same high price per unit. In contrast to such service industries, it is rather labor intensive. Certainly, the more client assets the institute manages, the greater the deals it gets from suppliers. Alternatively, if a client advisor manages 1,000 accounts instead of 300, he or she is usually paid the same salary. In spite of these mechanisms, we must not forget that in particular in private banking customers expect an individual and intensive care. Another advantage of firms with a strong international franchise is that they have the capacity to subsidize their international growth initiatives with other lucrative businesses.

As discussed so far, there is certainly every motivation for banks to consolidate. Besides the importance of size and growth, acquisitions, on the other hand, import risks and a large organization. Although there are forces that support size, scale, and global reach, large companies may imply a need for bureaucratically led rigid organizational structures. The challenge is to capture the benefits of growth, while at the same time staying alert, agile, entrepreneurial, client-centric, and global in thinking. This kind of business model implies a management style, which reinforces values of partnership, of collegiality and of teamwork. In general, companies should only be open for acquisitions, as long as the potential acquisitions meet the firm's specific hurdles. These include strategic fit, cultural fit, financial attractiveness and, most important, outweigh the benefit of repurchasing the firm's own shares.

Usually, banks with less aggressive international growth strategies focus on their home market. This becomes apparent if we look at Switzerland, which is one of the three largest wealth management markets (after the United States and United Kingdom) with assets under management of US $6.4 trillion as of the end of 2007. This accounts to about a tenth of the world's total assets under management. Switzerland is acknowledged as home base for private banking and is to remain a key pillar. Swiss private banks are traditional and respectable institutions. The service quality provided is not something that can easily be copied by competitors or adapted to other markets. Focusing on the domestic market and benefiting from size in Switzerland, as smaller banks may seek to sell out, might be an opportunity instead of taking risks abroad. One could say that smaller and specialized wealth managers, headquartered in Switzerland, have no need for global expansion. The consolidation in the industry tells a story closer to the Julius Baer case, where they strengthen their business in Switzerland and use the strong domestic position as hub for global expansion.

## *Competitive Positioning*

Top performers have learned from own experience and watching the market. They know exactly how to activate the levers of asset pool sizes and growth rates to generate value. Their strategy is to simultaneously grow organically, make acquisitions, and improve performance and capital allocation. The firm's capacity to access asset pools and extract sufficient value through the right distribution model is as important as managing a business portfolio. Latter means to establish growth platforms by acquiring small local players to build complementary capabilities and then leveraging own knowledge. Overall aim should be pushing profitability above cost of equity. This strategy to value creation has been recently evidenced at a number of large players. Usually, the logic of shareholder value-oriented firm is to grow and then return capital to shareholders. In fact, in the absence of the need to finance acquisitions, a firm can choose to return excess capital to shareholders by buying back its own shares. This form of optimizing the firm's capital allocation by returning it to their shareholder is what keeps them investing. Consequently, equity will further decrease and earnings per share increase with a relatively constant market capitalization.

To grow and thrive on competition, governments and regulators are jointly responsible. They are asked to advance and push the competitiveness of their financial centers. A strong and efficient financial industry is ultimately hiking a country's economic growth. To see the connection, just look at Germany's once impressive Deutsche Bank. Twenty years ago, Deutsche Bank was Europe's largest bank. It has gradually lost competitive edge and is today, ranked by market value, hardly a top 10 bank, far behind banks from the United Kingdom or rising French and Swiss giants, not to mention the Chinese banks that are currently the largest in the world. Even new competitors from Italy and Spain – products of banking privatization and deregulation – are threatening Germany's financial industry. The reasons for the new economic dynamism can be explained with deregulation and consolidation throughout Europe that has created profitable banking conglomerates. This is in contrast to Germany where banks hovered along, frozen out of two-thirds of their own home market by some 450 inflexible public banks and additional over 1,500 other financial institutes. A coalition of politicians has managed to fend off deregulation and globalization, but the price for the unwillingness to change and open markets is high.

## *Learning to Grow with a Chief Growth Officer*

Corporate performance over the long term indicates that growth is the most important driver of value in the capital markets. The dilemma, though, is not to let short-term goals undermine sustainable growth strategies. To oversatisfy analysts expectations short term, chief financial officers are tempted to hold back on discretionary, spending such as research and development for product and service innovations or advertising and marketing if they were in danger of missing quarterly profit numbers. We learned that a more disciplined approach to growth is needed, in which short-term financial pressure should not undermine initiatives that will pay off in the longer term. To make this clear, underinvestment in growth does never pay off, as it would impair a firm's products, services, and brand. Therefore, we strongly suggest detaching the financial authority from taking growth and innovation decisions and adding a new box on the organizational chart with the mandate to develop the right structure, conduct, capabilities, and culture for growth.

Although growth has recently risen to the top of corporate agenda, just a few firms installed dedicated functions that are determined to become true growth leaders. However, some forward-looking firms have realized the importance and have carved out a new executive position. This so-called *chief growth officer* supports the chief executive officer (CEO), as most CEOs are experienced in assessing people and organizations rather than ideas. The first reaction to that new role, coming from manufacturing firms of the United States, might be mild, especially in Europe and the rest of the world but a closer look shows potential. The main purpose of the chief growth officer is to identify and target new global growth initiatives and to deliver profitable growth by creating substantial platforms for businesses on that the firm can grow. Besides the responsibility to find value-enhancing revenue opportunities, he or she acts as a role model for sustainable and profitable growth. The chief growth officer is a portfolio manager and in charge of prioritizing the firm's short-term and long-term opportunities. Therefore, he or she must oversee sales, marketing, technology, product and service development, and new business ventures with focus on the most promising growth initiatives, and weed out the least profitable ones. This requires not only extensive line experience with operating responsibility, but also good diplomatic and negotiation skills as financial executives and risk manager will always challenge growth strategies. What separates growth leaders from their peers is the ability to create better organizational capabilities and a sustainable supportive culture. In such culture, the team is greater than single ideas. The team evolves an idea based on what it learns about customers, opportunities, and capabilities and brings it as fully fledged proposal through the chief growth officer to the top management of the firm.

In November 2006, Zurich Financial Services Group, an insurance-based financial services provider with a global network of subsidiaries and offices, appointed the former group finance director to the group managing board in the role of the chief growth officer. He will particularly have responsibility for managing a newly created growth council and assuring alignment of critical business processes with the company's growth targets. The announcement of this new position is based on the firms rigid cost-saving history over the past 5 years. While Zurich Financial Services almost exclusively focused on initiatives to increase efficiency, the insurance neglected innovation and growth strategies. Certainly, the firm managed a successful turnaround but it lost competitiveness. This becomes clear if we look at Axa – one of its main competitors. Axa has gained a good reputation of being a real leader in profitable growth, increased live assurance premium by about 20%, four times more than Zurich Financial Services. Since Axa delivered a total shareholder return over the past years that outperforms that of the Zurich Financial Service beyond means, it is time to change and shift the behaviors, capabilities, and culture for growth. The chief growth officer may be a first answer to develop cultural conditions necessary to foster growth but also innovation and brand building as these disciplines are adherent.

## *Keep Focused and Develop the Brand*

One consequence of merger and acquisitions is often brand confusion. The brand shows the size and power of a company and intimate client relationship. Brands reflect desires and propositions. They steer our behavior and influence our opinion whether we trust, buy a product, or use a service of a certain company or not. There are different sets of branding in private banking, those that project themselves as wealth manager units of international banks such as Citigroup Private Bank, Credit Suisse Private Banking, or Deutsche Bank Private Wealth Management and those smaller wealth managers whose brands are named after their founders such as Coutts, Julius Baer, or Pictet & Cie. Where the universal banks attract mainly prospects that are new to private banking, the others typically promote their heritage and attract old money and families that seek discretion and prestige. Branding is becoming increasingly important in private banking as they operate in the luxury business. It is particularly important in attracting and retaining profitable clients. Looking back to the 1970s, Pictet & Cie, a renowned private bank in Switzerland, had no logo, no advertisement, and the name Pictet did not even appear on their buildings. It was common practice to be discreet. The bank evolved and moved, over time, from discretion to greater visibility and is today recognized as a major brand in private banking. This transition was a cultural revolution, as Jacques de Saussure, Partner at Pictet & Cie noted. What started at Pictet in the 1990s to make the brand reflecting the firm's evolution is nowadays a generally accepted communications strategy. This means that the brand must reflect constant values such as reputation, integrity, excellent quality, discretion, and long-term survival but also the firm's agility. As banking has been changing, it is a challenge to ensure a constant adequacy between the brand and a firm's business activities. In particular, if global expansion is part of the strategy.

Most brand rankings assess the risk profile of earnings forecast. Interbrand, for example, examines brands through the lens of financial strength, importance in driving consumer selection, and the likelihood of ongoing branded revenue. The analysis also includes market leadership, stability, and global reach – or the ability of an organization to cross both geographical and cultural borders. Including all these factors generates a discount rate, which is applied to brand earnings to get a net present value. It is believed that the net present value comes closest to representing a brand's true economic value. If we look at the recent table of 2008, it is remarkable that the first ranked companies of the service sector – in spite of the financial crisis – are exclusively banks. Although far behind top-ranked companies such as Coca Cola, Microsoft, or IBM, Citi was ranked on 19 with a calculated brand value of US $20 billion. Citi's success can be explained with the launch of their new brand campaign in 2002. Once the world's largest bank, Citi unveiled its new image through a global campaign that highlights the unparalleled capabilities of this vast and unique business. The advertising campaign emphasizes one or more core strengths that bound together with the new tagline "This is Citigroup, tell the complete Citigroup story." Citigroup's quest to generate more revenues from international markets is leveraging its brand value to emerging markets. If we pick out firms in the financial service sector from the brand ranking, HSBC (27), Merrill Lynch (34), JP Morgan (33), JP Morgan (37), Goldman Sachs (37), and UBS (41).

Opinions are divided over this issue. Some argue that multibranding strategies remain typical for more product-driven industries. Companies must always view brands through the eyes of their customers. In fact, companies might think that they own their brands, but customers think that they have a stake in them and hence branding managers need the customer's permission to make changes – at least to a certain extent. Henri de Castries, the CEO of Axa, recently emphasized the importance of their one-brand strategy. Because the brand must be respected as it is part of the firm's culture and history and valued by customers and employees, he will not act like Napoleon. Nevertheless, he stated that it is a question of time until the name Winterthur disappears from the corporate landscape. The trend toward a one-brand strategy is reflected in the financial service industry by a number of large firms such as Axa, Credit Suisse, Merrill Lynch, or UBS just to name a few. Other multinational firms are to follow these examples. In contrast, the Royal Bank of Scotland, for instance, retains multibrand strategies, at least for some of their businesses. HSBC as well has adopted a slow approach to consolidation of brand recognizing the importance of specific brands to clients.

Main criteria for the decision to collapse brands of a group and focus on one name are factors such as innovative products, competitive prices, or technical primacy, and above all, customers want a bank of the size and expertise they can rely on. Generally, a firm's adoption of a single brand for all its businesses illustrates the ultimate ambition to client focus for expansion and innovation. It is clear that rebranding is accompanied with enormous marketing efforts. In addition, firms have to adapt structures, processes, and services thoroughly down to application architectures and shared systems. Customers all over the world benefit from these improvements, in the way that they can access services provided by the various business units of the same firm without even noticing it. Seamless resource sharing is often reflected in integrated client service models, as one attempt to leverage a *one-firm* philosophy. Although the improvements coming from an integrated firm are difficult to quantify, significant strategic advantages can be achieved through resource sharing among different organizational units. More about the benefits and threats of integrated banks is discussed in the last chapter of this book.

## *Leveraging Innovation to Grow*

To recapitulate, growth has always been and still is the ultimate goal of companies – at least in a capitalistic economic system. There are a number of growth opportunities. Stimulating client needs, winning new clients, improving the service level of existing clients, or growing through cross-selling is just one building block for growth. Another building block can be seen in the area of products and services. Developing new products and services, improving existing products and services, or bundling them to new value-adding solutions might accelerate demand. In addition, there is potential for growth by developing new distribution channels and exploring new markets. Here, collaboration with suppliers as well as distributors must be part of strategic thinking. A key challenge for managers is balancing organic growth and growth by acquisition. What strategy ever we emphasize the importance of profitable growth.

Within this section, we also attempted to explain brand value. To portray brand value in simplified terms, it is the recognition how stakeholders perceive a company. It offers an extra value, i.e., one in addition to the company value or product or service. It is assumed that the success of a company's growth strategy is linked with its brand value. Understanding sustained and profitable growth just by looking at the brand value rankings or annual reports is impossible. We need to concentrate on the process that created those results and influenced shareholder to invest in a brand. As shareholders, clientele, workforce, products all are spread around the globe, we need to dive into communications strategy. Therefore, firms that aim to expand internationally need to slice its advertising campaigns along dimensions such as geography and customer segments. This sounds logical but we often recognize global marketing campaigns without considering market specifications or customer segmentation schemes. For successful global expansion, we must understand and respect the cultures of the individual markets.

On the long run, sustainable growth can only be achieved either by increasing the labor hours that is required to produce a product or service or by increasing productivity. This is particularly difficult for developed economies with almost full employment, high labor hours, and productivity at high level. Leveraging these drivers is therefore hardly possible. Pursuing innovation with the primary objective to grow is suggested as the solution. Some companies have been strengthening their innovation activities for good reason – it simply turns out. Innovative companies have superior long-term stock market performance as a study by the Boston Consulting Group shows (see Fig. 2).[9] Accordingly, global innovators that encompass the top 25 most innovative companies overall had a median annualized shareholder return of 14.3% from 1996 to 2005, a full 300 basis points better than that of the S&P Global 1,200 median. The survey confirmed for all regions that innovative companies have the capacity to generate more total shareholder return. The reason for that outperformance was these companies' ability to expand margins at a superior rate without sacrificing growth.

Considering innovation as key driver for growth seems to be the logical conclusion. We must understand the process itself that tells us which innovations lead to new growth. That is important because growth can only be achieved if aligned with innovation strategy. The aim of the next section is to first explain innovation and then align growth strategies and innovation strategies.

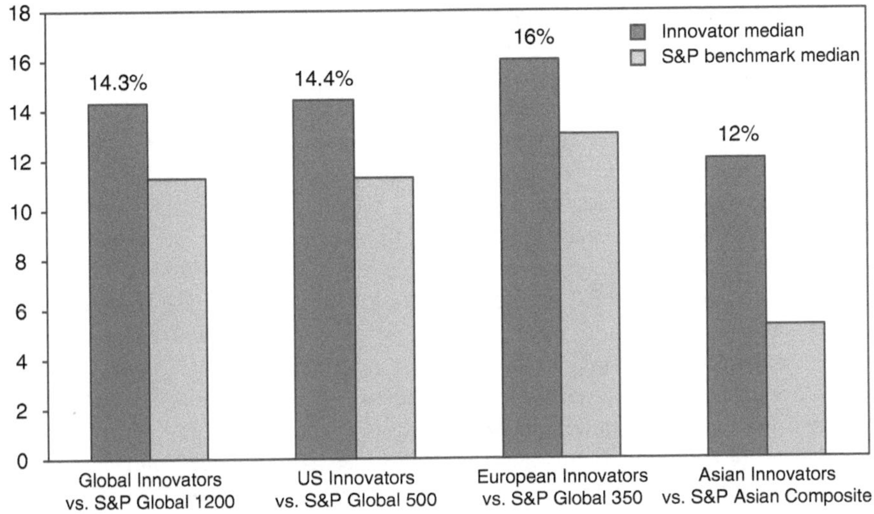


**Fig. 2** Ten-year annualized total shareholder return for innovative companies vs. relevant benchmark from 1996 to 2005

# The Power of Innovation

## *What Is Innovation?*

The term *innovation* is understood diversely and therefore a variety of interpretations is found in the literature. Without going into deep discussion about the Latin verb *innovare*, which means "to make something new," it can be said that innovation is a term broadly used for any kind of novelty. In terms of business, it commonly refers to the act of introducing a new product or service into the market or improving existing things. Whatsoever, innovation is used not only for products and services but also for concepts, strategies, and paradigms. Innovation comes in many different forms, from the truly revolutionary to the almost mundane. It involves the creation of new designs and ways of doing things, their commercial exploitation, and subsequent diffusion through the rest of the economy and society. Innovation is one of the main engines of long-run economic growth and structural change and has always driven economic progress. Innovation is the cornerstone of the Lisbon strategy, which was drawn up by the European Council in March 2000 to render the European Union, the most competitive and dynamic, knowledge-based economy in the world by 2010.[10] Accordingly, we understand innovation as:

- The renewal and enlargement of the range of products and services and the associated markets
- The establishment of new methods of production, supply, and distribution
- The introduction of changes in management, work organization, and the working conditions and skills of the workforce

We state that innovativeness is the property of being an innovation. But the understanding of innovation depends on the perspective from which it is viewed. From a general economic point of view, the innovation must increase value for the firm, the consumer, or the producer. For consumers, innovation means higher quality and better value goods, more efficient services, and a higher standard of living. Enterprises, on the other hand, expect more efficient production processes, improved business models, or new products and services, which lead toward sustained, improved growth, and higher profits for owners and investors. Employees may see benefits such as new and more interesting work, improved skills, and higher wages coming out of innovations. From an organizational perspective, firms without innovation would not survive because new products and services, and new or improved ways of doing business are vitally important for business continuity and growth. Hence, failure to innovate equals failure to differentiate equals failure to gain the profits needed to attract investors. In sum, innovation is about creating value and increasing productivity in any industry or economy. Innovation can deliver increased revenues, enhanced value added, and stronger sustainable competitive advantage. Since the creativity and inventiveness of companies are a country's greatest assets, for the economy as a whole, innovation is the key to higher productivity and greater prosperity for all.

It is essential to understand that innovation has its origin in almost all imaginable areas. These include not only management and leadership styles, processes, product and service development, but also the meanings and beliefs, which employees assign to organizational conduct and corporate culture. Later show how innovation influences individual's motivation and the way they behave. It is essential to understand how innovation helps to develop a better understanding for reaching and servicing customers, production techniques and methods, product quality, approaches to information and knowledge management, forms of partnerships, or management and stakeholder participation.

As the economic benefits of the successful exploitation of novelty are captured by enterprises rather than by universities and research laboratories, companies are constantly forced to innovate by pressure and trends, notably competition and growth. In respect of the different strands of thoughts on innovation, we believe that novelty is vital to companies and occurs from the four main routes, namely invention, value innovation, imitation and adaptation, and open business models.

## *Invention*

The industrial economic model of investing into innovation is through research and development (R&D). The exploitation of invention arising out of the research laboratory is an important and much studied route to innovation. Research is a major contributor to innovation, generating a flow of technical ideas and continually renewing the pool of technical skills. Invention as a source of innovation is commonly associated with *technology push*. This means identifying an interesting technology, making a product out of it, and finally, searching for a marketplace.

To specify, inventions produce the technological push for the development of new products, processes, and services. In theory, the rate of research and development expenses should correlate with the rate of revenues. To prove the sustainability of the current business model, the two curves should grow similar. Research and development is therefore a fundamental component of innovation-led growth. This is vital because new products and services or improved processes drive competitive advantage in companies. While the R&D model has a long tradition in manufacturing, it cannot easily be adapted to services due to the absence of a physical product. We will discuss these differences later on in this book.

In general, we can say that innovation is not dependent on invention in any direct manner. Companies have not necessarily to invent to innovate. Regarding history, a prominent saying is that innovations come and go while inventions stay. Nevertheless, innovation has played a more important role in economics and business than the concept of invention as Josef A. Schumpeter claimed in the 1930s.[11] Accordingly, the social process, which produces innovations, differs economically as well as socially from the social process that accounts for inventions. Schumpeter identified innovation as the essential function of the entrepreneur, along with credit and profit maximization and repeatedly emphasized that innovation is possible without anything we should identify as invention, and invention does not necessarily induce innovation but produces of itself no economically relevant effect at all.

Although innovation is often confused with invention, the latter is nothing more than the first step in a process of bringing new ideas to widespread and effective use. Innovation is about adding value to inventions. Think of the invention of the credit card in the late 1960s. Besides the creation of a global partner network, a number of innovative services such as insurances and loyalty schemes finally increased value and made the credit card to an accepted payment method.

## *Value Innovation*

Value innovation places an equal emphasis on value and innovation for consumers, customers, and the company. The aim of this concept is to create growth strategies, new products, and services or just reconfigure existing products and services to present a radical change that will be perceived by customers as offering more or better value. The logic behind this is simply to do things completely differently or to change things radically. Value innovation explains new and fundamentally different ways of competing in an existing business, i.e., one that conflicts with the traditional way. In view of this, a strategic innovation occurs when a company identifies gaps in the industry and attempts to fill them. These gaps can be newly emerging customer segments and needs that are not served well by competitors, or new ways of producing, delivering, or distributing existing as well as new products and services to existing, or new customer segments. Thus, it breaks with past practice in at least three areas: value chain, design, and conceptualization of customer value and identification of potential customers. In particular, understanding customer value with sufficient precision is vital for companies that aspire to growth leadership. On the bottom line, it is the difference between benefits as perceived by customers and the price paid for a product or service.

Value innovation is not about striving to outperform the competition, nor is value innovation about segmenting the market and accommodating customers' individual needs and differences. Value innovators ignore current industry conditions, the competitive environment, and conventional strategic logic and look for blockbuster ideas and quantum leaps in buyer value to create new markets. They suggest placing the buyer (client), rather than the competition, in the center of strategic thinking. If smaller firms in the banking industry for instance act as value innovator, they accept that they cannot beat firms such as Citigroup, Bank of America, HSBC, or the like by playing their game. But it may be possible to prosper and survive by playing an entirely different game. Therefore, the only realistic hope of survival in a very competitive retail banking market that is taken by very large banks can be a strategy that is truly customer centered and focused on local needs.

The concept of value innovation is in stark contrast to competition-driven strategies as championed by Michael E. Porter in the 1980s.[12] Defending competitive space within the Porter model has been constantly eroded in today's dynamic and global economy, as entry and mobility barriers are relentlessly assailed. The proclaimed advantage of creating new marketspace as a result of redefined customer's hidden demand or to create totally new demand is in contrast to *market-pull* strategies. For the latter, a marketplace is first identified and then a product or service developed which meets that need. In the case of value innovation, companies are driven by the market. They accept the market structure as given and do not aim to change markets. Concentration lies on analyzing and understanding customer needs. Once this is known, products and services will be produced that satisfy the expressed desires of the customer. This consumer perspective points to the power of the market, where the market is the hub for the demand that inspires innovation. For example, in commercial banking, innovations in ATM and Internet-based offerings helped to create new value by breaking traditional compromises with respect of availability, reaching, and servicing customers. This corroborates the thesis that technological innovation and value innovation combined contribute to value creation.

## *Imitation and Adaptation*

Referring to Schumpeter, imitation is the third force of innovation after invention and innovation that involves commercialization of the invention. Although he warned that "swarms of imitators" can erode profits for pioneers and that imitation is a nonstrategic approach that leads to the diffusion of innovation, it is accepted today as a strategic route to innovation. Imitation is known as the approach where an initial innovation is taken from the same industry, developed, and improved further to the firm's advantage. Adaptation is close to imitation and is often used within the same breath. Adaptation is the approach where a company takes an idea from other business sectors or industries and adapts it for use in its own production processes or market. Adaptability is in essence the ability to reconfigure internal activities and processes to cope with the demands from its environment. One form of adaptation is adapting customer behavior. Some might have heard from the "adaptation–innovation theory,"[13] in which individuals tend to be either adaptors or innovators. This though can, of course, be adopted for organizations. Research found that banks in the 1980s and earlier generally developed their services by reacting to customer needs and adapting those needs to fit the bank's existing framework.[14] The adaptation approach is often pursued unconsciously whenever benchmarking is performed. As organizations strive for better performance, benchmarking has become increasingly important. In practice, this means observing, adapting, and copying best practice from others within the same industry as well as other industries and even other sectors. Thus, generated knowledge about current practice is often seen as precursor to changing and improving that practice. The fact that companies must benchmark to improve their activities and their competitiveness explains the increasing emphasis on organizational effectiveness.

The rationale behind imitation and adaptation is the fact that new product and service development ab initio is costly, risky, and time and resource consuming. Copying the latest technology, products, services, processes, or state-of-the-art practice and management strategy may be a useful approach for overcoming the uncertainty for doing things that have never been done before. Especially if other companies have been successful with it, there is no point in reinventing the wheel. Every success leaves clues and organizations are sometimes better off by just looking at what others have done, what worked, and why it worked and then copying the concept, and adapting it to make it their own. Former leading industrial enterprises, therefore, often find strong competition from innovative newcomers such as Intel, Microsoft, Sun, Oracle, Cisco, Genentech, or Amgen that conduct little research on their own. Imitation of R&D-intensive goods in the manufacturing sector is faster and less costly than in-house R&D. Even with patent protection, imitation occurs regularly and not long after innovation. The Japanese industry in the 1970s and 1980s evidenced that imitation can be a strategy that outperforms *real* inventors or innovators. In banking, we see that time for imitating and copying a competitor's product is shortening. This practice has been growing in recent years with structured investment products, which are designed to meet specific investor's needs that cannot be met from the standardized financial instruments available in the markets. Such packaged investments using derivatives to replicate market performance, sometimes linked to a money-back guarantee, are in Europe sold by national post offices, and in the United Kingdom even by supermarkets to their customer.

Although there is a plethora of simple structured investment products available, there is room on both the life insurance and the banking side. Nevertheless, launching products for distribution at the mass retail level calls for firms that do things differently, rather than just do things better. Imitation and adaptation alone are therefore not enough. Thus, all firms have the ability to break out of what may have become an inhibiting traditional modus operandi – and such ability could, in competitive and high-velocity markets, be more advantageous than in others. A later argument highlights the importance that firms should consider new business opportunities simultaneously.

## *Open Business Models*

Business model and strategy are confusing terms that are often used interchangeably. For both, there is no universally accepted definition of the term. The business model is distinct from strategy; however, understanding each of its components and how they interrelate can help managers to make better strategic decisions. Main difference is that a business model starts by seeking and creating value for the *customer* while strategy is mainly concerned with *competition*. A business model is an abstraction of a business, which identifies who the customers are, what the customer value is, and how the business makes money. Principally, it describes the mechanisms by which a business intends to generate revenue and profits. Thus, it provides a cognitive framework – a mental model on how inputs are transformed in value-adding outputs or economic value. Correspondingly, outputs are products and services that are performed by the processes and operations of the business. Ultimately, a business model is concerned with how to create *value for the business*, in contrast to strategy that seeks *value for the shareholder*. While the business model forms the underlying rational for being in business, the strategy is the plan of how to put that business model into action. The business model must create value in its ecosystem and must capture a portion of that value for the innovator, so that additional advancements will be forthcoming.

The pace of change has become so rapid that companies have to monitor the changing business environment continuously, and evolve and adapt their business model to reflect the changes. The crux is to balance these streams, otherwise it may cause a dysfunctional mismatch between today's business environment and the business models. Therefore, we suggest a more dynamic, open, and flexible approach to business models. Business models are used in strategic planning and have an impact on every organization, regardless of whether it is a new venture or an established large multinational company. One might argue that when a new business model changes the economics of an industry and is difficult to adapt or imitate by others, it could by itself create a strong competitive advantage. Many executives see their business model as a more important source of competitive advantage than their products as these particularly in the banking industry are becoming increasingly commoditized.

The effects of business model innovation are hard to predict. Moreover, they emerge over time and can transform the full breadth of the economy. For example, in recent times the shift from *marketplaces* consisting of sellers, buyers, and physical places where the two come together, to *marketspaces* where transactions take place free from the bonds of time and space has fundamentally altered the way companies interact with their customers. As the radical shift from physical places to virtual (information) spaces requires a shift in thinking on how to add value, companies have to adjust their strategies and business models accordingly and find out when virtual is virtuous. New business models are often driven by customer needs, technological innovations, or other changes in the business environment and affect a number of different types of innovations. In an open business environment where firms look outside their boundaries for ideas and knowledge, they can bring in, as well as license or provide their intellectual property to other firms. Henry Chesbrough talks in his latest book "Open Business Models" within this context of "division of innovation labor."[15] He states that an open business model utilizes this division of innovation labor for the creation of value but also to capture a portion of that value. Overall, *open* business models create value for customers as well as for the company by leveraging many more ideas, due to their inclusion of a variety of external concepts. It is therefore important to create new ideas with outside stakeholders by embracing open innovation and knowledge sharing.

## *Different Types of Innovation*

Having discussed the routes to innovation, there are after all different types and concepts of innovation. The understanding of various types of innovation is important, as there is a correlation between the type of innovation and organizational performance. Schumpeter, again, was one of the first to mention five types of innovation, namely product innovation, production process innovation, innovation in organization, new market behavior, and new raw material.[16] The current understanding is that product innovation is destined to resolve, circumvent, or eliminate a technical difficulty in manufacture or to improve services. Process innovation can be assigned to innovations for the purposes of saving inputs such as energy conservation or automation. Innovation in organization as the third major category aims to improve the conditions of work, in particular innovations in methods and management.

While product innovation is about what a company offers, process innovation is about the way of effectively and efficiently producing and bringing these offerings to markets. The general aim of process innovation is to reduce costs, improve efficiency, raise productivity, and increase profitability. These process innovations may affect and change industry and society radically as evidenced in history. First endeavors to improve processes in manufacturing had been made by Frederick Winslow Taylor who measured and reformed work processes around 1878 at the Midvale Steel Company in Philadelphia. His contribution to more efficient production processes became later known as *Taylorism* and changed management strategies and production significantly. Henry Ford's success with the Ford T-Model 35 years later was based on Taylor's concepts. Ford just designed and implemented processes and techniques that could be repeated identically and indefinitely. The *assembly line* as the next great process innovation was born. A recent application of Taylor's concept of separating the design of work from its execution is the *business process re-engineering* approach.[17] Focus here is on an organizational rather than an individual level, whereby any organization regardless of size, type, and objective operates fundamentally by transforming a collection of raw material for manufacturing industries and raw data for service industries into required outputs such as products or services. The pure focus was on fundamental rethinking and radical design of business processes with the objective of improving the quality, service, cost, and speed of core processes regardless of cultural or social values. The application of business process re-engineering transformed whole industries and has been considered retrospectively as a too mechanistic and radical approach by a large number of opponents. The main critique of this approach was that it ignored the importance of people, describing them as objects who handle processes. Retrospectively, we know that such view can have devastating social and macroeconomic consequences.

The two main types of innovation – process and product innovations, respectively, underlie different concepts. While innovation in the area of processes and business models is often seen from a strategic point of view and assigned to the concept of strategic innovation, new product development is often marketing related. However, later should not be mixed up with *marketing innovation*.[18] While the term is related to the improvement of customer-touching processes or consumer transactions to stimulate demand, others see it just as innovative design and presentation technique for new forms of positioning advertising, and differentiation. Marketing innovation is usually claimed to be the part of innovation strategy that reflects the recognition of new ways of organizing work in all areas of a company.

There is dispersion and variation in the interpretation of routes to innovation and types of innovation. In the next section, we would like to discuss innovation in an industry-related context.

## *Innovation in Different Industries*

Considering what the most innovative companies are, we often think of Apple, Google, 3M, Toyota, Microsoft, General Electric, Nokia, Sony, IBM, or Starbucks Coffee. Surely, these brands have dominated many rankings and press releases or have been used as case studies for numerous MBA studies and advanced management program. *But what does it take to be consistently recognized as top innovator and why are there no service firms or even banks?* Innovation capability and its management are clearly sector or industry specific, if not firm specific. Most attempts to explain innovation are based on research in the manufacturing sector. Further, innovation of intangible products and services is hard to measure. Tracking and assessing inputs, outputs, and innovation processes regardless whether we talk of incremental or radical (breakthrough) innovation require a set of metrics to measure them. Measurement of innovation in the service sector has low priority and what is more, few companies tie incentives to innovation metrics.

Our intention though is to emphasize the importance of the service sector and to discuss how different industries within this sector approach innovation. Therefore, we divided broadly two sectors, namely manufacturing and service. Table 1 compares the characteristics of sectors and shows differences that remain significant when conceptualizing services. Having understood the traits of the service sector, we turn to next and discuss innovation in the financial service industry. We then dive deeper and explain the characteristics of services in banking, and finally attempt to find answers how to measure success in service innovation.

**Table 1** Innovation system traits of manufacturing and service

| System trait | Manufacturing | Services |
|---|---|---|
| Product characteristics | • Tangible<br>• Easy to store<br>• High transport and distribution costs | • Intangible<br>• Easy to multiply and transport |
| R&D organization | • Project-oriented<br>• Budget-driven<br>• Research and development units aligned | • Chaotic<br>• Costs often not assignable<br>• Research often outsourced |
| R&D approach | • Systematic<br>• Scientific | • Ad hoc |
| Intellectual property rights | • Strong, patents | • Weak, copyright |
| Technology orientation | • Technology-push<br>• Science- and technology-led | • Technology/market-pull<br>• Consumer/client-led |
| Innovation approach | • Mainly in-house resources (except high-technology industry in certain clusters) | • External and internal sources combined |
| Innovation cycle | • Short | • Long |
| Innovation form | • Attempt to be radical | • Mainly incremental |
| Commercialization strategy | • Prototyping and testing | • Direct to markets |
| Knowledge condition | • Make use of existing scientific knowledge | • Create new service-specific knowledge |
| Time to market | • Short to very long (depends on industry and product) | • Relatively short (little need for research or acquiring scientific knowledge) |
| Innovativeness characteristics | • Big<br>• Technological | • Small<br>• Social |
| Spatial scale of system or reach | • From national to global | • From regional to national to global<br>• Many services are national because of law an regulatory constraints |
| Labor productivity | • Depends on industry (from very high in high-technology, computer, and software to low in heavy metal industries) | • In most industries very high (highest in financial services) |
| Physical capital | • High<br>• Ownership of production | • Low<br>• Outsourcing/leasing |

# Innovation in the Financial Services

## *Key Innovations That Changed Businesses*

Assuming that a product is anything that can be offered to a market for attention, purchase, utilization, or consumption that satisfies a desire or need, it can include physical goods as well as intangible services. The specificities of innovation in services are in the innovation types. Under financial innovation, we understand the design, development, and distribution of any new financial product or service. But financial innovation can also mean the change that advances altering or modifying the role of financial institutions in general. Financial innovations aim to response to globalization and risk or to regulation and tax issues among various other areas. In any case, it is an ongoing evolutionary process. To reduce complexity, we categorized innovation for the financial service industry into three generic forms. This includes product and service innovations, process innovations, and innovations common to organizational function and service delivery. Later innovations include open business models and affect organization and management. The definition of innovation in services is difficult because product, service, and process innovation are sometimes overlapping. In addition, there is no strictly linear, sequential process, but rather there exist interaction and feedback at several stages of the innovation process. To gain a better understanding what innovations in the financial services could be, we listed key innovations in banking between 1960 and 2007 from various sources. Some landmark innovations such as credit cards, automated teller machines (ATM), Internet banking, or open architecture changed not only customer behavior but also banking businesses fundamentally (see Table 2).

By going through the listed key innovations, you may rightly ask whether that is all what banks delivered. Firms in the service sector and particular banks are not innovative at all compared to the manufacturing industries. That is correct but we must differentiate the various businesses of the financial services to gain a better understanding of innovation. To simplify, we focus on banking and distinguish between five main businesses, namely retail banking, commercial banking, private banking, investment banking, and asset management. These businesses all have different market segments, structures, cultures, strategies, business models, and offerings. Retail banks are institutes that undergo transactions directly with consumers, rather than firms or other banks. They offer savings, accounts, credit cards, mortgages, personal loans, and so forth. Commercial banking or corporate banking refers to deal with deposits and loans from corporations. Private banking, on the other hand, refers to the customer service being rendered on a more personal basis than in mass-market retail banking. Private banks, labeled interchangeably as wealth managers, usually provide comprehensive advice and a broad range of investment products and services tailored to the complex needs of wealthy individuals. Solutions include wealth investments, inheritance advice, tax planning, pension planning, trusts, and foundations. Investment banks are dedicated to serve companies and governments. They typically provide financial advisory, debt and equity underwriting, capital raising services, as well as issuing and selling securities. Much of their business is about giving advice on transactions such as mergers and acquisitions. One prominent financial innovation of investment banking is the mortgage-backed securitization that started in the middle of the 1970s, when its architects found that a system is missing that has the capacity to free up enough money so that almost anyone who wanted a mortgage could get one – even people with no securities. After a number of deregulations, the mortgage-backed securities

**Table 2** A selection of key innovations in banking

| Category | Innovation | Adoption date (est.) |
|---|---|---|
| Service delivery or access to financial markets, i.e., new products and services | Bond | 1960s |
| | Eurobond | 1963 |
| | Credit cards | 1969 |
| | Junk bond | 1970s |
| | Convertible bonds | 1970s |
| | Money market deposits | 1970s |
| | Money market mutual funds | 1970s |
| | NOW account | 1970s |
| | Collateralized mortgage | 1970s |
| | Derivates | 1970s |
| | Cash management account | 1978 |
| | Certificate of deposit | 1979 |
| | Mortgage-backed securities | 1980s |
| | Adjustable rate mortgage | 1980s |
| | Variable rate mortgage | 1980s |
| | Self-directed IRA account | 1980s |
| | Sweep (asset management account) | 1980s |
| | Debit cards | 1987 |
| | All in one account | 1990s |
| | Direct payroll deposit | 1990s |
| | Structured products | 1990s |
| | Credit derivatives | 1993 |
| | Exchange-traded fund (ETF) | 1993 |
| | Trackers savings account | 2000s |
| | Weather derivatives | 2000s |
| Organizational functions, i.e., processes | Risk management systems | 1970s |
| | Automated voice response systems | 1980s |
| | Automated check | 1980s |
| | Computerized loan document generation | 1980s |
| | Discount brokerage service | 1980s |
| | High-speed image processing of check | 1980s |
| | High-speed image processing of office documents | 1980s |
| | Truncation of check handling process | 1980s |
| | Telephone banking | 1983 |
| | Automated mortgage origination | 1990s |
| | Centralized loan application process | 1990s |
| | Customer information file | 1990s |
| | Electronic trading of shares | 1990s |
| | Loan tracking system | 1990s |
| | Profitability analysis by customer | 1990s |
| | Straight through process | 2000s |
| | Customer needs-based segmentation | 2000s |
| Common to both organizational function and service delivery | ATMs | 1967 |
| | Home banking | 1983 |

(*continued*)

**Table 2** (continued)

| Category | Innovation | Adoption date (est.) |
|---|---|---|
| | Electronic fund transfer (PoS) | 1985 |
| | Branch automation | end-1990s |
| | Transaction portal | end-1990s |
| | Internet banking | 1997 |
| | Mobile banking (GSM and WAP services) | 1999 |
| Miscellaneous types of innovation | Lockbox system | 1980s |
| | Treasury workstation | 1990s |
| | Lobby automation (video banking) | 1990s |
| | Loyalty schemes | 1990s |
| | One-stop banking | 1990s |
| | Online financial management system | 1990s |
| | Personal banker | 1990s |
| | Open architecture | 2000s |

market that radically altered the United State investment landscape rose exceedingly from the end of the 1990s until 2006. Today, there is a huge debate whether the financial innovation of securitization mortgages was right or whether it damaged more in the last 2 years as it contributed over the last 20 years. Asset management is obligated to the professional management of investments across asset classes, including equities, bonds, fixed income, commodities and alternative assets such as real estate, hedge funds, or private equity. If we closely analyze asset management, we must acknowledge that these institutes have recently developed a large number of structured investment products for institutional and retail investors. These complex financial constructs compete with traditional funds of funds and simple capital guaranteed funds that have driven most of the growth until now. However, listing all the structured products innovations would go beyond the scope of this section. The evidenced innovativeness in investment product development is in contrast to, e.g., retail banking. Retail banking has become commodity business because there is moderate growth and institutional barriers inside these traditional firms to real innovation are immense. Retail banks and to a certain extent commercial banks too mainly do things that are minor or routine, and produce few breakthrough innovations. Because of cost pressure, they may be more challenged to improve their processes and application architectures. Strategic programs to renew entire platforms are huge efforts and coupled with much more than just technology. Even though, it is commonly not considered as overly innovative. For investment banking, innovations here are not of radical nature either. Over the years, an accumulation of hundreds of small innovations has changed businesses and processes in investment banking. If we look at wealth management, innovations are rather in the area of client segmentation or advisory. Since wealth management has become an increasingly lucrative business with significant growth potential, we can observe innovation in business models of many banks. Innovations in the area of wealth management are discussed in-depth later on in this book.

## *The Characteristics of Services*

There is confusion between products and services; especially for the term *services*, itself, there is no common shared sense in academia or practice. The International Organization for Standardization (ISO) defines *service* simply as a subset of product.[19] A process, whereby the customer output is generated in this dedicated process, generates a service. The definitions in theory and practice vary and are often used interchangeably. A more comprehensive and accepted definition of what a service is might be useful at this point. It is provided by the United Nations.[20]

> Services are not separate entities over which ownership rights can be established. They cannot be traded separately from their production. Services are heterogeneous outputs produced to order and typically consist of changes in the condition of the consuming units realized by the activities of the producers at the demand of the customers. By the time their production is completed they must have been provided to the consumers.

To gain a better understanding, the distinctive characteristics of services such as their intangibility, inseparability, perishability, heterogeneity, and ownership have to be elaborated further.[21] Inputs and outputs of services can hardly be separated in contrast to products in the manufacturing sector. Explained as *inseparability*, services are produced and consumed simultaneously and cannot be separated from their providers, regardless of whether the providers are human beings, institutions, or machines. While products are, for most industries, physical goods, services can be any activity or value that one party can offer to another that is essentially *intangible* and cannot be stored, referred to as the *perishability* of services. It varies according to the provider of the service and does not result in the *ownership* of anything. Service institutions consider products as intangible offerings to their customers and services as a service process for their customers. This is because of the fact that everything they produce is intangible, regardless of whether it is characterized as a product or service.

One remarkable feature of intangible products and services has to be mentioned. While physical products are prototyped and tested before being taken to the market, this is barely possible for intangible products and services. This is one of the weakest facets and dilutes the quality of the execution of launch. The standardization of services has been another crucial issue for years. For services, it is more difficult to ensure the same level of quality as with goods, which leads finally to a greater heterogeneity in terms of conformity and quality. Another characteristic of services is that newly developed services can easily be imitated and replicated. While intellectual property rights and patents are an indicator for invention rather than innovation, the successful exploitation of knowledge and other intangible assets is increasingly recognized as indispensable for innovation in industries such as IT hardware, automotive, pharmaceuticals and biotechnology, electronic and electrical industries. These industries are, at the same time, the top investors in R&D. This is in contrast to the service sector as it has different propensities to inventions and patents. As new services have no technical component and rarely involve the explicit expression of a new idea – which would be a requirement for copyright – patent protection does not apply. Intellectual property rights, therefore, only offer loose protection from illegitimate copying.

## *Products and Services in Banking*

In contrast to industrial companies in the manufacturing sector, financial service institutions do not provide physical goods but intangible products and services. For banks, these consist of liquidity, information, and transformation services. It can be said that the credit risk of a bank corresponds to the investment risk of any other company, and liquidity risk corresponds to the capital structure risk. Banks are also facing interest rate risk due to maturity transformation, and a bank risks having to refinance its long-term loans at rates that exceed the rate of interest on the loan if the interest rate structure changes. Because every single business needs a bank for their financial transactions, insolvency of a bank can have significant external impact on the overall economy. This effect is potentially more serious than if an industrial company were to go bankrupt. What in bank jargon is called *systemic risk* means that if there is a run on a bank, a chain reaction might be the consequence and could result in the collapse of other banks. A similar situation prevailed when many banks securitized credits through complex financial products. This product innovation together with the worldwide network of global financial systems and sophisticated communication technologies leads to a behavior similar to that of a shoal. Hence, all participants are caught in the same network and act and react identical. In normal times, interest rates rise and fall where the one or the other institute profits from it. This *system* is in equilibrium as long as there is trust between the market participants. Through the process of the credit crisis in 2007 and 2008, trust has gone and hoarding of money was common. Because credits were not simple credits, instead complex securities, the system collapsed. These threats justify the call for more attention on regulatory supervision in the banking industry.

The terms *service* and *product* are often used interchangeably in the financial service industry, which may lead to confusion. To clarify, several banks commonly mean products as well as services if they talk about product innovation. Notwithstanding, a distinction must be made for technical reasons. This means that a clear distinction is a requirement for the cost and revenue allocation to management information systems (MIS). We observed that most banks have recently installed global product catalogues accessible over the Internet. Through the process of studying such catalogues, the definition of products and services becomes clearer. We observed that some banks use the term *module* but found that this is rather a technical issue than something that a relationship manager would mention in front of customers. Conclusively, we categorize products, modules, and services as follows:

- *Product.* Something that a client can purchase *stand-alone*, e.g., private account, savings account, all kinds of credit cards such as classic, gold, and platinum. For instance, a credit card can be purchased without having a bank account. A product is the smallest element still of use to the customer which the bank can reasonably calculate in its MIS.
- *Module.* Something that a client cannot purchase *stand-alone*. A debit card, for example, is dependent on an account (product) and cannot therefore be sold without having an account at the bank. *Module* is a very technical term and used rarely in common communication.
- *Service.* Part of a product that is too complex that it could be automated. It therefore requires in any case an interaction with the customer. Services for direct clients include financial planning or portfolio management. Services that same universal banks provide to other financial service institutes include cash currency services such as clearing and mass payment or security services such as custody and clearing and settlement and many others in the area of asset management, private banking, corporate finance, and trade and export finance. Regardless what customer type, a service is a process that generates benefit for the customer.

The strategic choice of the appropriate products and services is key in banking. In addition to accounts, cards, and lending, structured investment products typically account for a large part of revenues. Investment product ranges from equity and bonds to alternative asset classes. Today, many banks have invested their clients' portfolios in alternative asset classes with hedge funds, private equity, real estate, derivatives, and special capital guaranteed products. In particular, mutual funds have increased in popularity as they pool money from thousands of small investors. The fund manager then invests this money into equities, bonds, or other securities. By contributing money into a fund, investors attain a diversified portfolio that minimizes their risk. Besides the conceptualization of innovation in different sectors, the knowledge and information intensity of services have specific features, i.e., they underlie innovation cycles that differ from manufacturing. The next section attempts to give you an idea about the differences in the development process of services.

## *The Product and Service Development Process*

To answer the question, we would like to focus on new product and service development and elucidate on how financial service firms manage their product innovation processes. Note that both product and service development use similar underlying processes. Accordingly, the development of new services encompasses the following phases: idea generation, concept (development and evaluation), development, and implementation (product and service launch). The phases are conducted sequentially and partly in parallel. The process is completed with a number of marketing, sales strategy, and execution activities. Despite this structured process, there are studies that found that banks did not make systematic efforts to collect new ideas,[22] while others corroborated the chaotic approach to innovation.[23] We have all experienced that ideas for new services emerge almost everywhere in the organization. Through the entire development process of new services, banks as well as insurance companies rarely involve customers, front office personnel, and intermediaries. This may be because of barriers such as functionally departmentalized structures, limited use of new service development tools, conservative organizational structures, and constraining information technology. However, we believe that firms with a more formalized development process have better chances of success.

In contrast to the ad hoc innovation process in the service sector, there are well-tested scientific methods for developing and refining manufacturing goods. Although services imply special characteristics, innovation concepts from manufacturing can be applied to services only to a certain extent. A good example is the concept of in vitro product and service testing, and in vivo experimentation of new business models.[24] As simple as it is, an experiment is just as good as the learning it produces. Certainly, the rate at which a firm can learn by experience depends on factors such as iteration time, the extent to which the experiment is run in parallel or series, or the total costs of designing, running, and analyzing the experiment. However, these factors and many more are all unique to the organization. Experimentation in manufacturing has been at the heart of all innovation for years, but we should consider the adoption of these concepts in services. Thus, service firms must develop and systematically evaluate prototypes of new ways of delivering their services to their customers. To do so, systematic learning is required to strengthen the consistency and productivity of service innovations. Learning through experiments can lower the risk of launching new intangible products and services. This approach to innovation is less hazardous and can significantly improve the innovation process for new services.

The Bank of America, for instance, has proved that service development can be as thorough and structured as product development.[25] Given the fact that they had no rigorous research and development processes, the bank created at the beginning of 2000 a new corporate unit called innovation and development (I&D) with the mandate to test new ideas. Their five-stage process to conceive and execute service innovation experiments is grouped into:

1. Generate and evaluate innovative ideas from internal and external sources.
2. Plan and design possible trials.
3. Rollout certain ideas within the prototypes.
4. Create a stable operating environment for testing new concepts and ideas and measure customer response over a given period.
5. Evaluate ideas and recommend launches in wider test markets.

Based on this process, Bank of America created an "innovation market" by setting up 25 out of over 200 branches in the United States within the existing network into prototype branches. As it would be difficult to conduct a diverse array of experiments within the existing designed bank branches, they reconfigured the prototype branches into various categories, each with dedicated physical setup, processes, and knowledge of employees. To give you an example, they created "financial centers"; calm and spacious branches where customers had access to latest technologies required for equity trading and portfolio management. Experienced service staff supported these services. The "express centers," on the other hand, were designed for customers that wanted to perform quickly routine transactions such as deposits and withdrawals. They also designed a number of branches as "traditional centers"; familial-looking branches that provided conventional banking services supported by new technologies and advanced service processes. Within these laboratories, they were running a series of service experiments with the attempt to find new service concepts for retail banking. The experiments conducted by a corporate research team with actual customers during regular business hours generated an unprecedented surge of creative thinking about how to increase branch excellence. The program has resulted in about 20 innovations recommended for national rollout and what is more, within the innovation market, customer satisfaction has improved significantly and even attracted new customers.

## *What Determine Success in Service Innovation?*

Performance as a measurement factor for success in service innovation can be assessed at three levels, namely product level (profitability, market share, and revenue), project level (time, cost, and function), and company level in terms of excess returns generated through sustained innovation capabilities.[26] Other approaches to measure innovation group factors into inputs (financial resources being committed, people, the number of ideas generated and the expected payback for each, and key capabilities); processes (resources expended per individual project and on average, cycle time for the entire process and specific parts, the number of ideas that are moving from one stage of the process to the next, the difference between the initial expected value of an idea and the actual realized value); and outputs (the number of new products or services launched, incremental gains in revenues and profits, cannibalization of existing product sales by new products, and the return of investment of the firm's innovation capability).[27]

Certainly, there are other indirect metrics such as knowledge gained or impact on the brand. However, if we compare successes with failures of new product development between the manufacturing sector and the service sector, there are similarities between both sectors. Often, they influence the factors, which distinguish services from physical goods, how organizations achieve new service success. The quality of the delivered service, on the other hand, might have important implications for performance-related outcomes such as customer satisfaction and customer retention. This is because the customer is part of the service delivery process and therefore, customer participation is crucial. The extent of the customer's involvement is vital for the added value and quality of the service that can be provided in, for instance, a banking relationship. The closer and better the relationship between the customer and the bank, the higher the satisfaction and retention of the customer. A comprehensive understanding of the client's service expectation, as well as variations in those expectations across different customer segments, is fundamental to deliver a superior customer value proposition. This, however, is what affects the overall quality of the service. Examining the extent to which the delivered service meets the client's expectation is finally the only meaningful way to measure service quality. It is the holy grail. The problem of measuring service success is a matter of understanding accurately what the client wants and what is important to him/her. Many service firms are often too concerned with process improvements based on assumptions what is important to the customers.

One common factor of success in service innovations, regardless of the industry, is the time it takes to bring a product or service to market. Speed in the innovation process, alongside with factors such as cost and efficiency, is crucial. Let us believe that time to market is a factor that is judged by most customers as important. At least, it is the perception of many of us.

## *Is Time to Market a Myth?*

On average, it takes between 6 and 12 months in the United States and United Kingdom for banks and insurance firms from a product being conceived until its being available for sale. While many companies hold the position that speed has a positive impact on revenues, some argue that benefits of rapid product development in financial services are largely intangible or that there is no significant link between time to market and revenue at all. On the other hand, early market entries with new products have become crucial and offer significant first-mover advantages such as charge premium prices for a lead period, gain information ahead of other firms about future customer needs, and reputation for being able to offer state-of-the-art products. Additional reasons for faster new product development can be found in the area of customer relation and loyalty, changing customer needs, maintaining revenue streams, and competitive pressure – all these factors force firms to improve their product development time.

We assume that all product and service development efforts may benefit from process innovations. Although process innovations might result in better performance and cost reductions, one might also state that the main driver behind such re-engineering efforts at financial service institutions is not cost reduction per se, but improving customer service quality. *But what are the barriers to rapid product development?* We see the main problems in unfocused strategy, insufficient senior management support, poor economic conditions, organizational inflexibility, and high employee turnover. Difficulties and innovation failures are often due to organizational rigidities and a lack of qualified staff. In addition, regulations may hamper innovation likewise. Product managers claim that the time from the idea to selling the product is mostly consumed during controversies between other business units such as marketing and market research and IT departments. The cause for coordination problems is often due to the lack of IT support for pricing, forecasting sales, and product profitability associated with new or existing products. In particular, inflexible internal systems and constraints call for a proactive approach to technology. The frictions between IT and business can be explained with the fact that both parties have in most companies different performance measurements. Further, there is usually no common communication level. Understanding is often diametrically opposed. Where product development is talking about business opportunities with new products, the IT department often sees problems in terms of application integration, data ownership (especially about client information), and resources for development and maintenance.

It has to be said that so-called first-mover advantages are difficult to assess. There are few benchmarks accessible in terms of the time it takes to develop a new product before a radical improvement initiative, neither are there statistical data that indicate the length of time it takes from development to commercialization. In praxis, comparisons before and after can hardly be found. Where a new MIS to measure and interpret distribution performance has been implemented as part of the new infrastructure, it will always be difficult to compare product development speed since a firm seldom develops similar products and services twice. On the bottom line, rapid product development and time to market have been objectives for many years in most firms. Various voices from the financial services market stated that it is all about the architecture – how flexible a bank is, how quick a product can be developed in-house, and how quick a third-party product can be integrated into the existing systems. Thus, quick *integratability* will become a crucial competence and key success factor in future. We will discuss the importance of service-oriented architecture as one possible solution later on in this book.

Another assumption that may accelerate time to market and reduce costs for innovations is the development of standardized products instead of tailored individual services. This interpretation, however, might be unrealistic as it is in contradiction to what the sophisticated and demanding clientele expect. Therefore, firms have to find the balance between customization and standardization. To achieve this, one critical success factor for innovation in services may be the firm's ability to create a systematized innovation process and leveraging product platforms across their businesses. We will touch these building blocks of success later on in this book.

## Conclusion

We observed that growth is vital for economies and companies and that innovation accelerates growth. Always bear in mind, sustainable growth can only be archived if we continuously monitor the risks associated with innovation and growth strategies. We discussed several routes to innovation and types of innovations. To recapitulate, we broadly divided product and service and process innovation and to a certain extent marketing innovation. Latter combines strategies for sales and distribution channels in existing and new markets. Marketing innovation also deals with client segmentation, bundling of products and services to value-adding solutions and strategic pricing. Overall, this discipline is in charge for innovative advertising, public relation, and increasingly for social responsibility. The direct drivers for growth are innovations in products, services, and processes. Where product innovation generates high quality and service, process innovations support production, logistics, marketing, and sales. Both affect the efforts to win clients through attractive offerings and quick and reliable services. Innovations in these disciplines lead to higher margins and economies of scale and hence increase the firm's profit. We learned that innovation in services and its processes are different to that in the manufacturing sector. Nevertheless, there are similarities in the interrelation of growth and innovation. We observed that the service sector has recently gone through issues that were negotiated in manufacturing 20 years ago.

To portray profitable growth and innovation strategy in simplified terms, exceptional total shareholder return depends on our capability to understand and align these disciplines. The constant growing of knowledge as a whole as we have experienced it in knowledge-intensive service businesses is appreciably driving growth. Having understood the mutual dependence of knowledge, innovation, and growth, we can now go further and explore the opportunities arising out of the open innovation paradigm. But before addressing that crucial topic, in-depth knowledge about the developments in the market is required. In particular, we need to understand what enabled the shift form a closed to an open innovation paradigm. That is why we explore the major developments in the financial service industry and discuss the implications of the trends identified for businesses in the next chapter before we turn to open innovation.

## Notes

1. The value of financial assets expressed as a percentage of GDP can be used to explain macroeconomic interrelations. For example, advances in technology and the deregulation of financial markets around the world have made crossborder capital flows (foreign purchases of equity and debt securities as well as other transactions) possible and given rise to a growing class of global investors. Striking that some 80% of global capital flows involve three regions, namely the Central Europe, United States, and the United Kingdom with average crossborder capital flows within the Euro zone between 2001 and 2005 totaled US $1.7 trillion. For more on the global capital markets, see McKinsey (2005) "Mapping the global capital markets", *McKinsey Quarterly, Special Edition: Value and performance.*
2. Definition of assets under management (AuM): There are widely differing views within the financial service industry on what the term means. Commonly, it is the total value of assets that a firm manages and administers for itself and its clients. Some financial institutions include bank deposits, mutual funds, mortgage loans, and institutional money in their calculations. Others limit it to funds under discretionary mandate where the client delegates responsibility to the company. The difference between two AuM balances consists mainly of market performance and net new assets (NNA) besides foreign exchanges movements and structural effects of the company. NNA indicate how much money from clients had been newly invested. NNA growth shows the NNA in relation of the previous AuM balance on

an annualized basis. AuM and NNA growth are an important measure for banks of success and comparison against their competitors, particularly for wealth management businesses.

3. Christensen, C.M. and Raynor, M.E. (2003) *The innovator's solution*. Harvard Business School Press, Boston, MA.
4. See Boston Consulting Group (2005) *Succeeding with growth: Creating value in banking*. BCG Report.
5. For the resource-based view on the firm, see the seminal work of Barney, J.B. (1991) 'Firm resources and sustained competitive advantage', *Journal of Management,* 17(1), 99–120 and Wernerfeld, B. (1984) 'A resource-based view of the firm', *Strategic Management Journal,* 5(2), 171–180.
6. *Hedge funds* are actively managed investment funds that use a wide range of asset classes and strategies such as options or futures that are not usually available to mutual funds and pension funds. Hedge funds are generally open to only a limited range of investors, primarily to institutions and high-net-worth individuals. The objective is to generate returns that are not closely correlated to those of the broader financial markets. The funds managers do not necessarily hedge their investments against adverse market moves. Hedge funds' activities are limited only by the terms of the contracts governing the particular fund. Consequently, many hedge funds have their legal residence offshore in countries unrelated to either the manager, investor, or investment operations of the fund (e.g., Cayman Islands, British Virgin Islands, or Bermuda) with the objective of making taxes payable only by the investor and not additionally by the fund. Fund managers are compensated based on performance rather than as a fixed asset under management percentage fee.
7. The capital requirement is a bank regulation, influenced by the Basleel Committee on Banking Supervision. Within its Basleel II capital accord, the framework of a country's banking capital requirements is set and defines how banks and depository institutions must handle their capital. One important measure is *Tier 1* capital that consists primarily of shareholders' equity. It shows a bank's financial strength from the regulator's point of view.
8. The Morgan Stanley Capital International (MSCI) Frontier Markets Index, launched on November 27, 2007, is reflecting expanded investment opportunities beyond traditional developed and emerging markets. By covering 19 countries, the MSCI Frontier Markets Indices are designed to track the performance of a range of equity markets that are now more accessible to global investors. For further information, see http://www.mscibarra.com/products/indices/fm/ [January 7, 2008]
9. Boston Consulting Group (2006) *Innovation 2006*. BCG Senior Management Survey.
10. Commission of the European Communities (2003) *Innovation policy: Updating the Union's approach in the context of the Lisbon strategy*. Communication from the Commission to the Council, the European Parliament, the European Economic and Social Committee, and the Committee of the regions, Brussels. For more information, see the official innovation and technology transfer page of the European Commission http://ec.europa.eu/enterprise/innovation/communication.htm [February 4, 2007]
11. Schumpeter, J.A. (1939) *Business cycles*, Vol. 1. McGraw-Hill, New York.
12. Porter, M.E. (1980) *Competitive strategy: Techniques for analyzing industries and competitors*. Free Press, New York.
13. For the adaptation–imitation theory, see Kirton, M.J. (1980) 'Adaptors and innovators in organizations', *Human Relations,* 3, 213–224.
14. Kirton's theory has been put into the practical context of banking by Holland, P.A. (1987) 'Adaptors and innovators: Applications of the Kirton adaptation–innovation inventory to bank employees', *Psychological Reports,* 60, 263–270.
15. Chesbrough, H. (2006) *Open business models*. Harvard Business School Press, Boston, MA.
16. Schumpeter, J.A. (1934) *The theory of economic development: An inquiry into profits, capital, credit, interest and the business cycle*. Harvard University Press, Cambridge, MA.
17. The first who conceptualized business process re-engineering were Hammer, M and Champy, J. (1993) *Reenginering the corporation: A manifesto for business revolution*. Harper Business, New York.

18. Marketing innovation has its own tradition based on the seminal work of Levitt, T. (1969) 'The new markets – think before you leap', *Harvard Business Review,* 47(3), 53–67; Levitt, T. (1962) *Innovation in marketing*. McGraw-Hill, Maidenhead.
19. For the term *service*, we refer to the ISO 9004-2 (1991) *Quality management and quality systems element – part 2: Guidelines for services* [Online]. International Organization for Standardization, http://www.iso.org/iso/en/ISOOnline.frontpage [November 22, 2003]
20. For a detailed description of what a service is, see United Nations (2002) *Manual on statistics of international trade in services*. Department of Economics and Social Affairs, Series M, No. 86, United Nations Publications, New York.
21. For a description of the characteristics of services, see De Brentani, U. (1991) 'Success factors in developing new business services', *European Journal of Marketing,* 25(2), 33–59; Hill, T.P. (1977) 'On goods and services', *Review of Income and Wealth*, 23(4), 315–338.
22. Vermeulen, P. (2004) 'Managing product innovation in financial service firms', *European Management Journal,* 22(1), 43–50.
23. For the chaotic approach to innovation, see Quinn, J.B. (1985) 'Managing innovation: Controlled chaos', *Harvard Business Review,* May–June, 73; Mintzberg, H., Quinn, J.B. and Goshal, S. (1995) *The strategy process*. Prentice-Hall, London.
24. For an analysis of in vitro product and service testing, and in vivo experimentation of new business models, see Hamel, G. and Getz, G. (2004) 'Funding growth in an age of austerity', *Harvard Business Review,* 82(7–8), 76–84.
25. See case study at the Bank of America by Thomke, S. (2003) 'R&D comes to services', *Harvard Business Review,* 81(4), 70–79.
26. Adapted from various authors, especially Brown, S.L. and Eisenhardt, K.M. (1995) 'Product development: Past research, present findings, and future directions', *Academy of Management Review,* 20(2), 343–378; Verona, G.A. (1999) 'A resource-based view of product development', *Academy of Management Review,* 24(1), 132–142; Wheelwright, S.C. and Clark, K.B. (1992) *Revolutionizing product development: Quantum leaps in speed, efficiency, and quality*. The Free Press, New York.
27. Boston Consulting Group (2006) *Measuring Innovation*. BCG Senior Management Survey.

# Leading Through the Changing Business Environment

- Anticipate trends and master the strategic changes in the financial services industry by developing an in-depth understanding of the business environment.
- Pursue multiple paths to gather new ideas and adapt to change rapidly as well as effectively.
- Embrace new regulations that usually gain weight in turbulent times as an opportunity.
- Satisfy customers through local expertise and tailor-made products and services.

## Radical vs. Incremental Innovation

The innovation expert Joseph A. Schumpeter manifested in his seminal works that increasing productivity produces discontinuities, creates new industries, destroys old ones, and accelerates global economic growth in the process. The punctuated equilibrium model of change used in organizational theory assumes that long periods of small incremental innovation are interrupted by short periods of discontinuous, radical innovation. These innovations can be minor incremental improvements in a particular industry or sector, but can also be so extensive that they transform existing markets and industries, and change society. In the following sections, we attempt to explain the link from innovation to growth at the macrolevel in free and open market economies. In particular, we identify the drivers for strategic change and explain trends and its implications in the context of the financial services industry.

The form of innovation can be divided into two broad categories, namely radical and incremental. Both categories can come from different routes to innovation and have different competitive consequences because they require different organizational capabilities. Radical innovation is concerned mostly with the exploration of new technology and often opens up new markets and potential applications. The emphasis is on the development of new businesses, products, services, and processes which entirely transform the economies of a business. Evidence is the rise to industrial dominance of the United States, Great Britain, and Germany that was mostly built upon radical innovation and secondary on manufacturing process improvements.

In contrast, incremental innovation is concerned with relatively minor changes and the exploitation of existing technology, with an emphasis on cost or feature improvements in existing products, services, or processes. This is best reflected in a number of concepts that pushed Japan to industrial power. Japanese companies adopted total quality management concepts of the West and developed the ideas further to continuous and incremental improvement philosophies. "Kaizen" – the art of continual improvement, just-in-time inventory management, or "Kanban," just to name a few lean production philosophies that helped Japanese industries to achieve global success in the 1970s and 1980s.

From a management point of view, incremental innovation can and should be planned systematically in every organization. It can be managed with prescriptive strategies in which detailed business plans are developed in advance for a longer period. Radical innovation, on the other hand, cannot easily be planned. Therefore, a vital activity for the management team is to provide a platform where radical ideas can flourish. Today, many multinational companies combine all the traditional process innovations and Japanese methods with radical innovation and are so able not only to develop new products but also to improve customer service, product quality, and on-time delivery continuously. This is important to yield increasing profits to unique excellence for a mass market.

History showed that after the last radical period in the 1990s driven by information technology and the Internet, incremental and continuous improvements have received considerable attention in recent years. We have seen sustained incremental improvements. Thus, continuous innovation has established as a steady-state activity with continuing interaction between operations, incremental improvement, and learning. Continuous innovation as a means to cope with discontinuities helps in managing *contradictio in terminis* by combining operational efficiency and strategic flexibility or exploitation and exploration.[1] The concept of continuous innovation suggests a middle course for balancing radical and incremental changes. This is important as agile companies, and continuously changing organizations are likely to be complex systems with structures that poise the organization on the edge of order and chaos and links in time that force simultaneous attention and linkage among past, present, and future. These firms seem to grow over time through a series of sequenced steps, and they are associated with success in highly competitive, high-velocity environments.

We have also seen that many companies that dominate one generation of, for instance, radical technology innovation often fail to maintain leadership in the next wave, namely incremental innovation. Christensen and Raynor discuss in their book two distinct categories that lead toward the "innovators dilemma" – sustaining and disruptive – based on the circumstances of innovation.[2] While sustaining innovation means incremental year-by-year improvements and competing in the low end of an established market, innovations that create their own market are considered as disruptive innovations. The latter disrupt the current market by targeting new or less demanding consumers with products that are not as good as currently available products. Typically, they are simpler, more convenient, or cheaper. These kinds of innovation mostly involve new technologies and require considerable change in customer behavior and markets. As soon as these new entrants get a foothold in the market, the improvement cycle begins with the goal to displace incumbents.

The changing environment means that firms must continuously renew themselves, by transforming businesses and by creating value through new combinations of resources. Being able to link environmental change to strategy and to modify this linkage over time is theorized in the literature of organizational design and renewal and organizational change. A distinction needs to be made between organizational change, which takes place within every organization and is inevitable; and strategic change, which is the proactive management of change in organizations to achieve identified strategic objectives. Where organizational change is constantly occurring, transformation, as the process of change, occurs only when there is a realignment of logics across organizational subgroups.

Strategic change transforms the organization over a period. This *processual* organizational change is in a broader sense what Schumpeter termed "creative destruction," where one force of innovation is the continuous internal renewal of the economic structure that unyieldingly destroys the old structures for new production methods.[3] In other words, transformative change can be seen as a means of creating fundamentally new and superior value in favor of making existing things and ways of doing things irrelevant. This process includes the implementation of new strategies that affect *people, processes,* and the *tasks,* which they perform and hence it is a multilateral discipline without a clearly defined set of boundaries. However, the drivers that are responsible for strategic change and the firm's strategic renewal have to be understood first. Let us consider the ability to cope with strategic change as a unique resource, which determines a firm's competitive renewal and hence competitiveness.

## Drivers of Strategic Change

Purposeful, systematic innovation begins with the analysis of the sources of strategic change, which are at the same time new opportunities. A number of external environmental factors and developments lead to change in internal organization structures, processes, and behaviors. As the dynamic business environment generates new ground rules, it also creates new opportunities for innovation. Enablers for change can come from external environmental pressures but also within the organization, namely through unexpected occurrences, incongruities, process needs, or industry and market changes. Common circumstances that have forced companies to rethink and restructure their business model are changing industrial practice and strategy, such as outsourcing, strategic alliances, mergers, acquisitions, and the deconstruction of the value chain. Figure 3 summarizes external environmental pressures that lead to fundamental organizational change.

A global study conducted by Accenture in 2003 found that innovative organizations are much quicker to adapt to external changes, and hence much better placed to take advantage of opportunities when the drivers for strategic change are properly identified.[4] Those companies find it far easier to balance between short-term oriented operationally effective exploitation, and longer-term strategically flexible exploration. Firms that specialize in exploitation will discover themselves becoming better and better at an increasingly obsolescent technology. On the other hand, firms that

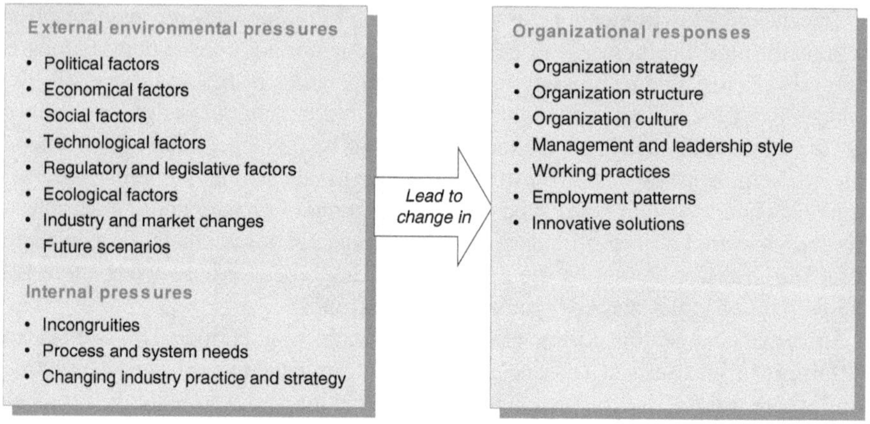


**Fig. 3** The external environment–internal organizational link

specialize in exploration will never realize the advantages of its discoveries. Exploration and exploitation are linked in an enduring symbiosis – each interferes with the other. The effective combination of both, exploitation and exploration, however difficult, should be a company's goal.

To be able to respond rapidly to external changes, executives should seek for help and structures that facilitate flexibility, creativity, and participation. The strategic imperative of radical change needs to be treated with caution as it may lose the benefits of more stable structures. On the other hand, bureaucratic structures may hamper innovation and organizational transformation. Such dilemma is omnipresent in today's dynamic and complex environment driven, most notably, by technology and knowledge. Although strategic change might appear complex, it has to be understood as a learning process. Therefore, it is required to gain a comprehensive understanding of the attitudes, behavior, social relationships, processes, and structures pertaining to strategic change. Such understanding can be produced through various methods, techniques, and best practices deriving from research as well as practice.

## How Can We Get New Ideas and Improve Businesses?

Two main paths significantly influence a company's strategy, namely consultancy and research. Management consulting, on the one hand, might be an analytical and rational discipline to provide benefit for organizations and its customers. However, other softer factors also have to be taken into consideration. Empathy and the need to understand cultural issues and the entire business environment holistically have become necessary qualifications for both consultants and researchers. We can also say that the complexity of a situation increases the higher we go up the organization's hierarchy. The explanation for this is that top-level executives are in charge of the strategic direction of the entire organization. A fortiori, their decisions are often politically influenced. Therefore, managerial decisions become unstructured, nonlinear, iterative, ambiguous, and incomprehensible for outsiders. To operate and contribute in such complex business environments, we need to see the entire situation with all interrelated elements multilaterally, rather than just analyzing a particular element. That is what management consulting stands for – advising executives in such complex situations. It is an eclectic and pragmatic discipline with the power to influence executives that are in charge of change strategies affecting the entire organization.

Besides consultancy, there is another external path open to organizations where they can get new ideas of how to improve their business, namely management research. The study of management has been approached from a variety of different disciplines such as strategy, organizational behavior, innovation, financial management, control, operations, process management, logistics, marketing, information management, international development, competitive strategy, and the like. Each stance has its own traditions and approaches to identify causal explanations and fundamental laws that explain regularities in human social behavior. Management research is a fragmented and heterogeneous field in which knowledge and research methods are often drawn from associated disciplines such as social and natural sciences. Therefore, no distinct ontological or epistemological philosophy is universal applicable. Subsequently, management research is a nonreductionism discipline that coalesces positivism and interpretive paradigms.[5] It is a transdiscipline, which needs quantitative and qualitative methods and it engages academic theories as well as business practice. The concern of management research is to understand the organization and arrangement of resources to deliver optimal task performance and social cohesion whatever the organization responses to change are.

Management research should be more than just technical troubleshooting for current problems, as this is the business model of many consulting firms. It is difficult to say whether the firm's management attaches more importance to research or consulting, qualitative considerations, or quantitative facts for decision making. There are a growing number of executives, who suggest the need for more qualitative research in strategic management. Management research is a soft, applied, and divergent field of study, which is not only about *knowing what* furthermore it goes beyond this to consider questions associated with *knowing how*. It is in its nature that *how* questions contribute to learning and knowledge, whereas qualitative approaches are considered as appropriate to explore *how* certain elements influence others.

For management research, one right to existence is the contribution it provides to practice although much of the research does not reach the practitioner audience or it is inapplicable. One might argue that management research is an applied discipline that is primarily *about* managers and social organizations instead of *for* managers. One intention of this book is to pursue the above notions and integrate theory and its managerial implications. To leverage management research, we should combine it with management consulting that is practice orientated and appropriate *for* managers.

Let us apply the assumptions above to strategic change. This means that we would yield better strategy implementation results if we understood a certain phenomenon comprehensively beforehand. Such a mindset implies that we should be open and accept new ideas from external resources. All firms within a sector or industry are going through changes that strike at the very core of their businesses. Although they are facing challenges that are unique to them, they all operate in the same markets, hence affected by the same developments. The conditions that lead to trends are hard to predict, uncertain, complex, and therefore dynamic in nature. Learning from the process of change means the systematic development of knowledge of what actually changes the business environment. In the context of the financial services industry, we observed drivers of change such as globalization, home country consolidation and convergence, regulations, technology, risk issues, innovation, and demographics. We structured the main trends into four areas, of which we believe that they will have the most impact on profits for the coming years. Note that some issues pertaining to one area may overlap and interact with others. Basically, they include market developments, changes in customer behavior, tighter regulations, and technological advancements.

## Market Developments

### *Globalization*

At the beginning of the last century, many firms used to produce and distribute on regional markets with local labor. They expanded slowly throughout the country and neighboring countries. After the Second World War, many expanded to other economic areas and continents. Thus, they adapted products, services, and distribution channels to a global market. Labor and finance became globally available, mobile, and exchangeable. The goal of internationally operating firms is to satisfy client demands wherever there is business. The last step in this process is what we today understand under globalization. A new competitive landscape has emerged on increasing globalization that has seriously affected established companies and caused a wave of corporate consolidation. New market entrants and flexible intermediaries that provide innovative products and serve clients on a global scale have become a threat that put revenues and margins under pressure. Thus, most managers fear foreign competition in domestic markets. At the same time, they have to expand their businesses on global markets. We see that major banks are building and enhancing their activities in growth markets such as Brazil, Russia, India, and China – markets that are expected to grow twice as fast as the global average.

The challenge though is to address the various markets, as there are a number of regional differences. We do not need to tell you that there are cultural differences but it becomes apparent if we just check some examples. The way things are now is that wealthy people in Asia and Russia coming mainly from entrepreneurs who have high-risk appetites. In contrast, to mature markets in the United Kingdom and

Europe where money has been passed on from generation to generation. Experience shows that old-established wealthy people have a more conservative risk profile. What is also striking is the sophistication level of clients. This, of course, has an effect of the offering provided. Clients in emerging markets keep their advisors busy by demanding personal advice, in contrast to clients in mature markets such as the United States where they settle much of their transactions through online platforms. As we will discuss later, the regulatory, fiscal, and political environment as well differ between countries and have a strong impact on client's investment decisions and private banking activities.

In Europe and the United States, strong relationship-based traditional networks, operating on a national scale, have been increasingly eroded. We see specialists operating globally in a highly competitive environment-gaining market share. This is because clients increasingly demand specialists with professional resources and the ability to harness the synergies of an integrated global platform. Globalization has led to increasing competition and has put purely national players at a structural disadvantage. Global players are forced to act in all major on- and offshore locations. Their managers must think globally and act locally. For mature markets, this means that firms must retain existing clients and attract new clients and at the same time, they must enter new markets and gain market share abroad. There is a strong fight for clients as everyone wants to grow above market share. Therefore, firms without substantial investment capacity, patience, and market-specific client value proposition are deemed to fail. The trend here seems to be clear. The question though is the scale that depends on the legislative velocity of the various markets, the capability of innovative and entrepreneurial thinking, access to resources, flexible organizational and technical architectures, and above all how visionary the top management reacts to all these challenges.

## *Competition and the European Union*

Financial markets and institutions are very competitive. London, New York, and Switzerland are the world's leading international financial centers. We would like to briefly introduce these centers and give insights why they are successful global financial players – although they could not be more different. The financial service industry in the United Kingdom employs over one million people and contributes to about one-third to the total gross value added of the country. The *City of London* is one of the world's leading financial centers and the largest center for many international financial markets. The *City* is characterized by deep, liquid markets, a concentration of industry-wide skilled workforce, and high-quality and innovative products.

After deregulation 1986, the United Kingdom became one of the most diverse and dynamic banking sectors in the world. Even though most industry observers predicted the end of traditional banking and established institutes after this "big bang," the City of London today has the highest concentration of foreign banks in the world. As of September 2003, London accounted for 19% of global crossborder bank lending, more than any other center. Total assets of the United Kingdom banking system are almost £5 billion, of which more than half belong to foreign banks. The assets of UK-owned banks are dominated by a dozen or so retail banks, with national branch networks, mostly serving domestic, personal, and corporate customers. Additionally, the United Kingdom has the world's leading insurance and reinsurance market, covering common motor insurance to space satellites. The London market is a unique international wholesale insurance marketplace, and is the global market leader in aviation and marine insurance. The UK insurance business, the third largest in the world before the United States and Japan, generates recurring strong premium incomes.

Advantages of the United Kingdom financial center are highly sophisticated and innovative management styles, techniques, and strategies, a skilled labor force and high-quality professional and support services, a liquid market with the opportunity to trade in large blocks of shares, and an open and liberalized operating environment combined with protection against abuses. These characteristics provide selling points for the banking industry. While London and New York are ahead in trading volume and in business areas such as investment banking, Switzerland is the established leader in private banking. The importance of the financial service industry to the United Kingdom economy continues to play an important role by contributing, together with the oil and gas industry, to most of the country's GDP. The high productivity per employee of about £80,000 is a competitive advantage as well as the fact that the United Kingdom is a member of the European Union, but does not share the European Monetary Union. It is well known that London is traditionally the center for international investment banking businesses. There are plenty of opportunities for the United Kingdom as a financial center, such as increasing the flow of pension assets from the European Union, asset management and mergers, acquisitions, and restructuring expertise. Additionally, major European banks have ongoing strategies to focus on global investment banking and, so far, locate their business in London. For further information about innovation, competition, and efficiency in the UK banking industry, we recommend the report by Daniel Cruickshank, which is regarded as the most accepted report about UK banking since the Macmillan Report of 1931 by John Maynard Keynes.[6]

New York is a global hub of international business and major center for finance and insurance. In 2005, New York had an estimated gross metropolitan product of US $1.2 trillion. With the New York Stock Exchange and NASDAQ, it represents capitalism. It is a command center for the world economy. Accordingly, financial services account for roughly 35% of the city's employment income. New York has a number of advantages, many similar to London. In addition, the United States is very good in terms of protecting corporate laws and of course, New York has a high density of collective financial brain power. Although Switzerland is not a member of the European Union, it is very well integrated. It has to be said that the European Union is Switzerland's most important partner, politically, economically, as well as culturally. More than three-fifths of all exports are sent to European Union countries and almost four-fifths are imports from European Union members. A close network of treaties, from the free trade agreement in 1973 to the bilateral agreements in the area of free movements of persons, agriculture, research, overland and air transport, technical barriers to trade, and public procurement, which have been in force since June 1, 2002, ensures that Switzerland is able to play its part in Europe as a financial center. The fact that almost all major international companies are present in Switzerland for tax reasons, some even have headquarters in Zurich or Geneva, corroborates international integration. According to a globalization index by AT Kearney, which includes rankings of 62 countries for 13 variables, Switzerland ranked as the second most global nation behind Ireland (the United Kingdom ranked ninth). Indicators included (1) political engagement such as the number of memberships in international organization, (2) information technology such as Internet users and investments, (3) personal contact in terms of international travel, tourism, and crossborder transfers, and (4) economic integration such as trade and foreign direct investments. On the other hand, large Swiss financial services institutions have long had a conspicuous presence in other metropolis, especially in London, where they are well-reputed and major investors and employers. The competitive advantages of Switzerland are the political, economical, and monetary stability, profound banking expertise, traditionally high standards of service and guaranteed protection of client privacy. In addition, Switzerland has been perceived as a tax and interest haven for decades. These factors, combined with the trustworthy banking tradition and international integration ability, make Switzerland to one of the biggest financial centers.

A politically open and well-integrated economy and a stable global financial system are prerequisites to remain competitive. Banking, so vitally important for economies, can only take full advantage if the structural framework remains favorable able in years to come, and if banks have the ability to cope with cost reduction in operations and growth at once. On a macroeconomical level, financial markets have changed rapidly, capital has become global, and interest rates in most regions of the world have reached a 40-year low. The low GDP and inflation rates in most industrialized economies and unpredictable equity markets account for lower expected global growth rates. Therefore, growth opportunities are seen in international onshore markets. Key countries with an estimated 80% of Europe's potential wealth investments are the United Kingdom, Italy, Germany, France, and Spain in addition to the rising of new financial centers, predominantly in Singapore, Hong Kong, and Qatar.

## The Changing Nature of Demand

### *Demographic Changes Renovate the Financial Services*

The changing customer attitude is a trend that all financial service firms have been facing within the last decade. Demographics usually define our destiny with retirement as one key milestone in our lives. Otto von Bismarck, the German Chancellor, designed in 1889 a breakthrough innovation that until today affects the financial system. He introduced social insurance in Germany to promote the well-being of workers and to keep the German economy operating at maximum efficiency. So, Germany became the first nation in the world to adopt an old-age social insurance program by setting the retirement age at 65 (at a time when the average lifespan was 45). Since then, much of the world has embraced a uniform assumption about the standard retirement age and productivity. One concern in the financial services is that a major demographical shift in the industrialized world is occurring. Woody Allen is not alone when he stated "I don't want to achieve immortality through my work. I want to achieve it through not dying." To make the point, the world's population is growing old and the baby boom generation is approaching retirement. Retirement is way below life expectancy today, in contrast as it was at the launch of the program. Most baby boomers with strong support of the orthopedics and pharmaceuticals industries are doing everything possible to put off the inevitable. Over the past 50 years, wherever baby boomers went, they pulled the cultural climate of an era behind them. When they left school, there was overcrowding, and with hitting puberty they announced the sexual revolution. When they went off college, there was unrest on campus and the beginning of the 1968 revolution. Record unemployment was noticed when they entered the job market. This was followed by record real estate prices when they started buying houses for the first time. Now as they are hitting the third stage of their lives, baby boomers will change the meaning of old age and retirement significantly.

This global phenomenon creates new policy challenges and investment realities. It also creates new business opportunities. If we observe the aging process of society, we soon understand that it is irreversible since the seeds of tomorrow's demography were sown decades ago. Fact is that people primarily in developed countries are having fewer and fewer children. The number of children has fallen below the threshold for generational renewal, which is generally considered 2.1 births per female. In addition, people are living longer. Based on macroeconomic theory of production, the impact of aging population will translate into fewer workers and more retirees. As the population gets older, the structure will likely affect the overall savings rate and public pension programs. Consequently, traditional saving products may shift in favor of pension plans and other investments. As simple as it sounds, we need to consider that savings and investment are theoretically balanced in a closed economy. A closed economy is defined as a setting without external trade and capital flows. In contrast, an open economy setting is one where saving is equal to the sum of domestic investments and the current account balance. However, reality shows that savings and investments in open economy settings are often correlated. This has an impact on capital accumulation within a country and investment flows between countries. It is obvious that people tend to exhibit different savings behavior during their life cycle. We know, for example, that overall saving rates will decline as nation's age. The impact cannot be simulated exactly as we have two extreme economic settings. In a closed economy, a declining savings rate would directly affect investment activity and reduce capital accumulation and growth. In an open economy, there would be independence of savings rate and investment activity because capital is completely mobile on international financial markets. As these are two extreme cases, the reality may lie somewhere between and differ slightly from country to country.

If we look at the impact of aging society and retiring baby boomers, we assume that there will be an increased demand for retirement savings and wealth management. Banks need to adapt to the changing behavior of their aging clientele. If they want to fulfill the expectations of older people, as they tend to be asset rich, banks will have to adapt their product suite. This ever-expanding group of people demands wealth preservation services and innovative financial products rather than risky equities. The shift out of equities into bonds is expected to benefit some asset classes at the expense of others. This makes sense as some bond funds managers invest only in near risk-free government bonds. One argument holds that as the baby boomers progress through their lives, they probably contribute to increasing asset prices. This may occur due to changes in the desired portfolio composition. The creation of reverse mortgage is a good example. This is a form of consumer loan financed by transferring ownership of an owner-occupied property, partially or completely to the creditor. The borrower keeps a life-long right of residence but their heirs get nothing. However, the asset management business benefits from the aging population in developed countries. The key driver for growth here is innovation.

We also want to discuss the controversy on the impact of aging on the financial service industry. One might argue that risk tolerance is loosely related to age and appears to be determined to a much greater degree to the socialization of the individual. Factors such as education, experiences, and knowledge of financial markets as well as income and former position in industry characterize an investor's stance. That retirees are rebalancing portfolios away from equities upon retirement is therefore just an assumption that can hardly be verified. It is further assumed that the phenomenon will affect companies with no international business harder than global companies. This is because global companies invest abroad and have increased the geographic diversity of their sales and cost structure. We know that many Western European companies already earn more in international markets than in their home country. Globally active firms in developed countries benefit from their recent investments in emerging market economies. Thus, demographic changes that may slow down economies of developed countries can be compensated with strong growth in emerging markets and should not necessarily affect their earnings.

## *Local Innovations with Global Impact*

Another driver for changes in customer behavior and demand are the impacts of globalization. The aim is to balance local innovation with global integration. Let us explain what we mean. Potential clients are not interested in a company's global strength, but rather in the relationship manager's strength in the national market where they live. Clients in the international market require tailor-made solutions. That is exactly what Citigroup experienced in 2000. Citigroup's emerging-markets division was expected to be the company's growth engine but the revenues from new products were declining alarmingly. The bank's problem was that the division did not clearly understand the local needs of its customers in emerging markets. Remember what we discussed earlier in this book where Citi closed its operations in Germany due to fierce competition from domestic banks that are more familiar with the needs of their fellow citizen. Being the largest bank in the world seemed to be not enough to attract and retain new clients. As a consequence of underestimating local needs, innovations were of low quality. In addition, the firm's decision-making process regarding innovation was slow and bureaucratic and as a result, best practices within the organization were not transferred among regions due to unstructured and irregular communication. Citigroup was forced to take action if they would not lose revenues from fast- growing emerging markets. First, it researched actual customer needs by intensifying relationship contacts. Through better interaction between customers and relationship managers and integration of clients into the product development process, product specialists were able to better grasp what clients really wanted. The emerging-markets division also increased transparency and accountability for innovation decisions. Besides regular mandatory innovation meetings for key decision makers, it introduced so-called "innovation catalysts" – a team dedicated to focus on transferring best practices within the organization. In particular, experiences made in, e.g., Asia could be integrated into other growth strategies for markets such as the Middle East. Because of these initiatives, a number of interesting new local products were developed and revenues in the emerging-markets division doubled in just two 2 years to US $1 billion.

The importance of making local needs imperative also becomes apparent if we look at the accumulation of wealth by the 1.2 billion Muslims. The market for Islamic finance in excess is ~US $450 billion with Islamic banking assets growing on average by 15% per annum, driven primarily by oil wealth. Moody's, the rating agency, estimates as of June 2006 that there are 250 Islamic funds with total assets of US $300 billion under management. In addition, 300 Islamic financial institutions are managing a further US $250 billion. A recent research report published by Morgan Stanley in September 2008 expects Islamic financial assets to cross US $1 trillion by 2010. This leads to new emerging banking markets with Pakistan as the key growth market, as it is the second largest Muslim-populated country after Indonesia. *Islamic banking* refers to a system of banking or banking activity that complies with *Sharia*, the Islamic law that guides Islamic economics. Based on the teachings of the Koran, the challenge in Islamic banking is the sharing of profit and loss. Precisely, it prohibits the followers of Islam from conducting any business involving *Riba* (interest). This means that Muslims cannot receive or pay interest. To compete with conventional modes of financing (interest-based financial instruments), Islamic financial institutions have developed a number of products that fulfill the Sharia obligation and provide the same value as conventional products.

*Mudharabah*, e.g., is an arrangement or agreement between a capital provider and an entrepreneur, whereby the entrepreneur can mobilize funds for its business activity. Any profits made will be shared between the capital provider and the entrepreneur according to an agreed ratio, where both parties share in profits and only capital provider bears all the losses if occurred. The profit sharing continues until the loan is repaid. The bank is compensated for the time value of its money in the form of a floating interest rate that is pegged to the debtor's profits. Another widespread practice for Islamic mortgage transaction is *Murabahah*. Instead of loaning the buyer money to purchase the item, a bank might buy the item itself from the seller and resell it to the buyer at a profit, while allowing the buyer to pay the bank in installments. However, the fact that it is profit cannot be made explicit, and therefore there are no additional penalties for late payment. To protect itself against default, the bank asks for strict collateral. The goods or land is registered to the name of the buyer from the start of the transaction. *Musharaka* is normally applied for business partnerships or joint ventures. It is based on the profit-and-loss sharing system where two or more parties combine either their capital or labor together, and they share in the profits and losses of their venture. The profits made are shared on an agreed ratio, while losses incurred will be divided based on the equity participation ratio. This concept is distinct from fixed-income investing (i.e., issuance of loans). Historically, Arabs practiced *Musharaka* long before the advent of Islam. It is therefore considered the most authentic form of Islamic contract. While the demand for *Musharaka* compared to other Islamic financial instruments is relatively low, it is expected that in the future to defend the system against criticism, more contracts will be established using *Musharaka* as the financing option.

Offering innovative and competitive Islamic financial products is a real challenge as there are different Sharia schools of thought that make it hard to develop a single standard product that can be sold in Malaysia as well as in the Middle East. This is because Malaysia adopts a more indulgent interpretation of Sharia law than for instance Saudi Arabia. But there are also advantages – once a Sharia compliant product is on the market, it cannot be copied easily by a conventional bank. On the other hand, as most conventional products employ some form of interest, they cannot be directly adapted or copied by an Islamic bank. What makes it more difficult is that regulations, legal documentations, accounting and tax implications, corporate governance frameworks, insurance, and so forth are all different from the bank's country of origin. Islamic banking plays into the hand of local players but there are a number of foreign banks that are keen to develop their knowledge and product ranges to meet the needs of wealthy Muslims. While some wealth managers, such as for example Pictet, entered the market by joining forces with local players, others like UBS have developed their own separately branded branch – *Noriba* that means literally no interest bank. HSBC, on the other hand, built with *Amanah* a global Islamic platform with subsidiaries in Saudi Arabia, Singapore, Indonesia, Malaysia, the United Kingdom, and the United States.

In spring 2006, the European Islamic Investment Bank Plc (EIIB) has received, as the first in London, banking and investment authorization from the Financial Services Authority, the UK's financial regulatory body. The Sharia compliant Islamic investment bank includes Gulf-based individuals and institutions, including a number of Islamic banks, as well as individuals and companies based on Europe. Offering products and services that range from Islamic treasury and capital markets, asset management, private banking, trade finance, and corresponding banking to advisory and corporate finance, EIIB has become an important differentiator in the market. Interestingly, if we compare conventional market indexes such as the Dow Jones World Index with the Dow Jones Islamic Market Index, the Sharia compliant Index performed better since 1996. This trend is also reflected in the FTSE-SGX Asia Sharia 100 Index, launched by the Singapore Stock Exchange in February 2006. The Index was developed by the FTSE London and the British Institute Yasaar Research and includes 100 companies that are Sharia compliant. Islamic banking is booming. It is a market that combines excellent growth rates with sound prospects.

The ability to adapt to the changing nature of demand is certainly a key of success for the survival and future of growth of a company, in particular in foreign markets. For expanding international onshore execution, offering local products and commitment to transparency and the highest prudential standards are just half the battle. What is more we need to understand that customers think differently, hence they have different manners and expectations. It is therefore vital to understand their activities and more specifically their investment culture. Being a global operating firm calls for the development and training of staff with local expertise. Such specific human capital development is essential for leveraging traditional structured investment products. The acceptance of customized local products is key for increasing exposure in complex emerging markets. The examples of Islamic banking demonstrate how vital credibility is. Thus, the development of relationship capital is very important. Engaging a top-notch Sharia scholar to sit on a firm's boards could open doors and make crucial connections to specialist in *Fiqh Almua'malat*, the Islamic Commercial Jurisprudence. The problem is the scarcity of Sharia talent and to find scholars that are respected in the religious community. Understanding modern finance and product development complexities and liquidity and risk management issues compared to conventional banking are other challenges. In addition, each market is unique and hence subject to its own culture. Ethics is vital, not only for the reputation of a brand but also in the way a firm serves its clients with compliant solutions.

The discussion made clear that growing in emerging markets is only possible upon the development of adequate strategies and innovative solutions. For that individual client preferences must always be taken into consideration. So much is certain, only banks that have the capacity for adaptation will be able to expand their footprint in the emerging financial centers of Doha in Qatar, Dubai in the United Arab Emirates or Singapore.

## Regulatory and Policy Changes

### *Do We Need Regulation?*

By reading the following examples, you will confirm that we need regulations. Looking back to Wells Fargo & Company times, banking was not regulated. There were wide-open fields with opportunities but also enormous threads because all it took to open a bank was a safe and a room to keep it in. Consequently, the Californian banking system collapsed in 1855 because of overspeculation. All financial institutions were forced to close their doors. Most did not survive the crisis. Some like Wells Fargo reopened soon, although they lost one-third of its net worth. Their strategy to keep sufficient assets on hand to meet customers' demands rather than investing or transferring it to New York offices paid off. What was a unique strategy by that time became later part of regulatory policy for all institutes with a banking license. Systemic risks and fragility in the financial services are definitely nothing new. If we look back, there are a number of events and periods of significant instability that led to regulations. These systemic financial crises have struck around the world. Just look at the most public examples: the stock market crash in 1973 and 1974 in the United Kingdom with a dramatic rise in oil prices and miners that went on strike; the savings and loans scandal of 1985 in the United States; the global stock market crash of 1987 (Black Monday); the bursting of the Japanese financial system (share and property prices) in 1990 which turned the country into a 13-year lasting deflation phase; the Asian financial crisis of 1997; and the ensuing banking crises in Brazil and Russia in 1998. In the twenty-first century, we evidenced the collapse of the Internet and technology bubble in 2000, the world economic effects arising from the September 11, 2001 attacks, the stock market downturn of 2002, and recently, the subprime mortgage crisis. Latter became apparent in August 2007 with a loss of confidence by investors in the value of securitized mortgages in the United States. Creating a secondary market for securitization of mortgages where banks in the United States could manage their loan portfolios and transfer risks to other market participants required changing laws and getting federal exemptions. It took more than 10 years, after the financial innovation of securitization mortgages was initially discussed to the first trades. The Tax Reform Act of 1986 applied only to housing, finally permitting real estate mortgage investment conduits, with multiple structures to be tax-exempt and allowing real estate investment trusts to invest in mortgage-backed securities. From that time on, institutional investors could invest in this new asset class and absorb the risk being shed by others. Without explaining the tide of events that eventually led the housing bubble burst, the subprime mortgage crisis showed that less control for complex instruments is dangerous for the financial markets and real economy. Where one may propose stringent international regulations for financial products, similar to that of the American Food and Drug Administration for the issuing of new medicines, opponents warn that overregulation hampers innovation. At this point, we can answer the question – yes, we do need regulations! It was the lack of regulation and failures made in the past concerning risk management that triggered the crisis to a great extent.

Besides the recent global financial crisis, where severe problems in one country are very likely to cause a crisis in another, there are also situations that have its origins in particular actions of policy makers. One cause that shakes the industry is money laundering and tax fraud. Increasing crossborder cooperation on taxation may even change offshore business models with institutes, providing tax-transparent solutions that share similarities with onshore banking. Many financial centers revised their laws and policies to shake off the label of being a money-laundering center. In European, even countries like Switzerland, Monaco, Luxemburg, or Liechtenstein have recently eased restrictions on bank secrecy rules and improved their cooperation to exchange information on foreign tax evaders. Look at Liechtenstein, a tinny and discreet bastion of gentility nestled in the Alps between Austria and Switzerland that with a population of 35,000 produces a per capita income of more than CHF 110,000 (Liechtenstein uses the Swiss franc). With its many banks, trusts and foundations that line the streets of the capital, Vaduz, Liechtenstein ranks clearly among the Europe's wealthiest countries. For decades, Liechtenstein offered foreigners to open private trusts anonymously by registering them through a local attorney or trustee. Although this practice is in line with international law, the scandal of February 2008, where a stolen customer list alleged hundreds of Germans to have hidden money in Liechtenstein to evade their own country's personal income taxes, showed the vulnerability of financial centers. The problem is mostly homegrown as Germany has above-average taxes. Please allow us to say that the responsibility of the German government is to first provide a better tax system before blaming other nations that have sophisticated and competitive tax systems. What initially enabled crossborder money flows is the openness of financial markets and innovations in modern information and communication systems where you can move large amounts of money with a mouse click. Whatever your opinion is, this example highlights the difficulty some nations have in keeping wealthy people from moving money to other financial centers. One thing is for sure, it will further stir up the debate on tax policies and regulations.

Today, it is the growing burden of domestic and international regulation that is considered as one of the biggest challenges facing banks in the coming years. In particular, globally coordinated regulatory and compliance pressure with focus on offshore businesses has vital impact for offshore financial centers. Regulation has put much pressure on the industry and will further increase costs for compliance as it is closely connected to developments in technology. To take an example, from the United States Security Industry Authority (SIA), the cost of compliance in the financial service industry reached an estimated annual total of more than US $25 billion in 2005. Thus, costs for compliance have almost doubled since 2002. We assume that the increase in expenditure will not lessen over the next years. One reason is that the stealthy developments of increasing complexity in regulatory issues always include governments as well as industries.

There are two types of regulators, the national government and industry bodies of which are important to the banking industry. As discussed earlier, in coming decades, most developed countries will be confronted with demographic shifts. Thus, pension reform is on the agenda of many governments across the world. Even in countries like the United States where aging is at an earlier state reform that is going to change regulations is under way. In Europe, the European Commission acts as a kind of central legal regulator, monitoring areas such as financial market supervision, tax amnesties, fighting crime, and antimoney-laundering initiatives, which are the main legal issues for the government. While most policies apply internationally, some are based on local laws. Pressure is expected to be on originating money due to the compound effect of withholding tax pressure and amnesties. International tax amnesties encourage wealthy people to repatriate their offshore assets. The aim of such tax amnesties around the world is to reduce the cost caused by illegal transfers of funds to other countries. Thus, bills declare that fiscal residents who have financial assets outside their tax domicile are obligated to transfer these funds back until a defined deadline. During this period, the payment on the reimported capital is usually low. For example, the Italian tax amnesty declared by the Finance Minister in 2001, *Scudo fiscale*, alone led to about €56 billion being repatriated from Switzerland to Italy. Regulations of such kind mean for Swiss private banks with a strong Italian client base the investigation of onshore solutions. The increasing complexity of customer accounts is a striking feature of wealth management. Thus, it is common that globally active clients have multiple accounts at multiple banks in a number of locations. The lack of a bank to know their clients' accounts creates vulnerability to tax evasion and money laundering. Consequently, it has become increasingly complicated for outside reviewer to identify all accounts belonging to an individual.

In terms of combat money laundering, the funding of terrorist activities, and the dubious assets of dictators, drug traffickers, insider dealers, and other organized criminals, significant efforts have been made on a national and international level. Events such as the terror act on September 11, 2001, forced organizations with primary responsibility for developing a global antimoney-laundering framework such as the Financial Action Task Force (FATF) to expand its mission beyond money laundering. In October 2001, FATF issued additional eight special recommendations to combat terrorist financing that became soon new international standards backed by the United Nations Security Council Resolution 1373 (prevention and suppression of the financing of terrorist acts). At the same time, the Basleel Committee as well as the European Union issued guidelines on monitoring money laundering and widened the range of offences. Post-September 11 activated many country and government bodies to develop a number of new regulatory and tax policies. Interpol and Europol, for example, agreed to exchange information on international crime, including money laundering and fraud.

## *The Swiss Banking Secrecy: A Sacred Cow?*

Various countries have legal or contractual confidentiality or privacy obligations, just to mention a few such as the United States Bank Secrecy Act, Banking Act of Singapore, or Banking Act of Luxembourg. The Swiss Bank Client Confidentiality Article 47 of the Federal Law on Banks and Savings Banks together with the Swiss Federal Act on Data Protection has been picked for further in-depth analysis as it is seen as the most hardwearing to protect client data. Therefore, it has a strong influence on crossborder activities. The soil of Switzerland has never fed its small population of little more than 7 million today. Switzerland is unique in Europe, as it has no iron, coal, gas, oil, or any minerals or seaports – all the resources a modern nation needs. Resource-poor, it should be a desperately impoverished country. As illustrated earlier in this book, Switzerland is instead a top financial center, where its population enjoys one of the highest standards of living in the world. Switzerland and its banks have a strange fascination. Voltaire, the French Enlightenment writer, noted in the eighteenth century, "If you see a Swiss banker jump out of the window, jump after him. There's bound to be money in it." Without entitlement but rather driven by enviousness, big nations have always tended to trivialize Switzerland's banking domination. In 1964, after the pound sterling was in serious trouble, George Brown, Economic Minister, and Number 2 in the British cabinet had the feeling that the pound was the victim of deliberate sabotage by Swiss bankers. So, he snapped after a meeting "the gnomes of Zurich are at work again." T.R. Fehrenbach published 2 years later his bestseller "The Gnomes of Zurich."[7] His book provided the first searching look behind the geranium-boxed barred windows of Swiss banks by tracing the rise of Swiss bankers and their relationship to the Swiss Confederation from the fourteenth century right through to modern times. With respect, let us perceive Swiss bankers as gnomes where they share many characteristics with the mythical woodland persons they are named for. Although they are seldom seen, they seem mysterious and appear to have great power. Their existence and their monetary dealings are spoken about in a hushed tone, whether the conversation is taking place in Zurich or outside Switzerland in the financial centers of London and New York.

Nevertheless, the country's discrete bankers have become legends just as the Swiss banking secrecy and numbered accounts. The Swiss banking secrecy, a subtle and sophisticated law, can be seen as one main cause of the rise although there is evidence that it waived the case of various criminal activities. At present, the banking secrecy is one of the most discussed issues as it has come under increasing external pressure to relax its rules. The banking secrecy is controversial, as it is seen from other financial markets as competitive advantage without a right to exist. However, its initial idea and historical background need further explanation. A narrative to introduce the bank secrecy and economic espionage laws of 1934 has been seen more appropriate than citing law texts or official statement from governmental side or any other banking association.[8]

The start of the Swiss bank secrecy goes back to 1934 right after Hitler came to power. In that dark time of German history, tens of thousands of Germans, concerned about the future of their freedom and wealth, were sending funds abroad, and much of this wealth went to Switzerland. To counter this asset drain, the German government enacted a new law ordering all citizens to declare their foreign investments. Failure to comply with this requirement was punishable by death. Even under the threat of death, most Germans did not report their Swiss accounts. Hundreds of Gestapo agents were then ordered to Switzerland in search of these secret accounts. They used bribery, fraudulent inquiries for account balances, wire-tapping, opening mail, and even posing as the supposed account owner to request funds. This Nazi onslaught against the Swiss banking traditions of respect for privacy and property prompted the Swiss government to enact the Bank Secrecy Act of 1934. Thus, it makes it a crime for a bank officer or employee to reveal any information about the customer's account to a third party without the written permission of the customer. Bank officers or employees are further prohibited from disclosing, even to the Swiss government, the existence, or contents of any bank account. Bank employees are covered under the law, even after they have left the bank or the banking business.

A violation is punishable by a prison term of up to 6 months and/or a fine of up to 50,000 Swiss francs. Even if the disclosure is by negligence, the fine ranges up to 30,000 Swiss francs. Therefore, bank account privacy and secrecy still exist in Switzerland, but not if you break a Swiss law or you are a major political tyrant or dictator and have committed crimes against your citizens. Still, depositors are protected in many cases. The Bank secrecy was never meant to cover up for money launderers and criminal organizations. Today, Swiss bankers must scrupulously identify their customers or risk a run-in with Swiss investigators. The original and continuing purpose for Swiss banking secrecy is to protect the innocent, not to shield the guilty. Indications from both Swiss government authorities and Swiss banking officials point to the continuation of this policy.

Unlike many countries where cultural traditions and heritage are often discarded and changed like used cars, real change comes very slowly to Switzerland. For example, the earliest written account of Switzerland was in the first century B.C. when Poseidonius, a Greek writer, described the Swiss as "rich in gold but peaceable." Five hundred years ago in *The Prince*, Machiavelli's classic on political power, he wrote, "Switzerland is known for her stability and military strength." Then in the nineteenth century, noted author Victor Hugo described the future of Switzerland when he wrote the following: "In history, Switzerland will have the last word." The past 700 years seem to affirm these conclusions.

Switzerland continues its long tradition of a belief in gold, stability, and political neutrality combined with a strong defense, and is on a path to continue these traditions. A widespread view of Swiss people is therefore, although controversial, that they are reluctant to give up their freedom in terms of foreign policies, after having fought foreign domination for 700 years. The recent warning of the European Commissions to Switzerland over tax breaks, which it offers to companies who have their headquarters there, undermines this stance. However, it seems that the Swiss gnomes still oppose vehemently – but with success.

## Regulations Are a Double-Edged Sword

For European countries, most regulatory issues have come into operation primarily under the increasing supervision of the European Union. For example, in November 2007, the implementation of MiFID (Market in Financial Instruments Directives) took effect. This requires European private banks to comply with greater transparency of best execution. Precisely, banks are increasingly forced to demonstrate transparency of risk conflicts of interests or pricing structures. As discussed, the impact of local regulatory changes is becoming more and more global. US antimoney-laundering regulations introduced under the PATRIOT act have had far-reaching effects for the entire banking industry. Another key regulatory body is the Basle Committee on Banking Supervision on capital adequacy that will require banks to guarantee system compliance and redesign processes. The new version of the Basle capital accord, so-called Basle II, attempts to set the minimum regulatory capital requirements by closely aligning banks' capital requirements with modern risk management practices. With regulatory capital converging with economic capital – the capital of how banks run the business – increasing profitability in the banking industry might be a consequence. Therefore, risk makes its way on supervisory practices and into market discipline through enhanced risk and capital-related disclosures for banks around the world. Many analysts see that banks increasingly focus on balance sheet structure, e.g., securitizations and disposal of noncore assets. As different banks have different lead times in coming to grip with the new accord, the impact will be felt for at least the next 2 years. Early winners will likely be large players with capital market operations. For less sophisticated players, we see opportunities for catching-up with acquisitions as Basle II offers acquirers' balance sheet as well as profit-and-loss synergies. Hopefully in future, we can observe lower levels of risk and higher levels of profitability at a number of banks. Some market participants even believe that a fully implementation of the Basle II bank capital standards could have partially prevented the recent subprime crisis, by forcing banks to provide capital backing for off-balance sheet funds used to invest in subprime mortgages and other risky asset-backed securities, corporate loans, and bonds.

Industry regulations can also have far-reaching consequences if we look at structured investments (synthetic instruments based on derivatives) that are in direct competition with mutual funds. In Germany, where structured products[9] enjoy their deepest penetration, with up to 60,000 capital market style certificates listed on the Frankfurt and Stuttgart exchanges, fund managers call for better regulations. They claim that structured products have an unfair advantage because they often avoid tax on income and are lightly regulated, quickly launched, and have no requirements to publish costs. In addition, it takes 2 months to get regulatory approval for funds in Germany, but a matter of weeks for certificates. This obviously creates a discrepancy. The complexity is increasing with the ongoing harmonization of 25 national laws of the European Union member states. In retail banking, a pan-European pension product would need equivalent tax treatment in each country where it is sold. For asset management, national and pan-European rules and regulations, such as EU-wide registration of funds, have increased complexity. This high fragmentation of jurisdiction has also a competitive disadvantage compared to, for example, the United States. As of the end of 2006, total fund assets were in the United States US $9.4 trillion and in the European Union €6.6 trillion. The average assets under management of a European fund are with €206 million much lower than for the United States with US $1.2 billion. This means that due to the 25 jurisdictions in Europe, the operating expenses are based only on a quarter of all assets. In view of that, Europe's asset management industry has a lot to catch up and a huge potential for consolidation.

To a certain extent, regulations are a double-edged sword. Once Switzerland and other dominant offshore financial centers adopt full information exchange, banking secrecy is effectively eliminated. Consequently, wealthy clients are likely to transfer their assets back onshore if there is a favorable tax amnesty. The tax developments represent a huge opportunity for traditional offshore wealth managers if they are able to adapt to the onshore model by improving their relationship management skills and upgrade their propositions and investment performance to ensure that they capture a high share of the repatriating assets. Without question, for fighting money laundering, we needed new policies on an international level.

On the other hand, regulations could, for example, decrease the approval period for mutual funds; to ease the entry barrier for firms, this however, would increase domestic competition. A further example is that of loosening legal obstacles for offshore businesses. This change would increase domestic competition likewise. While some argue that too much regulation hampers crossborder sales and damages profitability as well as paralyses innovation other bank manager claims that loosened regulations make it easier for foreign companies to offer their products on every market. Let us look to booming economies such as China, which is attracting the interest of global banks. However, prerequisite for the entry of international competitors is regulatory change. China that joined the World Trade Organization (WTO) in 2001 officially fully opened the banking industry to foreign competitors at the end of 2006. Reality is that the true extent of the Chinese Government's commitment to open competition remains unclear, while regulation is still stringent.

The examples examined the divergent opinions on regulations of Governments and industry bodies. Regulations have driven political and company agendas for years in an attempt to find the right balance between protectionism and open economies. We will see for how long Governments such as the one of China are able to restrain competition and an open market environment. The recent financial crisis provides an opportunity to rethink regulation of global financial markets. The Emergency Economic Stabilization Act, enacted October 3, 2008, commonly referred to as the bailout of the United States financial system and other injections of capital into financial markets by the European central banks, to prevent further damages or recession, are not enough. Governments and industry policy makers must take advantage of the crisis and provide banks with guidelines. But we neither need more laws, nor is regulation bad per se. What is required is smarter and more specific regulation. This affects banks as they are asked to improve their controls and to enhance collaboration and communication with policy makers. These reforms are necessary to sustain growth and to prevent future crises. The more, since the shift of direction – to borrow the metaphor *laissez-faire* by John Maynard Keynes – there will never be a completely free and self-regulating market.

## The Technological Imperative

Making the link to the previous section, compliance costs raised dramatically as new regulations force banks to overhaul their IT platforms or to buy new software to facilitate compliance work. It is estimated that large banks in the European Union spend between €80 million and 150 million alone on Basleel II implementation. Most are technology costs due to projects to improve monitoring and reporting functions and pertaining process changes. Besides compliance-related IT expenses, there are two other types of IT spend that act as key indicators for the potential for financial services in the different regional markets. One driving force for economic growth is productivity gains due to the diffusion of new technologies. The other confers competitive advantage by adding value to clients. Later is typically visible in the form of Internet-based services for clients or client reporting but also at client–advisor interfaces. The impact of technology to customers cannot be neglected. Recent advancements in technology have changed customer behavior and expectations significantly. Due to technological innovations, it has become easier, faster, and cheaper to obtain information about financial markets, products, and services. This increasing transparency of products and prices has led to lower customer loyalty and a readiness to switch institutions. Lately, because of this, capital is easily transferable electronically on the global market and switching costs and barriers are no longer a hurdle. Demanding ultra-high-net-worth individuals (UHNWI), those with liquid financial assets over around US $30 million invested, tend to behave like institutional investors. They hold products for shorter periods than they used to and, most notably, they want to select from a universe of "best-of-breed" solutions, regardless of where they come from. To sum up, customers are demanding a wider range of "state-of-the-art" products and services. Therefore, they require access information and place orders 24 h a day, 7 days a week from around the world through a variety of channels, securely and at low costs. Technological developments have always changed consumer behavior from the ATM to the Internet. However, all these factors pertaining to the changing nature of demand have led to advanced and complex services such as portfolio risk management, dynamic asset allocation, objective investment advice, and increasing investments in latest technology.

Besides these general changes, clients in international onshore markets demand different products. This consequence of international growth means for companies that they have to provide actual information about innovative products on the Internet. Sophisticated online product and service catalogues where potential clients can gather information get in contact with the bank, and placing orders is a challenge. We know that every company needs to be able to explore new business opportunities constantly while watching profitability. Profitability is a matter of creating the right product and client mix, while tightly controlling cost and the margins that drive profitability. In many cases, existing products and services and efficient processes are not enough to build strategic advantage in new markets, in the sense that strategic advantage is a unique resource that determines the firm's competitive renewal. For information technology, this means that there is an increasing recognition on the need to turn fixed costs into variable costs. Information and communication technology at large firms in the financial services industry typically represents between 15 and 20% of overall operating expenses. This is not only the second largest element, behind personal expenses it is more than double than other industries invest. This makes particularly banks the largest spender in technology vertical to telecommunications industries. This also explains why every tenth employee at global banks works in IT.

It is a given reality that financial service institutes do processing and communication of information rather than producing hardware. Technology is therefore a key driver for creating new open business models, improving processes, and product and service development. In recent years, the Internet revolutionized distribution channels. Making effective use of the opportunities of ICT and efficient information management is pivotal. Undisputedly, ICT has become an integral part of all businesses in a bank. The balancing act is to develop and integrate new business processes according to IT architecture standards quickly and at the same time operate the applications reliably and at low costs. The market developments in banking call further for developing and implementing new, faster, and smarter systems such as electronic banking, core banking processing, customer relationship management, or risk systems to keep up with increasing customer demands, legal implementations of policies, and industry initiatives. Besides the integration of acquired institutes, disintegration and outsourcing efforts, and, in particular, coping with regulation provisions, have led to extra expenses for organizational and technical adaptation.

All these factors enforce the process of updating or replacing core banking and other legacy systems that were designed back in the 1970s. Increasing awareness for a flexible architecture that is aligned with the business strategy has been observed. A number of other institutes are investing large sums into technology with the attempt to increase efficiency, distinguish them from other market players, and increase their competitiveness. There is no doubt that technology is one driving force behind new open business models. Just think of new Web 2.0 technologies, referring to the use of the Internet for collaborative information sharing and online service delivery. This technology innovation may set new standards for openness and forms of collaboration among firms and customers as it aims to maximizing collective intelligence through dynamic information sharing and creation. It is hard to predict Web 2.0 service adoption as it was just introduced a couple of years ago. To the present, many banks do not encourage Web 2.0 services because they are cutting costs and are incapable to grasp the potential financial returns.

Banking has changed radically within the last decades. It has become integrated with many banks evolving into global financial services providers. Requirements have altered accordingly. Product portfolios, too, have experienced substantial expansion, but entire core banking infrastructures had not been adapted. Driven by clear business requirements, we observe in the market that many firms run modernization programs. The driving force behind technological innovation in banking is rather a combination of business and market requirements and technological capabilities. There is a clear need to remodel the new business requirements using modern technology to increase efficiency in data processing, provide effective, future-oriented support for the businesses, and value-adding tools for clients.

## Implications of the Trends

A fundamental change is occurring in the way firms orchestrate innovation and value creation. The dynamic developments discussed in the previous section have had an enormous impact on the banking industry during the past 25 years. Based on the analysis of the industry environment, it is assumed that the discussed trends will continue to affect most global banks. As universal banks include different businesses, the trends do not challenge all businesses to the same extent. Banking is generally grouped into four areas: retail banking, wealth management, asset management, and investment banking. There are several factors determining the development over the coming 5–10 years. Wealth accumulation due to more capital-intensive activity in developed economies and growth in global equity markets will affect wealth management businesses. Additionally to these two factors, demographic shifts will accelerate retirement provisioning and asset growth and have an impact on global asset management activities. As a traditional bank's lending services have been replaced by securities trading and other financial market activities, corporate restructuring of crossborder consolidation and increased investments of assets in equity products have changed the traditional business practice of investment banks. Where retail banking is a domestic commoditized business with low growth, investment banking, on the other hand, is an international business with different business rules and culture. As the goals and expectations of wealthy, retail, or institutional clients differ, banks distinguish between different country-specific customer types. Services provided in their home market are often categorized for individuals, companies, financial sector, financial intermediaries, governments and public sector, and nonprofit organizations and charities.

The global highly competitive economical environment with low margins and unpredictable volumes has made it harder to generate the revenues necessary to provide good returns on products and services. Additionally, the increasing pressure to manage costs to improve profitability let institutes shift to new value creation models. There are two basic approaches to increasing value, decreasing costs, particularly high fixed costs, or creating new revenue streams. In banking, we assume that roughly half of total costs typically come from back-office overhead and investment management. Many global firms have a great deal of duplication of processes for equity, economic research, or third-party product selection. In particular, global operations lead to duplication of applications in customer relationship management, client and investment management, and back-office information processing. In contrast to back-office cost synergy opportunities, overall sales costs threaten to keep on rising, given the war for talents and especially continuous need for professional client advisors. Maximizing front-line effectiveness is therefore another crucial issue to decrease costs and increase value.

We think that the right organizational setup with concentration on core competencies and outsourcing of noncore businesses such as support processes in operation, transaction processing, and ICT are effective cost-reducing approaches. Applying a more structured and consistent sales and advisory process by providing the appropriate organizational setting with the right tools is suggested. In addition, we know that attracting and retaining top talent is a key driver for growth. Therefore, strategic hiring and human capital management of best people in terms of training and on-the-job coaching to front personnel are essential initiatives. Most private banks have also applied sophisticated compensation models that balance financial gains with other motivational factors. These suggestions, although just briefly discussed, should always be considered as general action fields.

For the second approach, namely creating new revenue streams, building and leveraging capability for innovation more efficiently and systematically becomes important. Several institutes in the financial service industry have changed their innovation processes. They consider new operating models that facilitate cross-selling opportunities. In addition, they eliminate company boundaries with the attempt of developing new products, services, and businesses in collaboration with partners, rather than making use of internal resources exclusively. On the distribution side, sharing revenues with third-party distributors has become a recent industry trend. This represents a clear shift in the value chain, in which banks substitute their own products with more profitable products offered by others. Moving from a fixed to a variable cost structure and working with other firms to spread risk and create new businesses are areas that will be changing the way in which banking business has been done for decades.

## The Challenges for the Financial Services

Leading through the changing business environment is a huge challenge if we consider all the vibrant dimensions discussed. Banks have to find solutions to cope with the changing nature of demand while satisfying their existing clientele. Today, mature customers wish to select products from an universal content. At the same time, they expect much more service from their bank. Product price and performance, advanced advisory processes, and relationship management are the crucial issues that we need to contemplate. To cope with these challenges, on the one hand, continuous development of innovative products to competitive prices is essential, and, on the other hand, there is a need to provide clients with third-party products that can be combined with the bank's own products and services. A number of banks are thus implementing new business models for selling products and services and, for adding client value on an international base. Drawing on market observations, there are several approaches to achieve sustained success. One approach is to open up product portfolios, precisely offering proprietary products in combination with third-party products on domestic markets. Another approach for satisfying demanding clients is to bundle products, services, and the advisory process to a solution that adds value to the client. To reach an international clientele, banks will further distribute their solutions through internal as well as external sales channels.

From a business viewpoint, there are always regulatory and legal obstacles that prevent banks from selling products and services in onshore markets. One way of doing business internationally is to develop the capability to integrate compliant products from local providers into their offerings. To add to these challenges, there is, particularly in mature markets, pressure from tax amnesties and concerns about tighter regulations. As we discussed earlier, issues like the banking secrecy might affect countries like Switzerland significantly. What used to be a competitive advantage for decades, if repealed, would drive assets back onshore. Although a number of bilateral arrangements have been made with Switzerland, as it is a major financial center but not member of the European Union, there have been concerns that these developments are leading to an increasing level of repatriation of assets booked in international markets. Several market participants expect to see a rapid growth of crossborder declared money that rely on tax arbitrage rather than secrecy. As the case may be, firms have to build up local branches to serve clients. The trust that clients placed in the bank when they had accounts and assets managed in Switzerland has to be established a new for offshore business activities. The latest acquisitions of local fund management and private client businesses across Europe anticipate those concerns, driven by growth strategies in the very fragmented wealth management market. Rebuilding trust in other cultures with other legal systems can be achieved more easily with the acquisition of local institutes. Just keep in mind that the barriers to entry in domestic private banking are higher than in offshore. This is because the costs of developing onshore operations imply the need for scale and expensive resources to achieve a leading market share.

Another form of increasing regulatory and stakeholder scrutiny has arised from the current credit and liquidity environment. The credit crisis calls for higher levels of transparency, better operational controls but also for breaking the siloed mentality toward a more converged view of risk that is aligned with businesses. As a reaction, institutes are forced to undertake projects to ensure a more systematically and comprehensively approach to risk management. Whatsoever, there is no doubt that policies and regulations affect any bank and might shift the competitive landscape radically.

The implementation of regulatory issues also affects solution delivery budgets with increasing expenses. Besides the mandatory implementation of regulations with information technology, there are various opportunities arising out of technological advancements. Information technology became the backbone of any activity in banking. It has affected all banking businesses likewise. We all know that information and technology for processing customer information is playing an increasingly crucial role in banking. Innovative applications may be the driving forces in the rapid development in the financial service industry. Banks paid less attention to information, particularly customer information in the 1970s and 1980s due to the lack of adequate technology to achieve this aim. This changed with applications like data-mining systems that allowed data to be stored, analyzed, and retrieved. Such applications have become an essential part of customer relationship management. However, the technology imperative can be discussed from various perspectives. It can be seen as a driver of demand rather than a consequence of it. For instance, ATM and Internet banking were originally a means for efficient information processing and increasing productivity. Both technological innovations changed customer behavior and revolutionized the banking industry more rapidly than anyone anticipated. Such innovations not only changed *where* clients do their banking, but also changed *how* they do it. Many banks realized that to leverage technology fully, it has to be aligned with the business intent. Technology and business interact and can only together increase the bank's innovation capability.

While the economy is global, financial market supervision and regulations are still organized nationally, alongside all cooperation and participation in international financial committees. There are active efforts to expand financial relations between European Union member countries. These issues are on the agenda of most board members and politicians, even if international collaboration with the aim of protecting a firm's or country's interest is not always without tension. Hence, some countries have been under constant political pressure, notably exerted by the European Union and the Organization for Economic Cooperation and Development (OECD) to relax and bring into line its banking rules with European regulations. New negotiations on further topics including combating international financial crime and fraud, the equivalence taxation of savings income, and issues regarding the banking secrecy might hit established financial centers. The Swiss combination of low taxes, bank secrecy, and political stability, once a competitive advantage, might face competition in the future, particularly in private banking from offshore financial centers such as Singapore and Hong Kong. It is expected that these emerging financial centers provide excellent conditions for high-net-worth individuals for the coming years. The example shows that leading financial centers can loose its dominant position due to regulatory developments within less than a decade.

The examination of the environment found that several trends are challenging the financial services. We learned that the entire financial service industry is going through a phase of forceful changes, particularly since the start of the 1990s. Banking has operated historically in a relatively stable environment that recently changed to a global business, driven by hypercompetition and high volatile markets. Consolidation is one effect of the increasing globalization. On the other hand, we observed quasi-nationalizations of suffering banks in the home of free-market capitalism – the United States. The fact that all G7 leaders agreed to direct government bailouts to be part of the solution to the banking crisis will change the controlling and voting right of these new shareholders. Other consequences of the trends are the disintegration of the traditional value chain and the reduction of production depth by outsourcing supporting processes or providing third-party products to clients. Although some businesses are affected stronger than others are, most large banks have included the recent developments into their strategic roadmap. Without understanding the trends, neither would proactive strategy be possible nor would quick reactions. We believe that the trends discussed are interrelated and have to a certain extent directed banking into a new business paradigm – the open innovation paradigm.

## Notes

1. For the concept of exploitation and exploration, see the seminal work of March, J.G. (1991) 'Exploration and exploitation in organizational learning', *Organization Science,* 2(1), 71–87.
2. Christensen, C.M. and Raynor, M.E. (2003) *The innovator's solution.* Harvard Business School Press, Boston, MA.
3. Schumpeter, J.A. (1975) [orig. pub. 1942] *Capitalism, socialism and democracy.* Harper, New York.
4. Accenture (2003) *The innovator's advantage: Using innovation and technology to improve business performance.* Study by Accenture, October.
5. The Cartesian dualism sought a native morality in the mind and a strict divergence of nature into subject and object, knower and known, observer and observed, and mind and matter. The epistemological epitome of rationalism and modern empiricism (Bacon, Locke, and Hume)

shaped the foundation for a neutral observation theory, which later influenced the development of positivism. Definite knowledge is based on scientific facts, derived from the observation of the empirical world through the accumulation of objective sense data as Compte argued in 1853. The philosophical doctrine of *positivism* declared that natural science and social science both are cohesive by value-free observation, description, explanation, and prediction of the external world. Empiricism, rationalism, and positivism all share the same ontological assumptions and build the basis for scientific law, in which social reality can be observed objectively, measured, recorded, and explained. Criticism of the above-discussed philosophical stances is that they commonly focus on the inappropriateness of natural–scientific methods for inquiry into the human or social sciences. The abandon of human subjectivity of positivism approaches in management research and business makes the discussion about opposed stances inevitable. On the contrary, there is *interpretivism* as it subsumes all or a part of a number of traditions, such as constructivism, phenomenology, hermeneutics, symbolic interactionism, and existential sociology. It is further believed that reality can best be understood by sound understanding and interpreting actors' perception of social phenomena. Overall, the author of this book supports interpretivism and the social construction viewpoint that meanings emerge through the verbal and social interaction of actors.

6. Cruickshank, D. (2000) *Competition in UK banking: A report to the Chancellor of the Exchequer.* March (ISBN 0115600752). Her Majesty's Stationery Office, London, UK.
7. Fehrenbach weaved facts and extensive documentation into gripping narrative to explain the rise of Switzerland to a leading financial center. He concluded that the Swiss banking secrecy has been one crucial success factor. Fehrenbach, T.R. (1966) *The gnomes of Zurich.* Leslie Frewin Publishers, London.
8. The section in the book is grounded on a narrative by Holland, R., Green, A. and Rukeyer, L. (2006) *Secrets of the great investors: Swiss gnomes and global investing.* Audio CD. Blackstone Audio, Oregon. For further information on the Swiss Banking Secrecy, see The Swiss Federal Department of Finance http://www.efd.admin.ch/dokumentation/zahlen/00579/00607/00621/index.html?lang=en [July 4, 2007]
9. *Structured products* are synthetic investment instruments that enable investors to receive an equity-linked performance that cannot be met from the standardized financial instruments available in the markets. They are used as portfolio enhancement tool to increase returns while limiting risk exposure of a portfolio. Equity-linked structured products generally combine an option component, which provides a unique payout, and a fixed-income security, which guarantees that parts or the entire investment will be reimbursed.

# Open Innovation: The New Business Paradigm

- Capitalize the key trends by enabling the transition from closed innovation to an open model of innovation.
- Tap the full potential of open innovation in the financial services early on as it will increasingly thrive your businesses.
- Be open to good ideas, negotiate open innovation mechanisms, lower organizational boundaries, and put all into practice.

## The Banking Industry at the Beginning of the Twenty-First Century

Many firms are transforming into flatter and more specialized organizations. They integrate their customers and link with suppliers and other businesses to form a larger, more open, value creation entity. The acquisition and consolidation activities of the largest firms to become even bigger are omnipresent and reveal that banking businesses are in constant flux. Let us, for instance, analyze the wealth management market as it continues to grow and offer many opportunities. It is a matter of common knowledge that competition has become global. Firms have intensified their search for best people around the globe. New growth markets are developing. And, the complexity of client demands has increased. Overall, the financial service industry will look different in 5 years. It will be more global with successful players having themselves established in emerging markets. Exceeding customer experiences will increasingly drive growth, where technology will empower customers. Innovative technology will be the centerpiece of a customer-focused strategy with personalization becoming increasingly important. The technological imperative will also improve back-office processes and provide better service and delivery to strengthen ties with a global clientele. The recent developments changed the very nature of products, processes, structure, competencies, and culture. To reduce complexity, factors that affect the bank indirectly or from outside the organization, such as the Euro, risk considerations, the financial markets, or the changing nature of society itself, although important they are not elaborated further within this book.

D. Fasnacht, *Open Innovation in the Financial Services*,

Induced by the trends discussed, the major phenomenon that will be driving change beneath the surface of banking for the next few years seems to be the transition from a closed to an open innovation paradigm. The term "paradigm" is used here in a similar sense to Thomas Kuhn, who referred to it as the *social context* such as accepted rules, standards, and practices that are deeply rooted and shared by individuals.[1] What makes Kuhn's position stimulating is the claim that there can be no strictly logical reason for the change of a paradigm. This is what we explained with the recent developments in the financial service industry. They have driven the shift to open innovation largely; however, there may have been other forces that facilitated the paradigm shift likewise. Open innovation is characterized by a new management style that facilitates collaborative operating models for innovation. One strategy is, therefore, the externalization of innovation processes and the incorporation of knowledge for each of the phases of the innovation process. Within the new open innovation paradigm, focus lays on the client. In particular, the advisory process rather than product innovation generates value added for customers. The operating model and the way people work, even the very nature of the organization itself has changed radically. Becoming an open, flexible, and agile organization requires overcoming organizational inertia. To achieve this aim, firms in the banking industry see one possible answer in what they termed "open architecture." This open and flexible operating model promotes collaboration with third-party product and service providers and in addition prompts the organization to think more flexibly, rather than bureaucratically and mechanistically.

During the 1970s and 1980s, most banks focused on product innovation apart from incremental innovation to increase efficiency. Rapid product development and bringing these products on the market were considered as imperative. The infrastructure for processing information pertaining to a product was expensive and complex to maintain. In addition, intermediaries and new market entrants were forbidden by regulation from entering the sector. Product innovation was an exclusivity of incumbent banks, whereby these banks provided a number of proprietary products to their clients. The developments in the banking industry, as discussed previously, changed the competitive landscape radically. Today, all market participants are able to process or outsource information management reliably and at reasonable cost. Although the nature of most banking products remains the same, they can be more easily imitated. The increasing variety has finally led to falling margins and moved basic banking products such as deposit accounts, loans, or credit cards from differentiated status to commodity. Consequently, customers perceive little difference between competitive offerings. Therefore, most differentiated firms attempt to bundle various products and services on a global level. These banks attempt to open up their operating models to allow customers greater flexibility. Thus, they shifted organizational boundaries and developed value chains across organizations. Processes actually go across boundary lines including the functions of several business partners. In the past, banks did not regard processes as a means to increase customer service as a complementary to their product offerings. One reason was that banks yielded good profits with the products they pushed to the market, and that focus was on operational process efficiency rather than process innovation for customers. This changed in recent years due to the fact that products became commodity and customers more mature. Most banks today focus on advisory processes to provide a significant amount of benefits to customers beyond just product sales. The advisory process is the real texture to the relationship and perceived by clients as value for money in the relationship with the bank. This process may include services from third-party providers wherever beneficial for the client and the bank. Operating open models for product and service innovation requires a smart advisory process as complementary. In the bid for differentiation, one business priority of a firm should be perfecting the client experience with the global implementation of a holistic client advisory process supported by seamlessly integrated tools.

Such strategic initiatives imply organizational renewal, as in most cases current structures are hierarchical, rigid, and bureaucratic in its nature. These organizational structures were legitimate to manage a centrally organized firm where strategies were dictated top-down and working one's way up. Old organizational structure was characterized by many hierarchical levels. Such structures were encapsulated in Alfred Sloan's General Motors and Harold Geneen's ITT. Perhaps, the mundaneness and regularity of bureaucratic and corporate life were best described in William Whyte's "The Organizational Man" from 1956,[2] in which the individual is taken over by the bureaucratic machine in the name of efficiency. However, traditional and vertical structures are not appropriate anymore. One rationale is that decision-making and implementing strategies are slow in addition to the changed perceptions of employees about career and incentives. Today's dynamic environment calls for structures that help banks to be more responsive to environmental changes and demands. Therefore, innovative firms implement more flat, flexible, process-oriented, and team-based structures that focus on coordination and collaboration across organizational boundaries. Flexible organization not only facilitates the development and implementation of strategic actions effectively and efficiently. What is more firms that adapt flexible forms are better set up if it comes to open innovation.

To deliver a unique client value proposition, transporting the benefits of the advisory process to the customer is essential. Therefore, front business areas should be relatively autonomous and support entrepreneurship. Managers, in general, must be free to decide whether they collaborate with external companies or use internal resources, products, and services. Client advisors are enforced to use their own judgment as to how they focus on current customer accounts or nurture new opportunities. The new type of organizational structure in banking is based on flexibility and developing new core competencies. The essential capability is believed to be adaptability. This means moving quickly toward new opportunities as well as increasing the speed of adjusting to changing business environments. The cause for this change can be explained with the fact that structure is preceding organizational conduct and is hence vital for a firm's agility.

If we look at technology as a means to support businesses, no sophisticated front system for managing customer information was available 25 years ago. In addition, there were no structured processes on how to capture and transform information manually. Consequently, knowledge was mostly kept in the heads of individuals rather than processed and disseminated with the help of information and communication technology. In particular, client advisors were not very keen on sharing information within the organization. Banks realized in the 1990s the importance of sharing and incorporating knowledge and developing human capital. This increasing awareness is reflected in a number of structural changes and in the installation of improved customer relationship management systems. Discontinuities and the uncertainty in the financial service industry called for evolving and developing competencies rather than static knowledge. Such competencies are not necessarily related to banking. The ability to utilize relationship capital is understood as a kind of soft skill that is used to integrate knowledge gained from clients with necessary, although captive, banking knowledge. It was observed that interactions of the bank's workforce with external business partners are increasing due to opening up operating models. Developing a unique set of dynamic competencies is what many firms consider as the main source for the management of transformative change processes. These core competencies are a *mélange* of knowledge that ties sets of other resources together. This include the ability to collaborate with business partners as well as the skills required for nurturing clients.

The theory and practice of organizational change tells us that the way of doing business as well as developing a set of new core competencies includes behavioral and cultural changes. Banking used to be a closed and traditional business for decades. Processes and structures that supported this paradigm have changed within the last year significantly. The open innovation paradigm with its nature of collaboration beyond company boundaries, even with competitors, requires an open and innovative organizational culture that emphasizes organizational learning. In an industry that seemed to be stable for decades, the change toward an entrepreneurial and open attitude is a challenge. Furthermore, adopting new processes, structures, and competencies is not everybody's native. Building a learning and innovative organizational culture across the organization is therefore considered as a key success factor for organizational change and renewal. This has become a top leadership priority for most banks. Firms have reacted with a number of initiatives. With the circle of excellence, for example, knowledge is disseminated diffused throughout the organization in the form of best practices. Another human resources initiative is empowerment of employees, a concept that gives them more scope for decision making as the bank attempts to encourage entrepreneurial and innovative attitude.

The changes in banking businesses imply new forms of managing innovations. Traditional and closed approaches to innovation are not appropriate anymore. We need to understand what changed and why and, in particular, how a firm can adapt to the new rules of the open innovation paradigm. In the next section, we show how open approaches replaced closed and traditional approaches to innovation.

## New Forms of Managing Innovation

We learned that innovation should be managed as a set of interdisciplinary processes, rather than as a single-function activity. The management of innovation is a crucial process for any firm. The innovation process is not restricted to the solution of a problem but includes a number of corresponding activities undertaken to bring the innovation to market. Successful innovation management involves taking a strategic approach to innovation, as well as developing and using effective implementation mechanisms and structures. Supportive organizational context and effective external linkages are other components of the innovation process, which must be carefully managed. Hence, the management of innovation is the purposeful orchestration and directed application of human capital in an organizational.

As innovation is about ideas, managing innovation is the activity, which structures the complete process from generation of an idea through the selling of the product to markets. Innovation in the financial service industry is more than just coming up with good ideas – it is the process of growing good ideas into practical uses that counts. This is a demanding and crucial activity in the process of developing ideas into actual products and services, or any other type of innovation. The innovation process is an interactive, often chaotic, intuitive, cumulative, and complex process. Therefore, innovation may occur through a diffusion process. The key in successful innovation is to take the right decision, or metaphorically, to let a thousand flowers bloom, then pick and nourish the most promising and let the rest wither. The challenge is to structure and channel innovation activities in such a way that creativity remains. Paradoxically, this is the "controlled chaos." It is the controlled (chaotic) approach, in which an organization provides a creative platform to generate innovation. Innovation can only prosper in a flexible organizational structure with little forms of standardization and bureaucracy.[3]

As the innovation process is broadly divided into phases such as idea generation, research, development, and commercialization, each phase requires distinct management. At the same time, the entire innovation process has to be viewed as a cohesive whole. A closer integration of an organization's research and development activities and the downstream (market-pull) and upstream (technology-push) process is suggested. The innovation process of the future is an interactive model with feedback loops and interactions between different activities. This thought interacts between science, applied science, technology, and interorganizational innovation-related activities. The management of innovation has become a nonlinear process, comparable to a complex system. This process can be managed with the right strategy. Structuring the innovation process for services, and putting its management on a strategic level might be initial activities.

The aim of the next section is to give the reader a broad overview about traditional approaches to innovation before we dive deeper into open innovation.

## Closed Innovation: The Traditional Paradigm

The approach in which organizations generate, develop, and commercialize their own ideas belongs to the closed innovation model. All innovation activities are performed within the company border and exclusively with internal resources. Closed innovation is a paradigm, which is based on control. It fit well with the knowledge landscape of the second half of the twentieth century. In the 1970s and 1980s, companies in the IT industry with its proprietary architectures and vertical integration represented a closed innovation philosophy. Research within this closed paradigm meant, without exception, internal research, as well as internal development. Consequently, companies such as Xerox and IBM invested heavily in internal research. Although they separated their research facilities, for instance PARC or a number of IBM Research Divisions from the rest of the organization, they focused on human resources to develop and maintain internal innovation systems, rather than making use of their core competencies.

Similar than in manufacturing, most banks focused on product innovation apart from incremental innovation to increase efficiency. Rapid product development and bringing these products on the market were considered as imperative. The infrastructure for processing information pertaining to a product was expensive and complex to maintain. Intermediaries and new market entrants were forbidden by regulation from entering the sector. Product innovation was an exclusivity of incumbent banks, whereby these banks provided a number of proprietary products to their clients. The developments in the banking industry, as discussed previously, changed the competitive landscape radically. Today, all market participants are able to process or outsource information management reliably and at reasonable cost. Although the nature of most banking products remains the same, they can be more easily imitated. The increasing variety has finally led to falling margins and moved banking products from differentiated status to commodity. That is why we see many banks bundling various products and services on a global level. These banks attempt to open up their operating models to allow customers greater flexibility.

Companies with an inward philosophy and persistent organizational structure miss a number of opportunities. External ideas, research and development, paths over the company boundary to alternative, and new markets are not destined in the closed innovation paradigm. As a result, many ideas were not realized and over time, this leads to a decrease in innovation power and finally impaired the firm's competitiveness. Besides the fact that ideas were cancelled due to the "not invented here" syndrome, there might also be other factors that guide resource allocation decisions, such as financial considerations among others. Most organizations across all industries were, until the early 1980s, good examples for a closed autarky system of innovation, where knowledge was simply added by sitting in closed entities within the organization. This was the appropriate strategy and was seen as "the golden age for internal research and development" as Chesbrough stated.[4]

With the transformation of the society into information-based, knowledge-intensive, and service-driven economy, business rules have shifted radically and with them in many industries, the logic of closed innovation has become obsolete. According to Chesbrough, firms must restructure themselves to leverage a distributed landscape of knowledge, instead of ignoring it in the pursuit of their own internal research agendas. Based on research in the manufacturing sector, several factors are responsible for the erosion of the closed innovation paradigm. For example, the increasing availability and mobility of skilled workers diffused the knowledge that companies possessed from the fortified towers of internal R&D to suppliers, customer, partners, universities, startups, and other third parties. Also, the separation of research and development in the product development process dramatically changed the internally focused approach to innovation. Other erosion factors are the venture capital market, which remains a reality even supposing the exaggerated days of the technology bubble. Lastly, the increased production experience, quality, knowledge, and reliability of external suppliers has led to the demise of the closed innovation paradigm and motivated numerous companies to take the step and open up their innovation philosophies. To unlock their full innovation potential, existing businesses as well as new ideas will need to be combined with external resources and ideas. This means that various forms of externalization and outsourcing of innovative activities should be considered.

## The Externalization of Innovation Processes

Externalization at its broadest level refers to the shift of a particular set of products or services from being generated within a firm to outside it. Externalization is therefore associated with collaboration beyond company boundaries for all phases of the innovation process. The rationale that encourages the use of external partners might be diverse. There is always an underlying theory such as market power or aggressive growth that gives good reasons for collaboration. If we look from a resource-based perspective on the firm, we can see many rationales like, for example, for collaboration. The value creation potential of firm resources, if they are pooled together. In addition, we can justify collaboration with the need to innovate or the lack of internal resources. Some companies simply contract their research or development work to third parties. If we understand collaboration activities from a resource-based perspective, it is driven by logic of strategic resource needs and social resource opportunities. Thus, a bundle of unique resources and relationships define a firm's competitive position. The need for collaboration can also be justified with the transaction-costs view of the firm[5] where we refer to the financial effort for activities that are performed for an exchange like selling, buying, or any other activity. Based on that theory, collaboration is justified when the transaction costs associated with an exchange are intermediate and not high enough to justify vertical integration. The transaction-cost economics of interfirm collaboration was, for a long time, the performance measurement concept *par excellence*. The main critique of this almost 40-year-old economics-based view for interorganizational collaboration, although it is one of the most dominant approaches, is mainly that it is too rigid and too focused on financials and therefore ignores value creation, which arises from combined partner resources. In general, we strongly believe that firms have to learn to create value through collaborative activities.

At the heart of the resource-based view and transaction-cost considerations, there is the scholar of core competencies that might influence the decision to outsource noncore activities to external partners.[6] Recently, it became clear that core competencies that focus on core activities might yield to competitive advantage.

A core competence can, in general, include tangible as well as intangible resources. It is the distinctive capability of an organization to exceed products and markets. Core competencies are embedded in an organization's modus operandi and show what a company does better, faster, or differently from any competitor. Simplified, core competencies are areas where a company must excel to maintain leadership. Thus, it is the company's capability to think, act, and operate differently. If a company systematically assesses what sort of competencies are worth developing and sustaining, and how it derives value from having them, then it has identified its core competencies. Imagine the global economy as a system. In such a system, all members are interdependent and are customers of each other. We saw many companies restructuring and downsizing to fund only those core competencies that are key to their profitable growth strategies and long-term survival. Essential part of this process is managing relationships not only with customers but also with employees, channel partners, and strategic alliance partners. If an organization is superior in such activities and capable of further developing and maintaining its relationship capital, it is well prepared for the global market.

One might argue that core competencies can simply be purchased on the open market. This is wrong; core competencies can only be learned from a partner. The phases of innovation, such as coming up with new ideas, research and development, and finally creating a market out of it, require all of its distinct set of capabilities. In an increasing specialized world, there is no need for a firm to cover diametrically opposed activities such as generating ideas or commercialization by themselves. They can do it with specialized partners. The transfer of resources and competencies between business partners may improve product development cycles. In other words, if organizations outsource key phases of the innovation process, they might speed up the process, lower cost, amplify impact, and above all offer continuous innovation and flexibility. Strategically, outsourcing innovation might save innovation cost and risk significantly. Outsourcing can be explained with the degree of uncertainty and complexity in R&D activities. To do so, we must categorize innovation from true uncertainty, such as fundamental research and invention followed by radical product and process innovation as well as major product innovation, down to very little uncertainty such as incremental innovation, product differentiation, and late adaptation of established process innovation and franchised operations in own establishment.

Because of restricted internal resources, focus on transaction costs and core competencies, as well as product complexity, shorter product life cycles, and risk issues encourage many companies to collaborate. A lot of innovation today has a collaborative nature, confirmed by the growing number of strategic alliances. This is in contrast to organizational structures and development philosophies two decades ago, which we described previously as the closed approach. Consequently, the core competencies of future-oriented companies have shifted and not just changed their processes and routines, but the very way they organize themselves, i.e., their organizational design. For example, empirical evidence from a number of cases suggested disaggregated organizational design in which firms separate business units based on the capabilities required. A recent study in the United Kingdom confirmed that this strategy could be successful. Accordingly, 62% of the sample companies entered new markets by establishing a separate business unit, and 68% of these built up a new company.[7]

It is important to understand that before we support externalization and outsourcing strategies, we have to answer the question "why innovate through collaboration?" The answer should be that importing new ideas is seen as a good method of multiplying the building blocks of innovation. Thinking about partnerships leads to a resourcing strategy that leverages the development of new and existing knowledge. Knowledge as a resource that offers a solution to a problem or a contribution in any other form is therefore available both within and outside the organization. Another benefit of collaboration is that exporting and importing ideas helps companies to concentrate on their core competencies and businesses and gives them a better instrument to measure an innovation's real value. The point of any form of externalization is, therefore, that a sustainable core business must have economic advantages such as lower cost or higher quality over other companies in the open market.

## Implications of Collaborative Innovation

As discussed in the previous section, collaboration is accepted as a form of resource exchange, in which leveraging, renewing, and refreshing existing knowledge resources are essential for the firm's competitiveness. Collaborating as one solution provides flexible access to external knowledge and facilitates innovation. Collaboration is an important knowledge-creating routine, which brings new resources and experience into the firm from external sources. External experiences usually enhance innovation by breaking down the thought worlds that arise because people with different expertise not only know different things, but also know those things differently. Charles Darwin noted "In the long history of humankind (and animalkind, too) those who learned to collaborate and improvise most effectively have prevailed."

No matter what the external and internal drivers are, the motivation for collaborative innovation is unlikely to be the same for both or several business partners and therefore might be motivated unilaterally. These modes influence the way the collaboration is organized. The most common form of interorganizational collaboration is an alliance, defined as a unique organizational structure to enable cooperation between companies. Alliances are unstable organizational constructions, which are constantly in flux but, on the other hand, can also be rigid structures. Alliances, which are more flexible, are the nonequity alliances or are alliances with no equity change or equity creation between the partners. We think that one of the greatest changes in how companies will do business in the future is the increase in relationships based on partnership rather than ownership. The flexibility in a partnership is needed to control risk, commit limited resources, adapt to changing conditions, and exit easily. On the other hand, rigid equity alliances, which include joint ventures, are required to align partners' interests, exercise strong control, discourage opportunistic actions, and provide a mechanism for distributing residuals.

All discussed theories such as market power and growth strategies, transaction-cost and knowledge-based view of the firm, core competencies, uncertainty and complexity theories, outside–in innovation, and virtual organizations touch on collaboration. Besides sound theories, executives must also address the issue of how external resources can be systematically integrated to enhance innovation in a knowledge-based economy without overreaching themselves with their desire to outsource. Combining some of the available theories to a consistent model would be necessary. One exception, which does so, is Chesbrough's model in which he suggested the importance of partners during the entire innovation process and their contribution in channeling external resources required.[8] His open innovation approach is a new way to address the management of innovation and the process of innovation. In particular, a *processual* view on innovation is suggested, as innovation no longer corresponds to a linear sequence of knowledge creation within company boundaries and its diffusion, implementation, and utilization outside its boundaries. The message given for a successful transformation into what Chesbrough called "era of open innovation" is to seek knowledge iteratively from various sources, such as suppliers, customers, universities, research laboratories, consortia, consultants, startups, new business units, and competitors.

## Open Innovation: The New Paradigm

### *What Does Open Mean?*

Based on Thomas Kuhn's understanding of paradigm, the expression "open" has been associated with a number of concepts in different fields. Note that sometimes "free" is synonymously used for "open." The Oxford Dictionary of Economics explains "open economy" as an economy, which has transactions with the rest of the world. These may include trade in goods and services, movements of capital, transfers of information and technical expertise, and migration of labor. The thought that labor is treated as commodity that can be bought and sold on the open market is going back to the Industrial Revolution. This commodification of man is what actually motivated Karl Marx to his proposed solution to transcend the profit motive by social revolution. Since everybody admitted the miscarriage of the communist-planned economy (except countries like Cuba and North Korea), most free economies are at least partially open for some of these forms of contact; but very few, if any, are completely open for all of them. But also reckon the other extreme. If financial markets are deregulated and too open, the pendulum of economic prosperity can swing back. The events of the past few months – centralizing banks by governments – represent a momentous break with decades of a free market philosophy. It was nobody else than Marx who famously advocated in his *Communist Manifesto*, published 1848, the "centralization of credit in the hands of the state, by means of a national bank with state capital and an exclusive monopoly."

Western Philosophy engrossed the term. In the nineteenth century, Henri Bergson developed the concept of the "open society" where political freedoms and human rights are the foundation of such an open society. In open societies, government is responsive and tolerant, and political mechanisms are transparent and flexible. The state keeps no secrets from itself in the public sense; rather all are trusted with the knowledge of all in a nonauthoritarian society. Karl Raimund Popper, who may be one of the philosophers of the science that is actually read and discussed in the management world, ensured that political leaders in an open society can be overthrown without the need for bloodshed, as opposed to a "closed society," in which a bloody revolution or *coup d'état* is needed to change the leaders. Going deeper into it, he stated further that such open society relies on skepticism as a modus operandi, refusing and resisting definitive truth.[9] Back to business, George Soros, who became a legend in the global world of finance with his Quantum Fund that has been the best performing investment fund in history, adapted the term for the explanation of "open society" as a form of global capitalism.

The computer industry, on the other hand, understands under "open architecture" a concept of hardware design that is publicly released. Open architecture is included into the broader ideas of the open source movements as a set of principles and practices that promote access to the production and design process for various goods, products, resources, and technical conclusions or advice. Since mid-1990s, when Linus Torwalds started with the development of Linux – a Unix-like operating system based on the open source philosophy, we understand open source as the source code of software that is made available to the public with relaxed or nonexistent intellectual property restrictions. This allows users to create user-generated software content through incremental individual effort or through collaboration. Open specification allows companies to manufacture analogical products that are compatible and typically compliant with one another. Open architecture in that sense would refer to the technology that allows multiple service providers to communicate and share data electronically. Respectively, a close architecture stands for a design in which the manufacturer will not enable other manufacturers to know about its specification. Therefore, it is not compatible and compliant with other hardware and software.

In the financial service industry, "open architecture" popped up around the Millennium as a disruptive business model. It has not much to do with societies or technical architectures. It was learned that the open architecture idea in financial services has its origin in fund distribution, whereby a bank delivers funds from third-party providers. Credit Suisse was one of the first banks that offered clients third-party products. The Fund Lab Web-based tool was launched in 1999 and since then gives customers an overview of investment funds with chart tools and facts sheets. What was completely new was that a bank that had its own funds to sell also included funds provided by its competitors in the range shown to customers. The idea was that investors could buy the funds that best suit their needs, no matter who the provider is. This open fund architecture was a revolutionary approach and warmly welcomed by the market. Today, the access to the world of mutual funds comprises more than 3,500 funds offered by dozens of asset management houses.

The term "separately managed accounts" (SMA) in banking stands for one prominent application of open (fund) architecture. SMA is a practice where financial institutes offer individual investment accounts, in which they provide their clients with advisory services and funds managed by independent asset managers. Open architecture is *en vogue* in the banking industry. It is considered as a key success factor and prerequisite for modern product and service innovation in banking. According to the Fédération Européenne des Fonds et Sociétés d'Investissement, the industry in Europe had ~€3.7 trillion in assets under management, where 8% are third-party funds and 92% are proprietary funds.[10] This number is estimated to rise to €6 trillion by 2014 with 30% third-party funds and 70% proprietary funds. These numbers indicate the growth potential for third-party managed funds and the trend into open architecture. Since more financial service institutes and advisors have realized the potential of the open architecture, demand for SMA is increasing enormously.

In fact, almost all wealth managers today offer multimanager products in terms of SMA. If we believe the customer's voice in the United States, about 90% of high-net-worth households wish that their financial advisor, broker, or bank offered products from various manufacturers. Such offers include not only managed mutual funds, individually actively managed fixed-income portfolios, but also financial, tax, inheritance, and charitable administrative services. Firms that refused the adoption of open architecture for their distribution platforms as seen in the 1990s and earlier, where they lost their customer base, must catch up and embrace open architecture. Developing platforms where clients can access best-of-breed products from multiple providers through a single point of distribution is crucial as it holds enormous appeal for wealthy clients. Hence, are the decision drivers leading to open architecture commonly client demand, client best interest, limited proprietary offerings but also fierce competition. As the all product through all providers model has clearly become the industry standard, a firm's proprietary products became less important to clients. The challenge though is the organizational adaptation with the intention to transform products from various providers and internal processes into value-adding services for customers.

Open architecture financial advisors offer institutional and other investors objective, advice without conflicts of interest, because they have separated the business of giving advice from the business of selling proprietary investment products. Closed architecture models, on the other hand, offer only proprietary products, while hybrid firms try to offer both outside and proprietary solutions. The American firm Greycourt, a premier provider of financial advisory, services to wealthy families and select endowments follow open architecture in its purest sense. Open architecture has been the guiding principle since the firm's inception. With an average client size of ~US $100 million, Greycourt serves private and institutional investors ranging from US $10 million in investable assets to a number of Forbes 400 families. The firm does not engage in money management activities – not even funds of funds – nor do they operate related business activities, such as custody, brokerage, or fiduciary services, or offer investment products of their own. Consequently, they are completely independent from the rest of the financial services industry and hence accept no compensation other than those fees paid directly by their clients. Greycourt's advisory services are not a product but a process – a process refined by continuous review and consultation and tailored to the unique needs of each client. The example of Greycourt shows that there is also a niche market for purely open architecture advisory firms. Such firms possess a number of distinguishing characteristics that set them apart from other firms – one distinct advantage is obviously their scrupulously independence.

## *The Open Model of Innovation*

Where banks have adopted open architecture as an operating model for products, we suggest extending open architecture ideas to entirely different fields, such as the dissemination of general knowledge. Therefore, we see open innovation as an approach to combine internal ideas with innovations and paths to markets from other companies, by systematically opening organizational boundaries. This viewpoint goes beyond that of just integrating third-party products. Rather, it is extensive including the entire innovation process. Accordingly, open innovation combines internal and external ideas into organizational architectures and systems whose requirements are defined by a business model. The business model in this case utilizes paths to create value, while defining internal mechanisms to claim some portion of that value. Therefore, the aim of the model is to develop as many potential ideas as possible, and release them as new products or services to current or new markets with the support of external resources wherever necessary. Within an open market, firms should embrace open innovation to bring the benefits of free trade to the flow of new ideas. We argue that a structured conceptualization of a collaborative innovation process enhances the more chaotic thoughts to innovation. The open innovation process is not a linear process where knowledge relevant to innovation comes from within the organization only. What is more innovation of any type involves the incorporation of both specialists expertise and tacit knowledge about existing practices from a wide range of sources. We further argue that open innovation should be viewed as a core process and put in the center of strategic management.

As mentioned, early adaptors of open innovation concepts can be found in the computer industry, in particular at companies with nonintegration or horizontal integration structures. Many other industries such as automotive, health care, communications, biotechnology, pharmaceuticals, consumer-packaged goods, and military weapons are in transition between the two paradigms. This is because multinational companies today hardly have the capacity to research, develop, produce, and sell their products with their own resources. If they used internal resources exclusively, they would cut themselves off from a continuing stream of innovation and the opportunity to react fast enough whenever a new value-added service appeared. For service industries such as insurance and banking, we see an increasing acceptance for open innovation as overall philosophy whereby open architecture has already been adopted by many institutes.

Table 3 illustrates contrasting principles of closed and open innovation, principally borrowed from Chesbrough. Most statements are valid to all industries but some pertain more to manufacturing industries with strong research and development activities.

**Table 3** Contrasting principles of closed and open innovation

| Closed innovation principles | Open innovation principles |
|---|---|
| • The smart people in our field work for us | • Not all the smart people work for us<br>• We need to work with smart people inside and outside our company |
| • To profit from R&D, we must discover it, develop it, and ship it ourselves | • External R&D can create significant value<br>• Internal R&D is needed to claim some portion of that value<br>• Generation of additional revenues from selling research outputs to other firms |
| • If we discover it ourselves, we will get it to market first | • We do not have to originate the research to profit from it |
| • The company that gets an innovation to market first will win | • Building a better business model is better than getting to market first |
| • If we create the most and the best ideas in the industry, we will win | • If we make the best use of internal and external ideas, we will win<br>• We are seeking constantly knowledge from others |
| • We sell only proprietary products and services | • Open architecture is part of our strategic thinking |
| • A solution excludes external value-adding processes | • Crossborder processes contribute to our client value proposition |
| • Customers are hardly integrated into the innovation process | • We invite the customer into the innovation process as a partner and coproducer |
| • We should control our intellectual property, so that our competitors do not profit from our ideas | • We should profit from others' use of our intellectual property, and we should buy others' intellectual property whenever it advances our own business model |
| • Little collaboration activities such as joint ventures and strategic alliances | • Network of collaboration partners from development to distribution. We believe that relationship capital contributes significantly to the firm's business value |

Open innovation has two dimensions: firstly, internal ideas, research and developments of products can be taken to markets through manifested internal distribution channels and secondly, through external, outside the current businesses of the organization. Later model clearly generates more value as it goes to the peripheries of commercial endeavors. The idea of the open model suggests the integration of external resources for each phase – from idea generation to research and development to distribution – to increase a firm's innovation power. The main proposition is that ideas can originate from inside the organization, but some of those ideas may seep out of the company, either in the research stage or later in the development stage. On the other hand, ideas can also start outside the organizational boundaries and then later move inside for research, development, or commercialization.

The organizational boundaries in the open model are more porous and flexible, but not completely open as Jack Welch of General Electric propounded in the 1990s with the "boundaryless organization." He believed that General Electric would be much more effective if the cultural, geographical, and organizational barriers that separated the employees become more permeable. Therefore, emphasis was put on the boundaries' ability to enable business. What such a recreation of boundaries would result in is *speed* instead of size, *flexibility* instead of role definition, *integration* instead of organization, and *innovation* instead of control. We would like to warn that open boundaries facilitate resource sharing but are also human edifices that can be beneficial. The "boundaryless organization" is therefore a myth because different bases for boundary creation and recreation will emerge as an organization faces different contingencies in the future. There is a need for a continual process of experimentation, learning, and adaptation. Organizational performance can be measured in terms of a firm's sustainable capacity to adapt, and that this capacity rests heavily on the organization's ability to innovate. Therefore, an organization's knowledge processing environment must be open. This openness principle in knowledge management is particularly reflected if adapted to open enterprises. Therefore, we should relate openness to transparency in the process of creating and adapting knowledge to fostering innovation.

In high-velocity and hypercompetitive markets, not everything that starts ends up fitting the organizations businesses later on. Many of the ideas, which companies work on, involve a paradigm shift to deliver value. Creating a value proposition or in other words architecture of the revenues for research outputs is as crucial as inventing the technology itself. As products are distributed to new or existing markets, it calls for a dual-distribution strategy in which companies deploy external and internal pathways to the market. There are companies that are keen to distribute both their own ideas and others. These firms identify profitable market ideas and try to bring those outside ideas in-house for commercializing. Within such business models, firms attempt to take the best idea from whatever source and deliver those offerings to their clients at competitive prices. In some cases, it may even be beneficial to set up separate legal units for distribution.

Let us tie together what we learned from the financial services and open innovation. Open innovation in the financial services occurs when solutions to address client's need are evolving openly. In addition, these ideas must be developed in collaboration, to safe time or because of the firm's outsourcing strategy. Finally, the resulting products or services are distributed through a flexible network of partners. As resources are drawn beyond the company borders, their integration and management require new competencies as well as an open innovation attitude. A network of business partners is an essential intangible part of a company's assets. Possessing such intangible resources and capabilities, known as *relationship capital*, and the effective management and exploitation is essential. Furthermore, partnerships are considered as a source for knowledge, which is required to develop and leverage the capability for innovation in a firm. Such networks create knowledge and learning, and have therefore become strategically imperative for many firms. Innovative firms characterized as knowledge creating can adopt such a model for increasing their competitiveness in the new paradigm. Overall, global firms can no longer rely solely on its own resources. They are, for instance, increasingly forced to acquire intellectual property on the market. Open innovation is a promising way to move beyond them. On the other hand, it is clear that the transition to open innovation entails radical organizational change. We need to understand the transition, even though it is a complex process. In the next chapter, we elaborate the building blocks of open innovation in the context of the financial service industry.

## Notes

1. One of the most influential books of modern philosophy of science in which Kuhn argues that scientist works within and against the background of an unquestioned theory or set of believes that he characterized as "paradigm." See Kuhn, T. (1970) *The structure of scientific revolution*, 2nd ed. Chicago University Press, Chicago.
2. William H. Whyte (1956) *The organizational man*. Simon and Schuster, New York.
3. See articles by Quinn for the "controlled chaos" and Mintzberg for the flexible organization in Mintzberg, H., Quinn, J.B. and Goshal, S. (1995) *The strategy process*. Prentice-Hall, London.
4. Chesbrough coined the term "open innovation" and conceptualized this insightful idea as a framework about innovation and creating new growth. He evaluated the two models – closed innovation and open innovation – and sees the future business model in open innovation. On page 29 of his book, he states that internal research and development as utilized in the closed innovation model is past. Chesbrough, H. (2003) *Open Innovation: The imperative for creating and profiting from technology*. Harvard Business School Press, Boston, MA; Chesbrough, H. (2003) 'The era of open innovation', *MIT Sloan Management Review,* Spring, 35–41.
5. For the transaction-cost theory of the firm, see Williamson, O.E. (1985) *The economic institution of capitalism*. Free Press, New York. For further discussion of the application of that theory, especially for collaboration models, see Hennart, J.F. (1988) 'A transaction cost theory of equity joint ventures', *Strategic Management Journal,* 9(4), 361–374.
6. The idea to focus on a firm's core competency exclusively was conceptualized in the seminal article of Prahalad, C.K. and Hamel, G. (1990) 'The core competence of the corporation', *Harvard Business Review,* 68(3), 79–91.
7. For information about firms that split their organization into new units for distribution, see Markides, C.C. and Charitou, C.D. (2003) 'Responses to disruptive strategic innovation', *MIT Sloan Management Review,* Winter, 55–63; Markides, C.C. (1997) 'Strategic innovation', *MIT Sloan Management Review,* Spring, 9–23.
8. Ibid 4.
9. Karl Raimund Popper (1945) *The open society and its enemies*. Routledge, London. In the two-volume book, written in political exile during the Second World War, Popper developed a critique of historicism and a defence of the open society, liberal democracy.
10. FEFSI (2004) *Investment funds worldwide statistics* [Online]. Fédération Européenne des Fonds et Sociétés d'Investissement, http://www.fefsi.org/Unrestricted_Area/frameset.htm [November 23, 2004]

# Transition Strategies to Open Innovation

- Foster collaborative innovation by integrating third-party products and solutions.
- Put the client in the center of the firm's value-adding processes to deliver holistic advice offerings.
- Enhance client satisfaction and profitability through a needs-based segmentation and analysis at the account level.
- Establish a flexible service-oriented architecture that leverages collaborative value creation.

## Offering Best-of-Breed Products

### *The Open and Unlimited Product Architecture*

As discussed previously, *open architecture* is understood in the financial services as an open and flexible operating model for products and services. Firms that operate modern product management models apply it. To recapitulate, the idea of open architecture is used for funds, mortgages, and a number of other banking products, but can also be applied for services and processes. Some banks have adapted this principle for the processing and settlement of securities transactions. Due to the characteristics of services, open innovation dissolves the distinction between the producer of services and the consumer of services. In particular, in the banking industry, this challenges many institutes to change innovation processes and their mindsets. It was observed that in recent years, open architecture has become *jargon* for a new business model that supports the offering of third-party products to clients, as well as distributing own products through third-party channels. The rationale for open architecture is evident as clients wish to select from a global plethora of products and get unbiased advice. In recent times, dedicated wealth managers come more to the fore, complemented, and extended by the philosophy of the open architecture. Taken to its logical conclusion, the philosophy leads to a banking model whose value is based primarily on its reputation as a hub for sales, quality assurance, and customer service, with the majority of the products and services sold, actually being bought in. The core competences of a networked bank of this kind would include equity research, product range policy, advisory services, sales, and advertising.

Although open architecture, in its initial form, proved to be the most popular distribution model among wealthy clients, many large universal banks enhanced the idea. Acting not only as a provider of products and services to other banks but also as a buyer from them strengthened their competitive position. Accordingly, they buy third-party products, incorporate them into their product portfolio, and sell them through their own distribution channels. The majority of smaller financial services institutions, however, are likely to operate as specialized suppliers, complementing their product range by offering targeted third-party products. As they act as suppliers, their business models are not designed to in-source external products and distribute them. To specialize, they most likely outsource classical transaction processing that is not their core competency to external firms with established infrastructure capacity.

In 2004, The Financial Times, Barclays Bank, and BNP Paribas host the Open Architecture Forum in London. At this event, banks share their view and experiences regarding open architecture. Thus, the vast majority of incumbent banks are considering open architecture because their clients prefer that their financial advisors or institutions offer best-of-breed products from multiple providers. The largest wealth managers, UBS and Credit Suisse, invest between 50 and 70% in third-party products for their managed funds portfolios. Merrill Lynch likewise distributes more non-Merrill Lynch products than its own products. Proponents of open architecture recommend an optimal profitability mix for banks of two-thirds proprietary and one-third external products. Deutsche Bank changed its distribution model in 2003 based on this recommendation. A more restricted distribution is known in the industry as *guided* architecture in contrast to *open* architecture. The trend toward an open architecture has encouraged most banks to sell their competitor's wares, wherever the competitor provides a better product or service to satisfy their customer's expectations. Metaphorically, open architecture is like a Swiss army knife. The knife, as a global quality brand, consists of several tools of which the knife is excellent, but scissors, screwdriver, bottle opener, or any other tool are of marginal use. However, the knife (bank) integrates other helpful tools (products) for the user (customer). The idea of a Swiss army knife with all best-in-class tools would be rather illusionary.

Open architecture is mainly driven by increasingly sophisticated customers that are demanding more choice, advice, and best products. There are rigorous regulatory and compliance burden that prevent institutes from offshore business. In addition, the global competition has led to margin erosion and moved banking products from differentiated status to commodity. These changes, among others, support the application of open architecture. Today, funds from an integral part of investments are – because of flexibility, diversification, and efficiency reasons an attractive alternative to direct investments. We observed that in the asset and wealth management area, clients wish to get unbiased advice. Reliable banks are only able to satisfy this demand if they combine third-party products with proprietary products. It would not work out, even mathematically, if all financial service institutes assured their clients that, on the one hand, they are providing unbiased advice and, on the other hand, they are selling their own products exclusively. This would mean that they had all best-in-class funds, which we all know is impossible.

A number of clients today, for instance, decide which funds they want from which asset management institute. Understandable that many institutes responded to this trend with open architecture. The client in this case splits the value chain. The house bank of the client merely acts in this model as client advisor and contact to third-party asset managers. The process is usually divided into two parts: client acquisition, and retention and distribution access. UBS as one early advocate of open architecture provides clients as a financial intermediary with a broad range of ~8,500 investment funds from 140 partners, including other banks, investment fund firms, asset managers, brokers, and insurance companies. A restrictive provider and fund selection process through which open market products are tested before being offered are eminent. Such process should include quantitative screening, in-depth qualitative analysis, and ongoing due diligence. Further developments in open architecture over the next few years to come could be to intensify and deepen relationships with third-party providers beyond just providing products. Establishing relationships with a few high-quality partners is important as the most profitable partnerships or distribution channels are those that remain for a long time.

## *What Is in for the Client and the Firm?*

One advantage of the open architecture for customers is "one-stop shopping," i.e., the flexibility of choosing products from a whole universe of contents in all fund categories with standardized pricing. Open architecture gives clients access to a wide array of prescreened, top-quality products from third-party providers that complement a bank's own range. The goal of many banks is to provide clients with the best solution – even though this might come from competitors. To a certain extent, open architecture can be associated with the thought of outsourcing. Developing that assumption further, the outsourcing strategy of a firm provides a complete product range to clients even though the firm does not have expertise in all areas. We concede it as the fact that regardless how big the bank is, it can hardly be specialized in all areas. It would be ineffectual if the organization tried to master everything. In fact, it would be simply impossible. While outsourcing certain products at the same time, the firm can focus on its strength and core competencies. For example, England, the financial center, has a good reputation for managing cash and bonds. Banks in the City therefore tend to manage these assets in house. But for equities, those banks prefer to identify and select the best outside managers on behalf of their clients. Following this approach, the relationship manager has the flexibility to offer clients a complete individual solution consisting of own manufactured and managed products, as well as products that are managed by third parties. The banking industry calls this a "multimanager" product or "multibrand" strategy. There is high potential in offering wealthy clients such flexibility.

Raised in the example above, a second rationale for being open to third-party product selling is the concentration on core competencies. This view is in line with middle office units responsible for product innovation. From a bank's perspective, open architecture is a way to increase entrepreneurial flexibility. This is because value chains are more fragmented today than in the past. Single elements are analyzed meticulously to find out in which areas the bank has core competencies, and in which it would make sense to find an appropriate partner. The management should take everything into account – core competencies, available internal resources, and efficiency – with the aim of generating volume for the firm. Consequently, internal sales channels, external sales channels, and internal products, as well as third-party products, must always be part of the strategy.

Drawing a correlation between time to market and entrepreneurial flexibility seems to be difficult. Through the process of the doctoral research of this book's author, this issue was discussed in-depth with a number of senior executives.[1] Based on the information gathered, some of the bankers expressed reservations for open architecture and said that time to market might be quicker if the bank incorporates external partners while others argued that it depends how efficient activities are performed. For the latter case, it does not matter whether they are internal or external. A managing director of a large European bank, responsible for product and services development, emphasized that he has had excellent experiences with external partners and that collaboration within the bank is sometimes more difficult. Others contradicted and said the same applies vice versa. It is clear that the bank loses strategic flexibility if collaboration with external partners is undertaken. In other words, if product and service innovation is done in-house, it is much easier and quicker to make any necessary adjustments during the development, production, and even commercialization stage of the solution. A responsible person for a solution would have the authority to solve problems with an internal phone call, rather than with time-consuming negotiations with external business partners.

The logical question though is what openness and partnerships for third-party products and services actually mean for a bank. Sometimes, it is difficult to detect regularities on how and when collaboration occurs. It is supposed to be a subjective, ad hoc and not a structured decision-making process, depending on the individual preferences of the responsible executive. What is for sure is that collaboration and relationship management is a kind of business secret as it contributes to the firm's relationship capital. To elaborate the effects of open architecture further, we introduce the collaboration between UBS and PostFinance in areas such as funds, cash handling, and lending operations.

## *Collaboration Between Banking and Postservices*

PostFinance is a fully fledged financial services provider within the financial services business unit of the Swiss Post. With 2,700 employees and total client assets of more than CHF 40 billion at the end of 2007, PostFinance has been doing well during the last years with open innovation models as one key element in its ambitious growth strategy. In May 2002, PostFinance entered the loans business, and now offers three types of "Yellow Mortgage" in collaboration with UBS, namely the Yellow Mortgage fixed, the Yellow Mortgage dynamic, and a combined product. Because of the current interest rate situation, the fixed mortgages accounted for around 70% of sales. PostFinance considers the collaboration with UBS as a good basis for gaining more customers for this type of arrangement in the future. In addition, PostFinance operations centers have been handling the major bank's paper-based payments from UBS since October 2005. The firm is putting its faith in products that are transparent and easy to understand. To compete on equal terms with other financial services providers, PostFinance is continuing to pursue its aim of obtaining a banking license one day.

The credit business has four elements in its value chain: distribution, balance management, risk management, and servicing such as consulting, pricing, contracting, and payment transactions. In Switzerland, UBS has core competencies in all four areas. An analysis found that an expansion of servicing would not be very beneficial for the bank. On the other hand, servicing has been a core competency of PostFinance, in addition to its very strong branch network. As PostFinance does not have a banking license that would be required for balance and risk management, they agreed that UBS covers the banking business, and PostFinance contributes distribution and servicing to the partnership. In this instance, the base for collaboration is the open architecture, in which the bank analyzes strength and weaknesses of its value chain, and collaborates wherever it its beneficial, rather than trying to cover the entire value chain with internal resources as a closed business model would claim. This business model innovation provides the bank with new routes for selling their products through partners, in addition to their established internal distribution channels.

## *Multichannel Distribution*

The PostFinance collaboration is an excellent example for multichannel distribution based on the open model of innovation, in which UBS acts as the producer of products, which are sold through a third-party distribution channel. In that case, the funds are sold through Swiss Post offices as its own products. Actually, they are managed and administered by UBS Global Asset Management – just like the funds sold by the Italian partner bank under its proprietary label in Italy. In addition, UBS acts as the custodian bank for the Swiss Post. The practice where products are sold under the partner's brand name is called "private labeling" or "white labeling." On the other hand, the bank also acts as the distributor of third-party products and as a producer for products that are sold over third-party distribution channels. Depending upon where the bank does business, in the domestic market or internationally, there are two perspectives to consider. The bank can sell its own products through internal and external distribution channels on the domestic market. In offshore

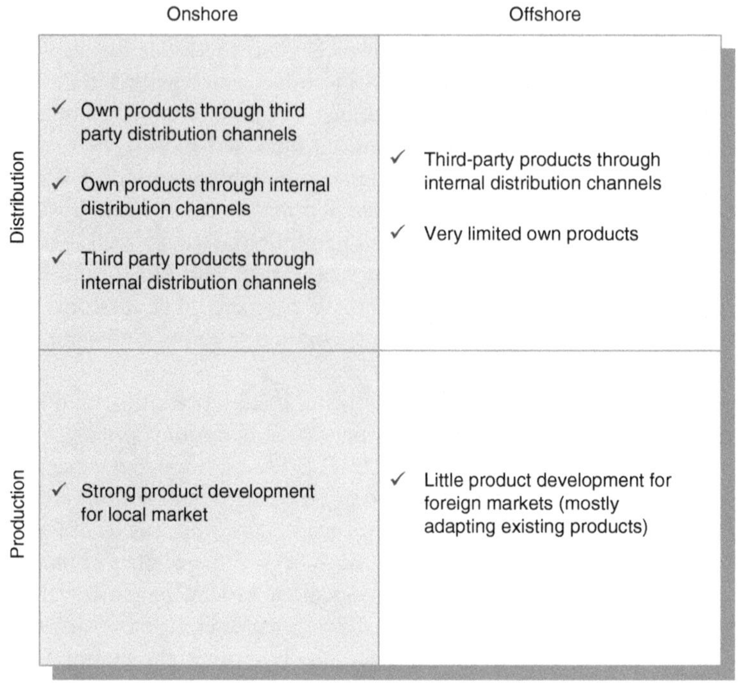


**Fig. 4** Open innovation quadrants

markets, the bank mainly sells third-party products that comply with local law, tax, and regulations through its branches. In other words, the bank develops products for the domestic market but only limited products for international markets. Figure 4 generically illustrates the distribution and supplier perspective in four quadrants.

If a firm integrates various third-party products in its proprietary product portfolio, we speak from a "multibrand" approach. Of course, there are other operating models such as "single brand" where only in-house offerings are provided or the "supermarket" where the customer is able to choose the best solutions from a complete market offering. We think that the single-brand operating model cannot be justified in the present market environment because the bank will never be the best-in-class for all asset classes. Such strategy denies a trustworthy sales approach as it results in a lack of objectivity in advising clients. The disadvantage of the other extreme, the "supermarket," is that customers need substantial product knowledge. It appears that the bank left their customers alone with investment decisions. The "supermarket" may also result in an oversupply of products, information overload, and lack of steering due to limited research and distribution capacities.

A good example of where firms employ the distribution perspective is in international mortgage business. Note that at this point of the book, we do not emphasize the subprime mortgage market, nor do we provide detailed analyses. Before the crisis, the mortgage volume in the United Kingdom is estimated to be

~£600 billion with a proprietorship of about 30%. We do not need to mention that the market is highly competitive with major players such as HSBC, Royal Bank of Scotland, NatWest, or Barclays just to name a few. Overall, the mortgage business in the United Kingdom was profitable for years. Recently, the growth forecasts have been revised downward. However, banks should see the current conditions as an opportunity as there are still reasons why mortgage business in the United Kingdom will stay important. While the United States clearly takes the laurels on numbers of wealthy households, the United Kingdom is expected to lead the way on concentration of aggregated wealth. Barclays Wealth, one of the leading wealth manager, forecasts that a quarter of UK households will hold wealth in excess of US $1 million by 2016 – considerably more than the following countries, Japan and Italy with both 22%, or the United States with 16%. One reason is that there is a stronger property ownership in the United Kingdom and in the long term, house prices are to remain buoyant. This situation is likely to drive wealth creation in the years to come and explains the correlation between wealth creation and mortgage volume. Let us come back to the question why foreign banks in the United Kingdom must collaborate with a local bank.

As the mortgage business will recover long term, recognizing its allure to the vast majority of wealthy clients, many banks want to sell mortgages in countries like England but cannot provide clients with its own products because of local laws and regulatory constraints. Because of these constraints, no product or service can be similarly sold in European countries. The foreign bank has to sell third-party products from the local market provided by local banks, building societies, or specialized mortgage lenders. That is why banks in the United Kingdom collaborate with institutions such as The Woolwich and Countrywide Credit Industries. Banks generally apply this outside–in approach for products where they are not specialized in. Thus, a bank might distribute insurance products from other financial service institutes or sells hedge funds from so-called "content boutiques" that are small but highly specialized firms.

There are general principles and selection criteria when to collaborate. Commoditized products in retail banking businesses, which are products that do not exhibit significant differences in quality or content, should, if economically meaningful, be offered from internal entities. On the other hand, in-house produced products should not be provided to third parties under more attractive terms than the bank's origination units. Responding to the question about the importance of the open architecture and being open for providing composite and complex products in collaboration, we can generalize and say that global wealth managers presuppose open architecture. If these banks acted narrow-mindedly in a world that is becoming more and more open and transparent, and where businesses and products affiliate with partners, they would no longer be able to satisfy their clients. They would lose business in offshore markets because of regulatory constraints. Even if they did everything within the bank, which from a resource-based view is ineffective and unrealistic, their competitors would cooperate with partners and promote products, services, and solutions that are more interesting to potential clients. As product information is globally accessible and easier to compare, clients became, in our time, more mature in their decisions. Therefore, banks with a closed approach would hardly have any business prospects.

We believe that the market pressure of being a global player drives banks into open architecture and collaboration. Firms that drive international growth strategies need innovative and local tailor-made products. In terms of openness, this means to have continuously the client perspective in mind. As mentioned, the mature and global client of today expects that a bank provides exactly the products that he or she is seeking and unable to find at other banks to good conditions – otherwise, the bank will lose them. The client wants the product from one bank, unless parts or sometimes the whole product comes from a third-party provider. This changed client behavior is reflected in increasingly effective cooperation between the markets. The advantages of being a global player in terms of providing third-party products, as well as offering own products via other financial service institutions, are obvious. As the client should in any case get the best solution, the solution may come from different business groups of a bank. This is part of the many integrated client service models. Without doubt, the best solution is not always own products. Again, if that was true, every bank would be the best choice for every single product, in every area. We suggest an open operating model in which banks can choose a partner who has a solution that can be combined with own solutions to fulfill their clients' needs, and to their clients' best advantage. The advantage of being a global bank is that they can choose their partners from the global market, and that they might add value to their partner with their strong and reliable brand. Conclusively, open architecture is vital not only for dedicated wealth managers but also for global market players, as it embraces a number of benefits.

## *Benefits and Challenges of Open Architecture*

Open architecture creates a possibility to combat legislation and regulatory obstacles in a country where the firm is not domiciled. It is an operating model that enables the bank to do business offshore, in addition to banking in the domestic market. Accordingly, third-party products and services that are legally compliant are sold to clients through a network of international branches. The global presence leads to a robust competitive position and seeks to create value for a greater number of stakeholders. Being dedicated to total value management on a global scale affects the sustainable growth of businesses within appropriate risk parameters. Not only this opens up new revenue streams for firms on a global scale, but also it is an advantage for the international clientele likewise, whereby they are able to access products and services in a number of countries from various providers through a single point of sales. In this case, open architecture has a positive influence on revenues, risk, facilitates the growth strategy of the bank, and hence it increases the value of different stakeholder.

Open architecture can also put the bank into the role of a producer of products and services. This supplier perspective is complementary to the distribution of third-party products offshore. For the domestic market, products such as mortgages are sold through the banks internal channels as well as through external distribution channels. In the latter case, the bank takes advantages of its brand value and uses the distribution network of other companies in domestic markets. Products that are not subject to regulatory and policy constraints such as funds are produced in-house and sold to other financial service institutes. The open architecture leverages the supply as well as the distribution perspectives and hence accelerates economies of scale (see Fig. 4). Within this operating model, the sales force is flexible in selling third-party products instead of own products. Thus, firms produce products and sell their products through third-party providers in addition to its internal distribution channels. The primary objective is to add client value through an optimal solution regardless of whether the products are internally developed or picked from third-party providers. As this model is in its first stage, there are also threats in relying on different business partners. One consequence is intraenterprise competition because of the fact that a proprietary product is only sold to clients as long as there is not a better similar product available on the market. While some argue that such an intraenterprise competition might motivate firms to monitor the market offerings more rigorously and improve their products continuously, opponents see in this philosophy threats.

In sum, the benefits of the open architecture philosophy have been debated vehemently in the financial service industry for years. In contradiction to all the advantages, several concerns regarding open and flexible operating models were observed. Disadvantages include losing strategic flexibility if collaboration with external partners is exaggerated. This concern matches with other critical voices heard at the Open Architecture Forum in London. Main claims are that open architecture, in particular for asset management, not only decreases margins due to fierce competition but also cannibalizes own funds. For instance, Deutsche Bank and DWS claimed that German funds are losing market share to foreign competitors on its domestic market. The compound annual asset growth for foreign groups is expected to be about 10% for the next 3 years. According to several asset managers across different banks, one reason for the foreign funds success is the trend away from fund distribution through internal channels, exclusively toward an open architecture distribution model.

Open architecture may also cannibalize the bank's own products. Gross margins of proprietary products, for instance for funds, across the wealth management industry are much higher than third-party gross margins. Considering the recent increase of third-party products at many institute's portfolio to over 50%, transforming third-party equity funds into internal equity funds can have a significant revenue impact. Data protection is another concern that might deter partners. If a firm's products are distributed through third-party channels, the business partner has the client contact and is privy to confidential client information. Similar applies if a bank sells third-party products. Even though both parties assure that client data are not used for internal marketing activities, there is always a risk. Building trust beyond organizational boundaries is becoming increasingly vital for sustained partnerships, especially for crossborder activities.

Overall, it seems that the advantages are outweighing the disadvantages. There exist many examples for open architecture in practice. The motivations for the transition to such operating models differ. Where the changing nature of demand and overcoming regulatory obstacles for international onshore business are often heard supporting voices, there are other more skeptical opinions from market participants. There is consensus that in particular, customer pressure for a wider choice of top-performing products is driving banks into doing what was once unthinkable – selling their competitors' wares. But a number of financial service institutes also believe that the trend toward open architecture is encouraging them to focus on their strength and improve their own performance. In contrast to the particular interests of bank managers for open architecture, opponents suggest that to succeed, they have to make the choice between producing proprietary products and services and distributing third-party products and services. Based on our current knowledge about the subject matter and studies in the area of ambidexterity, it is assumed that an either/or decision is not valid for universal banks. It is argued that firms have to balance cost efficiency and the need of customer demands. Many managers realized that if they wanted to satisfy their increasingly sophisticated customers, they had to run a dual strategy. This included developing quality products *and* providing third-party products simultaneously, in addition to offering their own products through a network of distribution partners. The strategic debate, whether to focus on production, distribution, or even combine both streams is in its early days. Well, the approach is to take everything into account – core competencies, available internal resources, and efficiency. In other words, internal sales channels, external sales channels, and internal products, as well as third-party products, must always be part of the strategy discussions.

## From Open Architecture to Advanced Open Business Models

Every organization in banking will have to embrace radical change in their operating models, just as manufacturing industries did 20 years ago in respond to East Asian competition. Most realized that open architecture not merely means opening up their organizational boundaries. Although there was a need to make boundaries more permeable through dismantling structures, there is evidence from the market that confirms the need to alter boundaries that enable growth, collaboration, flexibility, innovation, and learning. Open architecture offers economies of scale and is therefore currently and for years to come anticipated as the most efficient distribution model for financial products.

Now, let us go a step further and look how collaborative forms are continuing to evolve. We see open business models emerging out of the idea of open architecture with some banks even offering other financial institutions a wide range of modular services. This enables them to concentrate on their core competencies and deploy their resources more effectively. At the same time, the provider can make optimum use of its own capacities and expertise to meet the needs of its clients. A good example is the case of the Raiffeisen Zentralbank Österreich AG (RZB). The RZB recently became the 50th CLS (Continuous Linked Settlement) third-party client of UBS. CLS is a process enabling simultaneous foreign exchange settlement across the globe, eliminating the settlement risk caused by delays arising from time-zone differences. With this partnership, RZB and its subsidiaries will be able to execute and settle their crossborder foreign exchange transactions through the CLS global settlement system of UBS. In the current environment of rising fix costs and shrinking margins, CLS delivers a much-needed reduction in the marginal cost of doing business. The RZB's global treasurer commented that the quality of UBS's services and strengths in technology has given them the confidence to further increase the partnership.

Although collaboration is at its beginning in the financial service industry, in contrast to the manufacturing industry, first moving players may be centrally placed within the market and therefore more innovative. This is because they will be best positioned to structure the most attractive deals with the most quality brands. Successful firms have to demonstrate agility, openness, and innovative forms of service delivery regardless of where the products and services come from. It was evidenced that the adoption of open innovation approaches is the most likely route to business effectiveness and an efficient operation model. This is also important as open business models help to support serving customers with the optimal solution available on the markets.

Being open is an individual trait. Some experienced bankers may feel pressure on them. They are not used to the fact that pressure comes from colleagues in addition to pressure from external competitors. Changing the way of doing business includes behavioral and cultural changes. Not only does this issue need to be addressed with caution, but also the bank realizes that such additional cultural changes in addition force restructuring in the bank. It is believed that organizational conduct and culture originate from organizational structure. Developing an open innovation culture is a crucial and ongoing activity that so far has consumed much effort and time. On return achievements can hardly be measured quantitatively.

Our observation showed that many top managers are convinced that collaboration strategies and an integrated service–client model put them in an exceptional position to take advantage of the opportunities from open innovation. In particular, they justify open innovation by saying that it will be the *de rigor* business philosophy in the banking industry for the coming years. It was further learned that one important structural requirement of open business models is the adoption of a product-neutral advice that integrates the client.

## Sound Client Integration

### *Developing a New Understanding on How to View Clients*

Listening to the voice of the customer and differentiating customer needs suitably are vital activities and impact customer satisfaction. Therefore, in planning a product or service, we should first consider potential customer needs that the innovation should try to satisfy. Customer ideas about quality are often confusing and difficult to articulate. Certainly, there are many methods available for investigating the characteristics of customer needs. A straightforward approach for analyzing customer-defined quality and sorting the features of a product or service into various quality categories is the Kano method.[2] Accordingly, the different customer needs, namely *basic needs*, *performance needs*, and *excitement needs,* must be initially identified. Customers normally expect of the product or service basic functions or features. For instance, global acceptance and monthly balance statements of credit cards are taken for granted and so typically unspoken. However, if these basic requirements are missing, it will lead to customer dissatisfaction and result in complaints and lost business. Providing basic needs only shifted innovation to commodity. Performance attributes, although not equally important to all customers, are attributes that generally increase the level of customer satisfaction. For a credit card, we can think of low fees in combination with a bunch of services. Many credit cards offer free accident insurance cover for travel on public transport, access to exclusive airport lounges, or 24-h SOS assistance service offerings with on-the-spot medical advice worldwide. Finally, the excitement needs stand for enhanced benefits and prestige that delight and excite customers. An example is American Express that introduced in 1999 its Centurion Card that offers a bunch of elite services to a very limited number of customers that are eligible to it. Currently, it seems to be the most expensive and hardest to obtain card in terms of credit history, income, and assets. Only 1% of all American Express customers hold the prestigious black card. Cardholders qualify automatically for gold status at airlines, fine hotels, and resorts or car rentals. What is more American Express attempts to provide its exclusive Centurion clientele with business as well as lifestyle benefits, ranging from personal travel counselors to handle all travel needs, an own concierge or special deals with leading private jet firms and a space tourism company. Special perks can be an invitation to a viewing of a private Getty art collection or the like. Customers often cannot articulate these features, as they are unexpected. For the normal customer, we know the true promise of premium services if we get a flight, hotel, or car hire upgrade in connection with the product or service purchased. These kinds of experiences are what create customer loyalty. But beware that what excites us today is expected tomorrow. Once introduced, the exciting feature of a service will be soon imitated by the competition and customers will come to expect it from all the market participants.

Besides various methods and guidelines for product and service development, the way in which innovations are delivered is crucial. In services, it is difficult to satisfy all three customer needs categories as mentioned with market-push strategies. In other words, the time has gone where firms pushed their products and services to the market without involving clients. The new way of product and service development is to listen to the client or investor first and then find appropriate solutions. As discussed, it is obvious that innovations must start with the analysis of customer needs. It cannot be that a product or marketing manager while having an overly hot shower in the morning comes up with a new idea, runs to the office, develops that idea, and in the final step seeks someone who wants that product or service. To identify customer needs, we suggest pursuing a systematic approach.

We must analyze the customer's behaviors and then cluster this information into similar client groups. Understanding client needs and profitability drivers of a firm's customer base is key for developing new segments and value propositions. Since the book by Larry Selden and Geoffrey Colvin, "Angel Customers and Demon Customers,"[3] *client centricity* has popped up on the agendas of many senior executive. As easy as it sounds, the key idea is to place the client at the center of strategic thinking and innovate around clients. As you will see at the end of the book in the interview, Credit Suisse understands under client centricity a strategic framework consisting of client understanding, client innovation, and client profitability. In other words, it is about focus, innovation, and how customer service representatives listen to their clients and identify and address client needs with unique value propositions. This makes sense as all profits and value of a company come from profitable, high potential customers. Therefore, the opinion of leaders must be shifted. The company is not merely a group of offices, collection of divisions and departments, an array of products and services, or functions or regions – it is rather a portfolio of customers. Accordingly, every company's portfolio of customers must be managed effectively and efficiently to produce superior returns for shareholders.

Viewing customers in a new light and developing a comprehensive understanding what they really need cannot be stressed too strongly. For example, a bank client who deposits bonds worth millions and is satisfied with a low return does not have the same needs as one who wants to buy real estate and needs to grow his pension assets and take financial precautions for his family. Both require different types of advice and service. If we analyze the cases, it becomes obvious that the client with the bonds may be more profitable for the bank than the one with the real estate. Thus, a bank has to take better account of such divergent requirements. The purpose should be to know all clients well enough to be able to identify client groups with similar needs and to address these needs in a targeted manner. This has something to do with reputation, in which the clients' experience with the bank is positive.

## *The Quest to Find the Right Service Model*

The type of service model provided in different geographies impacts the economic attractiveness of clients in the market. There are two dominant models for the distribution of wealth management services: the broker/dealer model and the advisory model. Where the broker/dealer model is largely transaction driven with fee-based brokerage accounts and commonly used in North America, the advisory model emphasizes more comprehensive client servicing through open architecture, asset-based fees, discretionary portfolio management, and financial planning. The origin of the advisory model is in European countries with old money, once the main source of wealth. On the other hand, in the entrepreneurial-friendly United States and emerging markets, middle-aged entrepreneurs are the main drivers of wealth creation. These clients who have a complete different risk profile may be more dynamic and eager to self-manage their investments through brokers. They request access to a diverse set of products and services. From the bank's perspective, the margins of the advisory model are much higher than for brokerage services. The effects of global financial markets and impeding wealth transfer trends are becoming essential for servicing an increasing globally active clientele. Therefore, it is important to adopt the model prevalent in the region where the client lives. In addition, we must consider the cultural differences. Where clients in Europe are open to discuss their assets with their wealth manager to get holistic investment advice, in Latin America there is more suspiciousness. In general, Americans and Europeans are more likely to invest in domestic and regional businesses but, on the other hand, also have a greater appetite for global social responsibility-related-investments or to leverage their philanthropic investments to affect change on an international level. In Latin America, the history of political conflicts, corruption, and social instability has favored, for example, offshore banking business models. Security concerns may also be one reason that explains a higher demand in online channels for account information in these regions than in others. Clients obviously have different requirements and expectations, hence follow different business models. So do mature and sophisticated wealthy clients in the United States often solely draw on investment brokers and product experts where in Asia they seek a long-term trusted relationship manager that helps to advise and plan their financial matters. Although wealth management through advice in North America is gaining momentum, we do not expect the brokerage business to disappear.

What makes it even more complicated is the adequate servicing of communities in certain countries. To explain what we mean, just look for example to Peru with an increasing population of Asian ancestry born in Peru, or people who have made Peru their adopted homeland. One of the most prominent examples is Alberto Fujimori, who became the 45th president of Peru from 1990 to 2000 as a dual citizenship holder – Peruvian and Japanese. Other communities, like the Jewish in Venezuela, the Arab in the United States, or the nonresident Indian community in Asia, have all become key market segments as many of them are successful business owners. They are of great interest to wealth management institutions as they tend to be global in outlook, confidence about the countries in which they live and well informed about international affairs. These communities possess an excellent base for referrals because members discuss their investment experiences openly. Establishing trust by understanding, for instance, *Sharia* and its implications for investing and finance for the Arab communities outside the Middle East force firms to adjust their service models to the needs of a more globally aware and sophisticated clientele.

Firms must develop the capability to serve multiple client groups on a global scale and fulfill increasingly diversified needs. Uniform client service models are no longer appropriate. For instance, the bank wants to focus in Greater China on family-owned firms and in the United States on executives. Each client has very specific needs, but clients in these groups also have a number of common needs that the bank should address with an integrated approach. During this process, the bank should focus less on how much business these clients already have with them, and more on what they actually expect from their financial service provider. If the relationship manager succeeds in offering these clientele unique solutions through the combined efforts of active and integrated investment advising and corporate finance services, they will entrust the bank with a greater portion of their assets. This is essential, as most clients consider service quality as the most important factor for choosing their bank as well as for staying with their bank.

## *Needs-Based Client Servicing*

With the increasing global activities, attitudes, and needs of clients, banks must clearly focus on delivering relevant value propositions to targeted groups. Talking about these groups, we use the term *segments*. Many banks still segment their clients primarily by their wealth level, in terms of their net worth or invested assets. Interesting to know is that profit margins for so-called ultra-high-net-worth individuals (UHNWI) – those whose financial assets exceed US $30 million – are significantly lower than for the segment with investable assets of around US $1 million. The low gross margins at the top end, on average between 40 and 70 basis points, are due to relatively high cost-to-serve and competitive pricing. Across regions, very rich people are generally better informed about their investments than lower segment customers are. Thus, they tend to demand more sophisticated investment products such as hedge funds, venture capital, private equity, or philanthropic contributions, some often linked to their business affairs. They also seek for integrated advice and complex services such as international tax and wealth planning or global custodian services. The wealthier they are, the more price sensitive and tough negotiators they are. Research indicates that the UHNWI segment has grown at ~10% per annum over the last 5 years, and is expected to grow further much above the other segments.[4] This segment accounts for about one-third of the world's financial wealth. Forbes estimates that there were about 1,000 billionaires globally at the end of 2007 with a combined net worth of US $3.5 trillion, equating to US $3.6 billion each.[5] Deeper analysis shows that the average billionaire is 62-year old and that they are getting younger each year. In many ways, very wealthy people make investment decisions ahead of market trends. Their behavior holds important lessons for the other segments and financial institutions alike. High-level segmentation focus matters – even though UHNW clients are less profitable, they are the most important segment for growth. Table 4 compares the traditional approach and the postulated needs-based approach to client servicing.[6]

Even though there is no right or wrong method for client segmentation, traditional segmentation by assets under management does not adequately address the individual needs of clients. This is also because clients within the same wealth band can have different requirements and expectations. Nevertheless, high-level segmentation can be used to indicate and show the access levels to wealth management services. It is also frequently utilized for reporting and statistics. As the needs have become increasingly complex, the development of new client service

**Table 4** Traditional vs. needs-based client servicing approach

| | Traditional approach | Needs-based approach |
|---|---|---|
| Client segmentation | • Assets under management<br>• Primary demographic characteristics, e.g., age, gender, race, ethnicity<br>• Generic value proposition on corporate, product or service level<br>• Risk ability and risk tolerance | • Total wealth<br>• Detailed profile, e.g., education, professional status, family situation, status within community<br>• Personal concerns and business issues<br>• Past, current, and future investment plans<br>• Personality and psyche<br>• Value proposition with each segment characterized by specific, homogeneous needs<br>• Monitor risk profile and adjust client product portfolio |
| Product | • Focus on product sales with rudimentary preceding analysis of client needs<br>• Products offered based on wealth band<br>• Marketing material based on wealth band and/or asset classes | • Provide best-of-breed products based on client needs through open architecture<br>• Focus on sophisticated solutions rather than product picking<br>• Marketing services tailored to qualitative and psychographic segmentation |
| Client service model | • Clients placed into service model based on assets under management<br>• Static servicing unless changes in assets under management occur | • Needs drive client coverage and service level<br>• Level of interaction as desired<br>• Individual communication and delivery channels |
| Organization | • Product-centered organization<br>• Client repository distributed across the firm<br>• Vague knowledge about related client identification files (CIF)<br>• Business and technology architecture not designed around the concept of servicing | • Client-centered organization<br>• Single-client repository<br>• Central client database<br>• Client profitability and potential drives level of service and resource allocation<br>• Key account management concept for UHNWI<br>• Flexible service-oriented architecture |

models – models that move beyond just invested assets – is essential. We must also acknowledge that in a global and dynamic world, specific needs change over the course of a client's relationship with the wealth manager. Quite simply, client segmentation has become a strategy for differentiation. A method that has proved to be an effective means of understanding and penetrating clients is to employ secondary forms of segmentation based on qualitative and psychographic criteria such as *behavior type*, *source of wealth,* and the *life-cycle phase* of the client. Various approaches emerged from a number of firms but experience showed that clients predominantly choose their investments and display different levels of financial sophistication based on their age. The life cycle can be roughly cut into the following age categories, 20–30, 30–45, 45–65, and 65 plus, each with different situational needs. If we look where the wealth comes from, we can group clients into entrepreneurs, executives, professionals, landowners, heir or sports, and entertainment. This is crucial, as these subsegments take into consideration the lifestyle; hence, each category requires a dedicated value proposition. The largest segment at most global wealth managers is the entrepreneur with the most promising profitability for the bank. Entrepreneurs are usually self-made individuals with a strong personality. They seek financial instruments and advice to protect as well as grow their assets. Most clients with an entrepreneurial background wish to separate private and business in order not to provoke conflicts of interests. On the other hand, a frequent matter of concern is to discreetly optimize private wealth and if worthwhile link it with their business. It is a thin line between personal and business wealth advisory. As they usually do not put all eggs in one basket, they have several bank relationships. In general, entrepreneurs prefer a bank that delivers performance and flexibility through relationship managers that understand what it means to be an entrepreneur.

The behavior type of clients is another vital dimension. Adapted from various practices, there are mainly three distinct subsegments, namely *delegators*, *participators*, and *selectors*. The delegators tend to outsource all their financial activities to a wealth manager by giving their relationship manager wide discretion over their accounts. The parameters of service excellence are limited to a reliable and professional manager that yields the expected performance. Participators, on the other hand, are clients who enjoy the contact with their relationship manager. They seek permanent investment advice and often view investing as their hobby. Selectors are financially sophisticated clients that make their own key decisions. This group of self-directors uses the bank usually for execution of the products and services they evaluated. They expect reliable self-services and access through various channels but also innovative products with excellent performance.

With sophisticated secondary segmentation strategies as illustrated in Fig. 5 with the cube, firms are able to tailor their products and services to specific client segments and subsegments, thereby serving them more effectively. Such strategy is required to provide unique value propositions that open new growth opportunities. The advantages, in particular, in markets where competition is largely undifferentiated by price or other factors qualitative segmentation can help firms set themselves apart in the minds of their clients. Only if a wealth manager is perceived as an advisor that understands the unique needs of its clients, it can improve client experience further. Researching client segments is a continuous activity. It discloses how different certain populations are. Within this process, the bank gains expertise which products and services are needed most and can make appropriate offers.

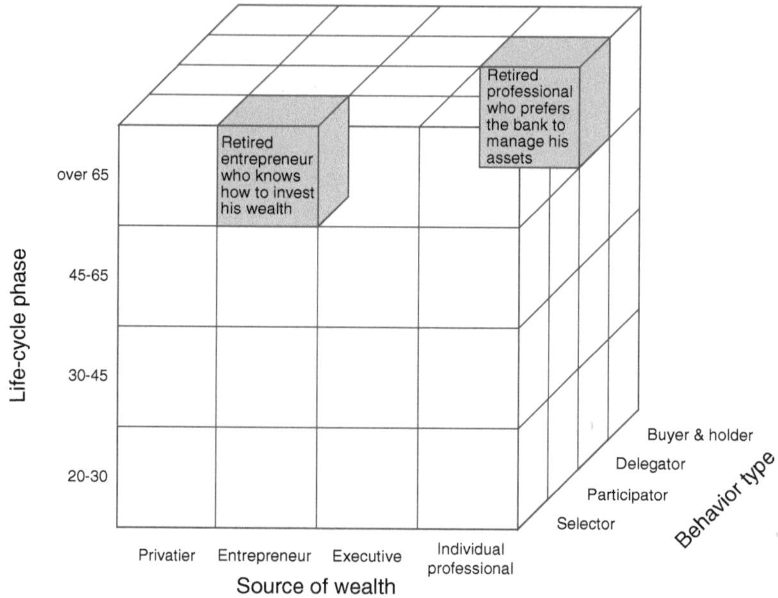


**Fig. 5** Segmentation by qualitative and psychographic dimensions

## *Increasing Profitability Through Smart Client Segmentation*

Many executives still do not know which customers are profitable and which ones are not. We believe that client segmentation can help to increase profitability – given that relationship managers go systematically and periodically through their client portfolios and analyze resource allocation, potential, risk, and growth. Based on that analysis, they can define client strategies. Goal is that they always know the strategies for their top clients, client profitability, business potential, and business volume at risk. In particular, the profitability of customer segments within a firm often varies radically. For example, in-depth research at the Royal Bank of Canada – one of the most advanced customer-centered firms – found that just 17% of customers account for 93% of the bank's profit.[7] This is why product managers often waste a lot of resources on the wrong products and clients and leave much money on the table by not fully meeting client's needs. Client centricity is all about the effective management of these two issues, namely client needs and client profitability while looking at opportunities with both new and existing clients. Transparency about economic profit would improve client profitability regarding various steering levers. Therefore, the gathering of as many information about clients is fundamental. Only if we know the economic profit of a client, we can adapt the product and service mix and prioritize marketing and sales activities or allocate advisory time more efficiently. In addition, special terms and tariffs can be granted and traced based on economic profit of a client rather than on gross margins of products and services or even arbitrarily.

The aspiration here is to establish how profitable clients are and how much potential they have. For a universal bank, this means that it identifies common clients with significantly overlapping expectations from different businesses such as corporate and investment banking, asset management, private banking, and retail banking. But before doing a financial analysis of clients, we must implement a standardized economic profit calculation scheme across all businesses. Note that high revenues do not necessarily result in high profit and good relationships. Also consider capital cost. They are highly important as they can significantly lower profitability. The economic profit can relatively simply be calculated as shown in Table 5.

If there are unprofitable clients identified, as we know most firms have, actions are inevitably. However, it does not mean that a firm should get rid of unprofitable clients, but it should rather think about how to turn them into profit contributors by providing services they will value and pay for. Taking a 360° view of the clients needs and aspirations and then applying solutions from across the product and service portfolio including third-party products is what yields profits. Thus, it is essential to generate a value proposition for the customer first, and then to develop a value proposition for the innovation as such that satisfies the customer's needs. If the value proposition has potential, the product management team comes forward with a proposal for implementation. The innovation is no more than a value delivery. In other words, adopting a client centric approach means delivering value propositions tailored exactly to the specific needs of the client.

It is important though to assess the entire value chain and to decide which parts are to be performed within the organization and which parts are for partnering would be more profitable. Final stages are the rollout and maintenance of the innovation. The discussed form of new product development is integral part of true client focus. Following such an approach means doing and implementing new things and improving existing things rather than just thinking up new things. Above all, client profitability as well as budgets, targets, and expected ROA must be segment based. A firm must respect client needs, risk, and behavior profiles to differentiate from competitors and reach advantage in the fierce competition for new clients and assets. Consequently, client satisfaction increases and clients will recognize and appreciate the value delivery and hence steer more of their business to the firm.

**Table 5** Generic calculation example for client economic profitability

| |
|---|
| Revenue |
| – Relationship manager costs split according to time consumed (inclusive bonus) |
| – Product and service costs |
| – Marketing and advertising expenses |
| – Support costs |
| – Capital costs |
| – Tax |
| **= Economic profit** |

## *Client Integration Means Organization Around Clients*

The advantages of integrating clients are so clear that one might ask, *why didn't most firms do this long ago?* Part of the answer is precedent and habit. In the closed innovation paradigm, most businesses were based on physical assets. Companies were captured by the intricacies of this business paradigm where lenders and equity holders wanted a careful accounting of how their investments were performing. This has not changed basically. What changed is that with the increasing dominance of the services sector, the match up of a company with the physical product it produces is hardly possible for intangible products. In particular, in the service economy, the practice of "what gets measured gets managed" has pervaded. We would like to elaborate that further. For example, one firm yields high profits with just a few customers where the other has probably ten products and a million customers. The point though is that almost all firms across industries and of any size are organized around product groups. For many businesses, putting the clients at the center of strategic thinking has been a challenge.

One reason why many firms have not been able to focus on clients was that the data demands could be overwhelming. Even if they could classify their clients into manageable segments with similar requirements, the challenge of continuously collecting and analyzing this customer information so that each client can be assigned to a proper segment is an enormous effort. Modern multichannel strategies where customers can access the firm by phone, fax, in-person online you name it increase complexity. In addition, clients and prospects wish an ease of use, navigability, and personalization. From the firm's point of view, there is another challenge besides giving their clients 24 h, 7 days a week access. Collecting and managing large amounts of customer information calls for aggregation so that data can be sliced and diced usefully. A number of remarkable technological innovations such as state-of-the-art customer relationship management or data-mining systems enable firms to do everything they must do to be truly customer centric. Many firms have recently spent heavily in their information and communication infrastructures, but just a few have gained return on net investment. Although technology to a certain extent might be the centerpiece of a customer-focused strategy, there are open issues. Many firms have figured out that the use of customer information extracted from their systems and transform that information into beneficial economic use is difficult.

Still, one problem of many firms, despite all the investments in technology and people, is that they have not been able to put the customer at the center. They are still organized around products, functions, and regions and that is why they typically fail. In fact, no single individual of the firm owns the customer, precisely the customer information. This entails that no one is accountable for customer profitability and loss. These companies usually make little effort to differentiate clients and to treat them differently. What makes it even more difficult is the seamless integration of assigned financial information. Responsible executives realized that customer relationship management systems, like many technological innovations of the past, require them to do something even harder than just make applications work. If we look at Royal Bank of Canada's structure, there are formal customer managers, as well as product and territory managers – all jointly accountable for profit and loss. The bank retained its old product-centered organization and put the customer-centered structure simply on top of it. Admittedly, this model would not work for all firms. Whether it works is largely a matter of how open, flexible, and adaptable a firm is. Organization around clients requires a comprehensive view on client segments.

## *Creating Organizational Entities for Women If Beneficial*

Some banks have developed an almost fanatical devotion to satisfy customer demands. Providing clients with exceptional value-adding services became the center of strategic thinking at many firms and hence the very core of their businesses. The foundation for targeted offerings and differentiated services was found in a kind of value segmentation. Examples that indicate this concept include art banking, philanthropy services, inheritance and succession planning, tax advisory and innovative services for sports stars, artists, and entertainers. Strategic advantage is interpreted as exclusive organization, which, in this case, at the same time increases competitiveness as there are just a few banks that provide such services on a global scale. Coutts, the English premium brand with a long tradition, is a good example of a successful wealth manager that tailored its services to suit assorted client segments. Client benefit at Coutts is thus generated by putting the customer into the center of strategic thinking. They so become a unique and valuable resource for building strategic advantage. Within this value innovation approach, the client provides the demand for innovation rather than the bank. We know that this concept is pushing product and service innovation to markets, which has a number of positive effects to the development of *buyer–seller* relationships.

Creating client segments and integrating them into the organization can go to extremity. Let us explain this with the example of women in private banking. Male clients have traditionally dominated wealth management businesses. However, the demographical and financial facts of woman's life are different from a man's. A number of reasons show why banks should focus on attracting more women as clients. In the United States, as in the most central European countries, the average life expectancy for women is around 81 years vs. 73 years for men. As they live longer, they inherit wealth, which is contributing to the growing number of wealthy female clients. Inheritance is certainly a major source of women wealth with the average age for widowhood in the United States of 55 years.[8] Additionally, divorce is increasing and a significant source likewise.

Social changes such as emancipation and equality have shown that men are more likely to involve their wives in financial planning. Accordingly, women are controlling more of the family money with the tendency to increase their knowledge about household finance, trust, and real estate. They have been empowered to become an active participant in planning their financial future. Women enrolling into higher education, flexible working conditions, and day nursery assist the growing number of wealthy female corporate executives and entrepreneurs. Today, female entrepreneurs in the United States make up about 30% and women's owned and co-owned business is estimated to be 48% of all US enterprises, amounting to ~11 million firms.[9] Interestingly, the majority of women business activity is within the service sector, which corresponds to the explanations made at the beginning of this book regarding the growth of services. These developments have led to a significant rise in the number of wealthy women attributable to independent money rather than the more traditional sources such as inheritance and divorce settlements. It is expected that by 2010, the amount of wealth controlled by women in he United States will swell to more than US $22 trillion, which will be half of the country's wealth. In the United Kingdom and Hong Kong, for example, wealthy women already outnumber men. It is predicted that by 2025, women may control 60% of the personal wealth of the United Kingdom.[10]

Some wealth managers have had a long history of traditional client segmentation. Although, today women make around a third of their business, they neglect women. They still believe that focus on style over content is what wealthy women are seeking. Pink and feminine Web sites and newsletters with topical issues regarding fashion, jewelry, or beauty are of interest to many women but may not be a propelling client value proposition to sell private banking products and services. Female-focused networking events, personal development trainings, and workshops that provide advice to women regarding birth of a child, inheritance, divorce, philanthropy, creating own business, and the like promise more benefits as these include financial decisions facing many transitions throughout a woman's live. The trend is clear; women will be largely underserved when it comes to financial and investment advice. They require treatment, different from that of traditional customer relationship management. Many female customers avoid talking about their money and financial plans, simply because they are not keen to sit opposite a sharp-suited banker who has little understanding of their needs. As women have more changes and transitions in their lives, they need more thorough advice from their bank managers and more understanding about career breaks. To gain market share in that new growing segment, wealth managers must adapt to this new customer behavior. They are forced to attract female clients.

Developing new services tailored specifically toward women is crucial but not enough. As declared in the open innovation paradigm, innovations are starting with the client. Thus, the basis for success is upon the development of women client segments. To attract wealthy female clients, banks must first integrate the segment *wealthy woman* into their organizational structure and client-centric strategies. New value propositions have to be clearly defined before starting with marketing and investing in the development of products and services. Through the fact that the United States are in a leading position regarding the size and growth of women wealth, it is not surprising that firms like Citigroup or Merrill Lynch are leading the way in terms of innovations in the female wealth management business. These banks have a specific segment approach. Citibank Woman & Co., is an organizational entity dedicated to address the unique needs of women. Its dedicated Internet presence offers access to education, financial tools, and a resource network that helps women to get involved into financials, find answers, save money, and make investment decisions. Overall, it supports them with the planning of their financial future. That the trend offers new business opportunities is evidenced with the start of the Frauenbank in Germany in 2005. It is the world's first bank for women with the aim of liberating female customers from dealing with patronizing, traditional bank managers. Positioned as a specialist service bank for women, the predominantly female employees offer short-, medium-, and long-term financial instruments, retirement planning including pensions, insurance but also networking, and business advice.

A crucial factor of dedicated organizational entities within a universal bank (e.g., Citigroup) in contrast to exclusively dedicated firms to unique customer segments (e.g., Frauenbank) is that valuable customer information must be treated consistently across the organization. The crux for dedicated organizational entities within the firm is to break through business and product *silos* and develop new capabilities upon cross-selling. This is particularly central for firms that have grown rapidly through acquisitions and neglected integration of organizational and technical architectures and cultures. Incompatible cultures, different risk profiles, and incentive schemes present common obstacles for collaboration. Established silos impede innovation and growth by blocking the free flow of customer information and insight. Silos prevent knowledge exchange in the form of best practices for innovation and new ideas themselves, which is contradictory to the open innovation philosophy. On the other hand, silos can result in a proliferation of innovation and growth initiatives. This means an increase in too many uncoordinated ideas that need to be funded and thus a dilution of resources available for the most promising innovations. With the recent developments, competition is becoming fierce and hence half-hearted approaches to customer segmentation without dedicated organizational entities and thorough value propositions may not succeed. The understanding of emerging customer needs and influencing customer value by integrating the customer's information and insights is a challenge faced by many firms that aspire to open innovation leadership. The example of the growing wealthy women customer segment showed that such opportunity demands that managers rethink the way they run their businesses fundamentally. Visionary leaders must shift their mindset, managing a portfolio of customer segments rather than putting products to the fore.

## The New Perspective on Product Innovation

Focusing increasingly on client value has changed product development. The role of product management has become more structured and standardized. Many firms improved processes and made organizational changes accordingly. They divided product development into renewal processes (product life cycle) and delivery processes (client life cycle). While renewal processes include idea generation, product planning, and product development, delivery processes include client acquisition and origination, business settlement (delivery), and client services. We observed that some firms empowered and enabled their staff to make decisions and to act based on their own judgment. Empowering product managers gives them the responsible for both the product life cycle and the client life cycle. The intention here is that they concurrently focus on service offerings, but are also accountable for reaching productivity targets. Building relationships within the organization with, for example, application developers and sales force, as well as clients for understanding and segmenting demand, became an additional key responsibility. It is believed that client-focused business initiatives can so be launched, executed, and finally implemented more efficiently and effectually.

These changes in the product and service development as well as delivery process imply an advanced technological infrastructure. A global product catalogue, sophisticated product calculation, and product profitability calculation systems are the new tools required for modern product management tailored to client needs. Eventually, the philosophy of product development and the role of the product manager changed. Product managers have new to understand the complete value-added chain, particularly as a generator of costs and revenues and optimize these. He or she acts along this chain as an institutionalized entrepreneur and has the duty to escalate counteractive events. This new role requires additional soft qualifications. Besides banking industry knowledge, an open attitude will also be important, where the product manager uses both external and internal benchmarks as well as third-party products and services. Assuming product managers are accountable for choosing content providers of value-added products to deliver investment product services to clients and client advisors, they faced competition both from within the bank and from external business partners. Leaders must acknowledge such competitive situations as opportunities. The new way of product innovation through open operating models leads to a transparent innovation culture. We will emphasize the importance of the open innovation culture in the last chapter of this book. We would like to continue with the notion that client segmentation and client integration strategies and structured and project-like approaches on product innovation are the fundamentals to develop competitive value propositions.

## Differentiate Through a Superior Client Value Proposition

### *Products and Services Are a Compelling Proposition*

To gain strategic advantage, firms in the service sector strive to increase their competitiveness with services that add value to customers. It is not the product itself the clients are interested in, but services, which the product can provide. This argument is conforming to so-called economics of complementarities.[11] The understanding that customers buy expectations of future benefits rather than just products has grown recently. We know from the resource-based view on the firm that most products require the services of several resources and most resources can be used in several products. What can be added for the financial service industry today is that besides the unpredictability of customer demands, most customers, for their investment decisions, take aligned services to product offerings into account. It might be argued that the open architecture *vogue* may obscure the fact that customers often value banking relationships more highly than access to a pantheon of products. It is a fact that especially retail banking products are commodities, but by no means the way of distribution. Therefore, it is argued that banks must build an emotional bond and long-term relationship with customers through excellent services. Many firms have put much effort into all the capabilities customers expect to find in the relationship with the bank. The client advisory process, which on the bottom line is perceived by clients as a bundle of services, contributes essentially to customer's benefit.

The commoditization of products, market developments, as well as client trends have challenged the front businesses of most financial service institutions. Reliance on improving market conditions is not an option. Firms must strive for leadership in effectiveness and efficiency. In particular, focus on the customer as a major characteristic of the open innovation paradigm calls for innovative processes to serve clients and leverage product sales. In addition, rigorous cost management, considered as essential to improve cost–income ratio and profitability, can be achieved with the optimization of processes.

## *How Processes Become Services and Add Value*

We learned that innovation can be seen as novelty (radical innovation) or improvements (incremental innovation) of existing processes or of products and services alike. Although this is accepted generally, the definition of process innovation is difficult in practice. Two concomitant factors are responsible for this difficulty, namely the fusion of products, services, and processes and the client-centric characteristics of processes. In the next sections, we would like to explain the increasing amalgamation of products, services, and processes. How processes become services that can be sold to clients is demonstrated with the credit asset transfer (CAT). Further, we discuss the effects of client integration with the client advisory process. Both examples stand for considerable major process innovations, which have affected organizational as well as technological infrastructures of many firms. Concerning the fusion of products, services, and processes, we found that it has become irrelevant to put independent emphasis on the definition of each of these elements. We believe that the achievements of product and service innovation, and the processes to accomplish these achievements, interact with each other. They are interdependent and should be perceived by clients as a coexistent bundle of products, services, and procedures or processes.

An interesting example of such a process that includes the distribution of a product and a complementary service is the CAT of UBS. Within this service, the bank provides a process that certifies the interface between the bank and its business partners. This CAT model enables UBS to use consulting centers and the sales forces of partners, such as PostFinance and numerous other institutions. The model operates successfully for mortgages where real estate promoters distribute UBS mortgages products while the bank handles risk and capital management plus refinancing through the purchase of accounts receivable that are all classical bank competencies. CAT does not come into play after the client debt has been entered onto the balance sheet, but rather transfers the client risk as soon as the mortgage has been concluded. The asset transfer does not affect the client relationship of the cooperation partner, which acts as originator – both partners remain independent. Interesting though is that the distribution perspective of the CAT model is based on the open innovation philosophy.

We state that a main characteristic of processes is that the client is part of the process. A deeper investigation into process innovation leads us consequently to the client advisory process of a bank. Since wealthy clients have become more vociferous than ever in their demand for integrated advice about all their financial concerns, they want certainty about their investments. Thus, clients require integrated investment advice for financial concerns, tax, pensions, and inheritance. A structured advisory process that integrates asset and liability management, considering both existing and future liabilities, is a crucial service that complements to product offerings. Such advice is knowledge intensive and based on trust and a good relationship between the client and the relationship manager. Advice has a great impact on the suggested products, and biases the clients' perception with every interaction or experience the client has made with the bank. Those who offer a superior client experience do so by leveraging their knowledge of clients and aligning the entire organization to manage and fulfill their client's current and future expectations.

On the way of developing new value propositions, it can be questioned what form of innovation this might be. As we have discussed earlier, innovation whatsoever might produce something new within a firm but must not be innovative for clients. Innovation in general and particularly process innovation regarding advisory services must therefore always be seen from a subjective perspective. There are situations in which a firm wants the client to notice the innovativeness, but there are other situations where the firm offers a product or service that might be highly innovative, but that the client takes as a service that just reflects basic needs. Going back to the UBS example, the bank promoted the CAT model as a true innovation where their clients understood the complexity of this service and its value. On the other hand, efforts of many banks to improve client advisory processes involve huge internal efforts, but are sometimes perceived by clients as just another banking service. Paradoxically, UBS can sell the CAT service, but struggle to alter clients' perceptions of the underlying value of their advisory services. The example reveals a basic phenomenon in the banking industry, which is that the nature of process innovation is complex and difficult to capture.

## *The Impact of Service Innovation*

As modern advice has the client at its center, it is the client, therefore, who can change the industry. An increased level of involvement in their investments and higher expectation of customer services are just two challenges a firm has to cope with. At the same time, a decreasing loyalty has been noticed in banking. The ultimate question nowadays is *what do clients want?* The industry not only faces a more mature clientele, what is more personal finance has reached a higher complexity. Clients have raised interests in integrated advice, as there is a growing demand for complex products, a greater search for security and reassurance, and increasing interest in third-party products such as life insurance. In addition to the impact from client side, we assume that industry trends such as regulatory and fiscal amnesties and corporate consolidation lead to increasing pressure to manage costs to improve profitability.

The discussed developments have affected process innovation. The changes gear many bank's business goals and priorities. We have to gain an in-depth understanding about what drive banks before investigating actions and consequences. Therefore, the main goal for every bank is the net profit before tax influenced by two streams; the *net revenue* including return on assets, invested assets and loans and *total costs,* on the other hand. Although these value drivers apply to every bank, the strategic goals might vary. Most banks define their strategic goals as return on assets (RoA), total client assets, net new money, loans, and cost-income ratio. These financial drivers can be delivered through focus on perfecting the client experience but also on industry leadership in operational efficiency. While client experience is a process that is complementary to product and service innovation, efficiency efforts improve processes in an incremental way. Incremental process innovation in this case focuses on operation and cost issues. Note that process innovations have always the intent to reduce cost and effort for internal and external customer. Through operational excellence, a firm may increase its competitiveness. Any initiatives regarding process innovation are, therefore, not primarily linked to products. On the other hand, a firm may increase its revenues with new and improved products and services whereby the organization has not necessarily to change its support processes.

Incremental innovations relate, therefore, not on client activities or innovation in terms of novelty. This is in contrast to mastering client experience as the other business priority as mentioned above. Improving the client's experience is based on process innovation that leverages product and service sales. Giving holistic client advice is considered as a crucial competency for relationship manager. They provide a customer-tailored solution from a universe of products and services supported by the open architecture. Overall, advice remains at the center of the wealth management business and can damage the reputation of a bank if not addressed appropriately.

## *Increasing the Client Experience*

Globalization forces firms to offer uniform advisory quality within the entire bank. This is crucial because many clients today operate in multiple geographies. Thus, they have one advisor in New York and another one in London, Zurich, or Singapore. Irrespectively, they expect the same service at all places. As clients have come to expect better services and intensified customer care, many banks have recently taken action and invested into their advisory processes. Some of us may have noticed that their bank has been spending more qualitative time with them. Consequently, one goal of many banks is to increase the time relationship managers spend with their clients. Delivering better service and becoming more customer responsive is vital but not enough. For gaining customer retention, an advisory process that guides customers reliably and seamlessly through the interaction with the bank is considered as very important. The implementation of such a process on a global scale and its continuous improvement is a challenge in its own right. To adopt the process and benefit from it, the front personnel need to develop new competencies. More empathy is indispensable for a better understanding about clients' expectations. It was observed that the emphasis on the client needs has shifted the way of doing business throughout the industry.

Questions like *how do clients choose – and why should they choose the bank?* can be answered because customers logically validate providers to gain emotional benefits. Many relationship managers assume that without meaning and appraisal, there is no emotion. Emotion, on the other hand, is important as it has an impact on client satisfaction. Clients seek attributes or features on factors to achieve benefits. Their definition of what constitutes a benefit for them comes from their perception and values. Many banks believe that their clients have high qualitative expectations about the nature of advice. This advice finally supports their decisions. Especially in wealth management, a number of banks attempt to combine logical and emotional drivers to achieve clients' confidence in their decisions and consistently deliver these values. If a relationship manager of a bank is able to consistently deliver this client experience, the bank will see return on assets and asset growth, as a result of the client's predisposition to consolidate their assets with institutions that give them confidence in their financial decision.

The term "experience" in that sense hits the mark since the clients' needs consist of a complex web of the concrete and the emotional, the articulated, and the unarticulated. For ensuring a superior client experience, a firm should put itself in the client's position and respond to the following client expectations:

- *Does the relationship manager understand my financial goals?*
- *Does the relationship manager take into account the needs of my spouse and children?*
- *Do I get what I want?*
- *Do they meet my expectations and financial goals?*
- *Can I trust the bank?*
- *Am I in control?*
- *Is security and privacy ensured?*
- *Can I access the bank through a variety of channels, 24 h a day, 7 days a week?*
- *Is this the right brand with excellent reputation?*
- *Is my money save at the chosen institute?*

The client experience in the end creates knowledge for the organization. This knowledge is very precious because of the fact that adaptation or imitation, without reproducing the circumstances and social context that led to its development, is difficult for competitors.

*What then determines how advice provides decision confidence?* Front personnel argue that the nature of the advisory relationship and the nature of the advisory process facilitate confidence for their clients' decisions. They have realized that client service is not about pushing products, rather about understanding their client's needs and providing advice. Relationship manager can only provide optimum advice if the clients' needs are covered as a whole considering all assets. A systematic and structured advisory process helps clients to understand how the investment decision is reached. It increases the transparency of advice and thereby creates an atmosphere of security and confidence. Banks, in future, have to differentiate through client relationships and the way they serve their clients, rather than just through the performance of products. Identifying client needs earlier than their competitors and reacting to these needs with innovative, competitive solutions that really do generate added value for the client are key to success. Intangible factors such as client trust and offering advice, accompanied by a strong brand, should come to the fore of a bank's strategy. The crucial questions then are *how can relationship managers execute differentiation with the advisory process?* and *why are relationships considered as sustainable differentiators?* As examined earlier, the product manager is responsible for creating a value proposition for the customer in the form of a product or service, or a bundle of both (product life cycle). The relationship manager in a second step is the one who delivers this value proposition (client life cycle). The relationship manager's professional role has recently become more demanding as he or she acts as an interface between the client and the entire bank's expertise. Thus, the relationship manager embodies the entire bank's core competency. Nowadays, the relationship manager is confronted not only with more complex client needs but also with shrinking margins. In addition, product managers and open architecture have increased product range. A stringent client advisory process might be one response to this changing environment, ensuring that the organization delivers the brand promised everywhere in the world, anytime, and in the same quality. It helps the relationship manager cope with new sophisticated client demands. Top executives are strongly convinced that in the bid for differentiation, holistic advice offerings are what provide the real texture to the client relationship and trust. The holistic advice offering to capture and economize client experiences and perception will become a new core competency of many institutes.

In wealth management practice, advisory processes commonly cover four to five basic steps. These are usually grouped into:

- Needs analysis
- Financial concept
- Client profile
- Investment strategy
- Implementation and monitoring

The initial step of the *needs analysis* is crucial, as clients perceive that the relationship manager listens to them and takes time to understand their needs. The objective of this first step is gaining a full picture of the client's situation. Additional client information about their assets and liabilities is crucial to serve clients with more individually tailored advice. This includes information about current invested funds and assets and inflows of assets such as salaries, bonuses, pension income, equities, bonds, licenses, and patents. What is also important to know is the client's wealth attrition. This relates to all expenditures such as living costs and regularly occurring payments such as taxes. Developing a *financial concept* for the client is the centerpiece of asset and liability management. It can be visualized through a private individual's balance sheet. The financial concept gives a detailed idea of the client's potential and delivers the key information that the relationship manager needs to define an individual investment profile.

At the heart of the *client profile*, we need to understand the client's risk ability and risk tolerance. Both are based on key figures derived from the financial concept as well as information gathered during the initial needs analysis. Where the risk ability defines clients' ability to cope with financial loses without noticeable effect on their standard of living, the risk tolerance describes the way that a client deals emotionally with investment risks. Further, it shows the clients interest and attitude toward financial assets. Clients that have a profound knowledge about financial markets and that are experienced in dealing with risk-bearing investments will probably understand market fluctuations better and thus accept temporary ups and downs. Since investment activity is often guided by emotions, the risk tolerance of clients is very individual and hard to grasp. It is very important for the relationship manager to develop an individual risk profile for every client and considering it for developing investment strategies. In addition to the risk profile – that can vary from low to high – the service profile of a client has to be developed. The client service profile helps the relationship manager to decide how intensively the client should be served. Some clients want to manage investments and make investment decisions either on his or her own or after consulting with the advisor. Others may prefer to assign the management of their portfolio to the bank based on their personal investment priorities and goals. This is called discretionary portfolio management mandate and usually offered to clients with assets in excess of US $1 million.

The *investment strategy and proposal* and other *solution implementation activities* where advisors provide comprehensive solutions tailored to the client's needs are the next step in most advisory processes. The crux is a perfect match of the risk profile of the individual client with the respective investment strategy. The risk profile is the result of collaborative work where the advisor together with the client agrees for a long-term investment strategy. Through allocating assets, the aim is to secure the highest possible portfolio returns for every client. A good investment strategy – regardless whether it is safety-oriented or growth-oriented – is dynamic and reflects the current and expected market developments. The purpose here is to continuously assess the markets. The outcome of this identifies which asset classes based on bonds, equity, hedge funds, or index-based structured products are attractive or less attractive. Selecting the right investment strategy that matches the client's risk profile is crucial for investment success. For instance, if a client has an increased risk profile and wants to give a substantial sum every year to a charitable foundation, he or she thus relies on a steady cash flow from the portfolio. Interest-bearing investments should therefore be overweighed in the investment strategy. This step of advisory is the prerequisite for the relationship manager regarding reviews and adjustments of investment strategies. For securing the long-term investment goal of the client, the investment strategy should always take account of the latest developments in the markets. Finally, there is a *review* phase, which is the process of systematically monitoring the client's risk and service profile continuously. The advisor conducts regular formal reviews with the client that covers the client's complete balance sheet, progress toward long-term goals, and necessary portfolio adjustments. This process safeguards the client's best interests and keeps the client informed.

To sum up, the differentiator factors that leverage competitive advantage in wealth management are representative for other businesses such as business banking, asset management, and even investment banking. Important factors for a coherent client experience include highest qualification of all people involved in client interactions, the advisory environment, intelligibility, the structure of the process, the time that the advisor spends with clients, the extent of client-centered activities on all solutions provided, proactiveness and monitoring of suggested solutions, and the quality brand of the firm. These factors corroborate the attitude to differentiate or die as differentiation will no longer rely on product level, or on back-office processing. Furthermore, the client advisory process will be the key differentiator for the future and has to be addressed as such. Hence, organizational innovation at many banks lies in the advisory process.

## *Initiating Process Innovation*

The way firms initiate process innovation varies. One approach is to constantly use benchmarks. Within this approach, the bank compares processes and successes between outstanding achievements and such that requires improvement. Besides surveys at regular intervals on all levels, top management is questioned equally. Building a circle of excellence, for instance, can be an incubator for innovation, whereby outstanding employees meet at least once a year and discuss various problems and threats. The aim is to develop creative solutions in heterogeneous groups. From the analysis, the attempt has been sharing best practices and in a second step to implement these within initiatives and actions. It is important that the initiatives merge into one another in a seamless transition. For example, the next initiative of the successive implementation of a client advisory process may look at product and service consistency.

Although these approaches appear to look like just additional methods for facilitating innovation, they should be part of a whole system of initiatives that go beyond innovation management. The aim is rather to systematically create and incorporate knowledge as knowledge about client experiences and the management of relationships is crucial. The continuous accumulation of knowledge in the form of best practices and case studies, and its explicit discussion may increase the learning capability of a firm across all their businesses. This is a process over a longer period, in which knowledge has to thrive and prosper through experience and cannot be built rapidly. Elaborating this further means developing innovation management system that must not be equated with initiative management or innovation management independently. More than ever, the success of process innovation is not depended on the quantity of initiatives but on the relevance of the initiative for clients and the effectiveness of how the innovation is implemented internally and communicated externally. Key is the interaction of innovation and a set of initiatives to develop and deliver the innovation.

If this attitude is not part of the culture and values of a bank's front personnel, their clients are unlikely to accept the bank as an innovative and trustworthy brand.

To support the unique banking proposition – that is to create client value and accelerate profitable and sustainable growth – firms should put emphasis on managing the team, managing the clients, and managing sales processes. Such an approach includes the sharing of experiences reflecting the advisory process in all origination units. Activities to manage the team may be regular coaching sessions, weekly sales meetings, leading indicator tracking, target transparency, or deputy procedures. The clients should be managed with stringent client prioritization and action planning, client contact management, and client profiling in addition to a sales process that includes optimized product campaigns and the organization onto product champions. These standard guidelines have to be used on a global scale and of course have enormous impact on cultural issues, processing and the use of applications and tools.

Since clients demand for a more comprehensive set of advisory services, firms must consequently promote its advisory process as a client experience, in which the client and the satisfaction of needs are in the center of the process. We learned that the number of initiatives to increase the client's experience should be perceived by clients as a matter of course. Delivering a superior client experience can increase sustainable client value added and hence customer retention among other benefits.

## *The Benefits of a Holistic Advice-Focused Business Model*

A wealth management model that focuses on the provision of comprehensive advisory services, including financial planning, and discretionary and advisory investment portfolio management, is what we understand under a holistic advice-focused business model. There is no question – an advice-focused business model starts with the utilization of a structured advisory process that facilitates globally consistent offerings and results in comprehensive advice and enhanced consultation transparency. If the client feels understood and secure, they will bring more business to the bank, in which the client has gained confidence. Providing a comprehensive set of services expands and deepens existing relationships and potentially attracts new clients. On the one hand, this is a revenue growth opportunity through increased referrals and, on the other hand, it can be an essential retention tool. More money inflow can result in a higher gross margin and improved total operating income. At its Investor's Day in January 2007, Credit Suisse presented that the gross margin in wealth management with advisory process was about 138 basis points in contrast to 118 basis points at clients without advisory process. Understandably, that Credit Suisse, like many other institutes, wants to boost the penetration of clients and assets managed with a structured advisory process. Besides the benefits for the firm, a structured advisory process also increases the relationship satisfaction between the advisor and the client.

We identified relationship satisfaction as a crucial determinant for what the customer perceives as value-added services. With each positive interaction or experience, the customer has had with the bank, the relationship is enhanced, and hence trust is increased. The importance of trust cannot be emphasized enough. Providing holistic advice is knowledge intensive and based on trust and a good relationship between the client and the advisor. As banks move to a more holistic advice delivery, advice becomes periodic and intangible. This makes the benefits hard to quantify and difficult to communicate. The advisory process helps to structure. Such process has a great impact on immediate investment products and biases the clients' perception with every interaction or experience the client has made with the organization. There are a number of studies in the banking industry that confirm the benefits of positive experience and participation in the banking relationship or trust.[12] The outcomes are striking and show that some banks evidentiary create an experience that increases customer value and loyalty. The reason is that experience is considered as tacit knowledge, which is developed through individual and shared experience. It is difficult to replicate unless the experience that led to their development is recreated, which is hardly practicable. The systematic capture of this experience and development of customer relationships can be viewed as a capability that, if incorporated, may increase organizational knowledge.

The role of trust in the development and maintenance of relationships in the financial service industry has become vital. It was observed that trust is especially important in wealth management, where the bank has the implicit responsibility for the management of its customers' assets, otherwise referred to as fiduciary responsibility, but also for specialist services. Clientele in this segment expect unbiased objective advice from their bank, whereby the advisor looks beyond the bank's in-house range and selects the best product on the market for them. Other important factors for gaining trust in the bank are a competent, reliable, and knowledgeable point of contact, the ability of the bank to get the basics right, open product architecture, and a general sense of value added including a stream of personally relevant investment ideas. As stated earlier, great importance should be attached to the understanding of customers, whereby a good relationship manager listens carefully and responds wisely by giving the best possible advice. Listen to learn, as a concept approach is crucial and may increase customer relationship social capital with the aim of generating trust. Listening tells customers that the relationship manager takes them serious. The bank in that case wants to do what is right for the client. Thus, providing better solutions than competitors is only possible if the relationship manager understands his/her client' needs.

## *Becoming a Trusted Advisor*

Wealth managers are evidently seeking to move up the value chain to become trusted advisors. Becoming a long-term trusted advisor is actually the overall intention of every bank since it is related to increasing revenues and profitability. Through this form of contact, both parties, provider and client, create trust. In the words of Julius Issac Baer, the founder and namesake of the Julius Baer private bank, who stated in the nineteenth century "If contact between people is based on trust and absolute integrity, then it is of benefit for both sides." This statement includes providing clients with holistic advice and acting demonstrably in the primary interests of clients, under consideration of other business and personal circumstances. As a result, clients will understand the value of advice and the value of service. Although there is much effort at most institutes to increase client value, client satisfaction is not always as high as expected. In fact, European private banking clients are dissatisfied, particularly with the levels of open architecture practiced by their banks. This is the conclusion of a survey that was conducted in Switzerland, Germany, and the United Kingdom by Booz Allen Hamilton and Reuters.[13] According to the study, clients feel that their advisors, even if they promote an open architecture proposition, attempt to sell them generic, proprietary products, and services. Furthermore, they are dissatisfied with service failures such as wrong transactions, suboptimal back-office processes, order fulfillment, and reporting. Many clients feel that their advisor is not proactive enough in providing them with investment ideas. The study also revealed that most institutions are not able to balance administration and customer service activities and that the time bankers spend with their high-net-worth individuals is as little as 5–10h a year on average. The results of defining excellence in private client servicing are astonishing. It is in contrast to what clients actually expect from a trusted advisor. Having an unsatisfied client base – some may even considering to leave the bank – a downturn at the financial markets with poor investment returns would decrease the trust in the bank. This would mean the deathblow for many firms.

Another recent study by Booz Allen Hamilton investigated customer expectations and satisfaction in retail banking based on four index parameters, namely branch services, product knowledge, customer orientation, and sales orientation.[14] The study found that Swiss banks came off best compared to banks in Germany, Holland, Spain, Denmark, and the United Kingdom. Retail customers in the United Kingdom are most dissatisfied with their bank's services. Although the advisors were assessed as knowledgeable and competent, the products offered were often not what the customers expected. Conclusively, retail banks have to improve their advisory processes toward a more holistic management, which includes providing best-in-class products and services of third-party providers as has been observed in wealth management and asset management businesses.

## *The Service Bank*

In general, regardless the business, today's financial services arena offers two long-term viable ways of achieving a sustainable strategic advantage, namely that of a *product bank* or *service bank*. There are two approaches for becoming a product producer. Where the commodity player focuses on a high-volume approach through low cost and standard products, the niche player differentiates through highly specialized products and services. The alternative involves focusing on client relationships and providing a high service level through addressing the needs and preferences of specific segments as well as serving these segments with excellent advisory processes. The dilemma of many firms is that they might stick in the middle, which might lead to a long running strategic dilemma. In other words, they will be neither a service bank nor a product bank. Either choice is valid and viable since most firms are not able to pursue both strategies simultaneously. Just a few very large companies can and do succeed both – as premium advisors and as providers of commodity products.

Considering the trends in the industry, predominantly more demanding and less loyal customers, commoditization of products, shrinking margins, and increasing competition associated with consolidation, it is suggested that banks must understand their clients well for being recognized as a service bank. What clients finally want are products and services that are not more innovative or differentiated, but simply meet their expectations and are better than others are. Against this background, the factors by which clients measure the quality of private banking services are that priority will be given to continuity of service, professional advice, and the social skills of their relationship manager, before the absolute performance of products. This assumption reveals that the importance of professional advice correlates to the increasing complexity of products. In particular, in retail banking, an often-heard quality criterion for client satisfaction is easy access to the branch, stability of the infrastructure, and speed and availability of banking services.

Banks, in general, must focus on differentiation based on value added to clients, in the form of quality and service so that clients are willing to pay a premium to cover higher costs or the specific knowledge pertaining to extremely specialized services. We should see banks from a value-based view, which means that unique value created is primarily reflected in competitive advantage. In other words, value created is defined by the buyer's willingness to pay minus the opportunity cost of the provider of the product or service. Let us add that value is derived from the effective and efficient application of the resources. Cost, on the other hand, is something that every firm can influence similarly. It is anticipated as substitutable, where reliability, image of the bank, and service quality are not. Numerous examples in praxis show us that the quality of services matters to customers most. Thus, it should be treated as differentiation resources. We know that especially in the wealth management business, one key criterion for the choice of a particular bank is the intensity of advice and the brand name before price. Note that in retail banking, the emphasis is more on the national presence of branches followed by price, brand name, and intensity of advice. Recently, we observed that focus was led on cost reduction and process automation; however, we suggest that investments should increasingly shift to customer-centric initiatives with the aim to improve customer loyalty.

If customers trust their bank, they will understand and accept that quality service comes with a price tag. Excellence in price management is, therefore, an effective lever for securing and increasing a firm's profitability. Corporate strategy provides the basis for defining pricing principles not only by considering clients' needs and readiness to pay, but also by watching the market and competitive situation as well as by constantly tracking production and risk costs. Focus on the customer is considered as crucial in banking because of the fact that innovation in banking lies more in process and organizational changes as in product innovation in a traditional sense, as research in the US retail banking industry and United Kingdom confirmed.[15] Focusing on clients with the continuous aim of perfecting the client's experience should be manifested in every bank's business priorities.

## The Future of Banking: Creating Passionate Clients

Some banks have recently reinvented the economics of its customer interaction. The implementation of a structured advisory process may definitely help to increase a client's experience across all channels of the organization. This may result in additional value for clients and the increase of overall customer satisfaction and hence loyalty. What is more, as clients in wealth management seek a high level of service and advice quality, so they do in retail banking. Here, customer intimacy becomes even more crucial. Retail banks need to create passionate clients who actively promote them. There are several ways on how to achieve this ambitious goal. We would like to show you the example of a small commercial and mortgage bank, Nykredit. Nykredit is a Danish mortgage and consumer credit provider with a long tradition. Since 2000, the institute has gone through tremendous developments in terms of innovative product and distribution strategies. Through its strong focus on Internet technology, it has become one of the leading multichannel service providers in Denmark. All its products are sold out of all channels with clear focus on cross-selling. Traditionally, the bank's clients are homeowners with mortgages. Recently, their clients increasingly open current accounts, ask for consumer credits, or buy home insurances. Their customer relationship management system is central where front office and back office share integrated customer information. New marketing strategies can so be launched based on the effectiveness of the different distribution channels. Coming back to comprehensive advice offerings, Nykredit follows a lateral thinking approach. They found that more than 90% of their current account clients prefer Internet banking, besides the fact that they sometimes need personal advice and prefer physical contact. This is in line with other expectations as Northern Europeans are clearly the most enthusiastic online bankers. If this trend were to continue, we could see an average adoption rate of 50–60% in the European Union by 2020. Besides Nykredit's advanced Internet banking services, they recently introduced a new interactive video communication – WebDesk. The Web-based video meetings allow the bank to do online meetings between their advisors and customers in the form of chat, audio, and video. So, documents can be securely and easily shared and discussed on the screen. Simulations over WebDesk help to explain results of the advisory tools offered on the Internet. Nykredit, as the first bank, introduced in the summer of 2007 blogging, podcasting, and idea-sharing. With these tools, retail clients have the opportunity to blog with an expert or a Nykredit executive or using podcasts to get the latest news about the financial markets.

To tap distributed knowledge through integrating their customers, there is an idea-sharing section where clients can send, vote, and discuss innovations for products and services. By using this channel to incorporate innovations coming from the open market, the bank has trod trails that before only firms in manufacturing did. LEGO, also a Danish firm, was one of the first that made its LEGO Gallery online available and invited customers to develop ideas or products interactively in its toy-brick business. Another similar approach launched Peugeot, the French car producer, when it asked people to submit car designs online. While LEGO financially rewarded the people, whose ideas proved marketability, Peugeot built a demonstrating model of the winning design to exhibit at automotive marketing events and integrated it even in a video game. Nykredit is probably the first firm in the financial services that offers these new ways of interacting with clients and integrating their thoughts. Encouraging customers to join the firm in cocreating innovations using new Web 2.0 technologies presents a true application of the open innovation paradigm in the financial services. It evidences that self-service Internet and personal advisory services are not mutually exclusive – it rather works and is a reality for the ambidextrous organization.

To create passionate clients, we suggest a bank to develop a framework to assess where the business stands in terms of client focus. The levels before a client becomes passionate are commonly engaged, understood, heard, and ignored. To climb up these levels, we must identify projects that analyze client views, client experiences, and client culture. Getting the clients view is crucial as through this process we can gain a fact-based understanding of clients and prospects through a number of client and market research techniques. Once the bank has gained an in-depth understanding of client needs, behaviors, and preferences, we must design and deliver a useful and enjoyable experience to clients. Certainly, there is a wide variation in the level of overall client satisfaction where some initiatives are more promising than others are. For instance, we know from a retail bank that developed a sensory concept for their branches that includes five senses: sound, scent, taste, visual, and touch. The success of such concepts in terms of financial return is hard to measure. But such innovative initiatives may help to increase client satisfaction, client loyalty, reputation, and share of wallet. Share of wallet refers to the amount of the client's total spending that the bank captures with its products and services. It is the new key performance indicator since wealth managers all want to become trusted advisors and gain new clients. The share of a client's wallet can be increased by offering new products and services or by cross-selling within the bank. One thing is for sure, it is always important to establish a client-focused business with a strong client culture to be nurtured. This requires initiatives that create awareness and motivate employees to consider the client view in everything they do. We will touch this subject in the last chapter where we discuss open innovation culture.

## Accelerating Client Integration

We believe that our interpretation of open innovation has become a necessity for those that want to orchestrate customer experiences. We suggest that if a firm decides to be a service bank, it needs to develop the ability of creating superior experiences for their clients so that they become passionate clients. The organization must truly put clients at the center of every aspect of the business so that the clients' needs drive the business. The open architecture combined with holistic advice offerings enables banks to provide clients with a solution consisting of proprietary and third-party products and services. This option gives clients the possibility of accessing products from a universal content and allows them to be involved in their investment decisions. As the bank offers third-party products, even from competitors, clients perceive this as unbiased advice. The auxiliary client advisory process, as a collection of integrated activities taken together, attempts to add value to clients. Thus, providing excellent service and being extremely useful, whereby the client defines usefulness, is what really counts. High-quality service further improves the relationship between the bank and its clients. A good customer relationship leads to customer satisfaction and turns into customer retention and customer loyalty. With the growing trust in the relationship, the bank receives the status of a trusted advisor. Maintaining a trusted relationship is much easier than building it up. It is, therefore, the ultimate goal of every relationship manager. Therefore, client value added through client integration and an advice-focused business model is considered as the main differentiation factors for wealth managers. Note that it is essential that all employees of the organization understand the value drivers as reviewed above. Only if they do, the firm can differentiate itself on dimensions that are hard to replicate by competitors.

The advice-focused business model that integrates the client is a mindset that requires radical strategic and organizational changes. Organizing around clients instead of products means changing from developing product strategy to developing client value propositions and managing product life cycle to managing client life cycle. From a financial point of view, such change implies tracking client profit and loss as well as calculating client net present value instead of that of products. This shift has implications to compensation models as well. Thus, best performing client segment heads should be best compensated with incentives that reward client profitability more than products. Most changes are associated to providing client value through excellent relationship management. All changes, however, have in common that they require investments and organizational adaptation. Some even may impede the firm in other initiatives such as cost reduction.

Developing the ability to align sales, service resources, and technology according to customers' specific value and profit contribution to the bank may lead to powerful path dependencies. Investing in human capital to promote customer integration and the new distribution model pertaining to open architecture is just one consequence. Client-focused organizational setups and compensation models could change employee behavior likewise. Imagine if employees increasingly want to be on teams that win with clients rather than in back-office functions. Within this setting, employees face three mutually interdependent challenges, such as more sales responsibilities, complex products, and stringent compliance requirements. These new skills need to be trained across the organization. The overall approach here should be neither a "me-too" reaction to what other banks do, nor a number of uncoupled ineffectual initiatives. Moreover, customer integration should be declared as strategic priority with top management commitment. It is impossible to be client centered if the management thinks product-oriented. A firm must be fully committed to client focus and following a stringent implementation of pertaining initiatives.

Client integration and holistic advisory projects and activities rely heavily on the alignment of organizational and technological innovation. The best processes, raising productivity by streamlining back-office operations, or reducing channel costs are worthless if we forget to put the client in the center, of strategic thinking.

Certainly, many business and IT executives as well as branch workers have a strong desire to better meet customer needs and provide them with value-adding services and processes. This was also confirmed by a global survey by Accenture and SAP published in September 2005. Accordingly, old, inflexible, and loose systems would have an impact on how banks do business, with branch employees spending 40% of their time on back-office processes instead of customer-facing activities.[16]

Many firms have recently invested heavily in advice delivery capabilities, including human resources and customer relationship management technology. The efforts to align organizational and technological innovations are increasingly becoming a key feature of their target infrastructure for the future of banking. Despite adaptability to the current business developments, achieving high levels of agility and enhanced flexibility is what is currently required. Leveraging open and flexible architectures to capitalize innovation is challenging. We would like to discuss this topic in the next section, also because we see flexibility as the basis for other transition strategies.

## The Flexible Enterprise

### *What Do We Mean by Flexibility?*

Although traditional organizational forms have worked well in relatively stable environments of past decades, the trends that we discussed earlier in this book have radically altered business rules for competing in the twenty-first century. The question though is *how does an open innovation-driven organization operate today?* In our hypercompetitive environment, firms are confronted with rapidly escalating competition that leads to constant friction between change and preservation. Firms must continuously increase the variety and speed of managerial capabilities. This calls for the development of dynamic management practices to address demands from the environment, as well as for the coordination of these capabilities collectively within the same organization when they would appear to demand different innovations. A possible solution to this dilemma is flexible forms that are between rigid and chaotic form of organization. With such flexible form, the firm can respond to a wide variety of changes in an appropriate and timely way. There are two broad different types of flexibility, namely strategic and operational flexibility. The basis builds the organizational flexibility, which consists of managerial capabilities to adapt the organization structure to suit changing conditions. Organizational flexibility is merely the ability of the firm to react upon hypercompetitive and volatile markets with new products, services, and processes on the basis of integrative organizational forms and a culture oriented toward renewal and learning. Operational flexibility includes all the operational activities and routines required to plan, produce, manage, and distribute products and services. Such processes are based on present structures. The more flexible they are, the better the firm can vary product volume and pricing, manage inventories, distribute through various channels, and maintain excess capacity in terms of financial resources. On the bottom line, operational flexibility enables quick changes for global, empowered, and service-oriented customers.

Strategic flexibility is the dynamic control capacity and responsiveness of the firm's management. It is related to the strategic objectives of the organization and an indicator of how rapid managers can activate this capability to adapt to changing conditions. Speed is a vital factor for both organizational and strategic flexibility. When the financial service industry is compared with other industries or sectors, observers often note that it takes too much time to adapt the strategic goals to technological innovation. Certainly, banks and insurers are marked by special requirements and obligations. These firms must earn the trust of their customers and business partners in the value chain as well as rating agencies, shareholders, or regulatory bodies. If this trust is impaired, business suffers and if destroyed no bank can survive. Thus, stability is also vital. Banks must achieve the benefits of flexibility as well as stability and leverage their innovative capacity with the aim to grow and increase productivity. Flexibility is opposed to stability. Since change cannot be predicted in an uncertain business environment, flexibility is strongly required. It is also not entirely new that if flexibility is to have value, it must be combined with stability.

Flexibility is the collective ability that enables an organization not only to react to changes but also to integrate intangible resources, processes, and systems to enact forms of connectivity that ensure endurance and accommodation to an unpredictable future. A large and rich flexibility mix dominated by strategic and organizational flexibility is also prerequisite for the alignment of organizational and technological infrastructures. Such alignment is important for growth, time to market, and premium customer services, and the tipping point argument is because almost all service industries and firms are now affected by the open innovation paradigm and its impact.

## *Organizational and Technological Infrastructures*

We observed that banking and insurance institutions seem more likely to introduce extensive changes into their infrastructures than any other service industries. In the banking industry where firms rely heavily on external resources to synchronize the speed of innovation and its delivery, more than just the acquisition and dissemination of knowledge would be required. Rather, it requires a fundamental organizational transformation in the approaches through which innovation is initiated, managed, commercialized, disseminated, and delivered. The capacity for transforming organizations is embedded in a firm's organizational and technological infrastructure. Such infrastructures require a high degree of organizational flexibility.

We discussed the need of frequently altering strategies and structures in response to environmental changes, and learned that rigid technological infrastructure could severely handicap innovation strategies. This problem can be solved with strategic alignment that includes business and information technology. In other words, organizational infrastructure should make information technology an integral part of the emerging strategic direction of the firm. Since people will always need to manage their finances, banks and insurances will always rely on technology to do business. Firms must utilize technology to expand and push into new markets and delight customers, to fend of competitors, or to cut costs. It is about a continuous and dynamic synchronization of the capabilities inherent in the information infrastructure, and the demands of strategy that facilitate efficiency and innovation. The gained flexibility accommodates strategic change quickly and at low costs. A flexible infrastructure further reflects the essence of developing generative learning in building transformation capability and a learning organization. The overall aim of such strategic alignment is to leverage technology for transforming organizations toward open innovation.

## *The Benefits of a Flexible Service Architecture*

The integrative and flexible capacity of a firm is based upon the development of a structure that represents the collective ability, derived from the seamless connection between back office and front office. This is crucial for every firm to survive and prosper in the new open innovation paradigm. Through increasing competitive pressure in the financial services industry, firms should no longer compete based on either low cost, best quality, or customer service. Sustainable competitive advantage derives from the synergy of the firm's various resources and capabilities. To make this clear, a bank must fulfill customer wishes by providing products with good performance at low costs. Sophisticated clients would not accept bad return on capital even if commissions were low. Firms simply need the flexibility to improve time to market, develop tailor-made solutions to clients across multiple segments simultaneously. We have heard all that several times. The point we would like to make is that for all these activities, integration has been a problem since time immemorial. In the 1970s and 1980s, the connection problem was solved by point-to-point integration, which means the linking of single points via individual and hard coding of interfaces. This worked fine as long as the number of linked points did not exceed two. In an increasingly complex world of networked businesses, multiple points needed to be connected to meet objectives. The increasing number of mergers and acquisitions even worsened the integration problem by several magnitudes. To simplify, different solutions or applications as well as old and new applications needed to be integrated quickly and at low costs.

The origin solution to find an elegant way to solve the integration problem came up from IT leaders. They abandoned the idea of point-to-point integration and inserted a new layer of intelligence into the technology stack. The fundamental principle is quite compelling – joining each application to only one central point referred to as the *hub*. The technological ingredient that makes the hub supple and flexible is the *service* – an exposed, self-contained, and platform-independent piece of functionality with a well-defined interface that can be dynamically located and invoked. Instead of customized and hardwired connections between applications, databases, or core banking systems, service-oriented architectures rely on standardized interfaces and explicit descriptions. Designing the business and technology architecture around services increases entrepreneurial flexibility and can improve business agility. In other words, a service-oriented architecture enables business processes to be addressed as independent units that can be assembled and disassembled whenever markets or customers are changing. One advantage is that it makes system or third-party product integration easier without friction or customization. This is particularly interesting for merger and acquisition activities. Another benefit of the fact that linkages between business processes and specific applications are no longer hardwired is that it enables businesses to assemble and orchestrate their business processes with greater flexibility in supporting business operations without neglecting customer services. What on a computer layer is the interaction between applications is on another layer the interaction between communities or the consumers and providers across company borders. New computer-to-computer solutions have arrived in the form of Web 2.0 services (e.g., payment service providers such as Paypal or Worldpay). With the increasing number of graduates that are arriving in the workplace with Web 2.0 collaboration skill, we will see more and more collaborative content sharing Web sites similar to YouTube, MySpace, Facebook, Bebo, Wikipedia, or Skype. We are curious how that is going to turn out in the financial services business context.

Services-oriented architectures utilize these technologies to offer the increased levels of openness, flexibility, adaptability, and customer integration. A key strategic issue though is whether an organization can balance efficiency and flexibility. We can see this from two perspectives: as a paradox of administration and as a paradox of flexibility. We learned that firms are forced to compete on several dimensions simultaneously. Large companies such as Merrill Lynch, Eastman Chemical, and General Motors have started to focus on service-oriented architectures with the aim to improve their service level and at the same time increase their flexibility and innovation capability. The recent initiatives of visionary big brands are creating optimism about the business appeal of this new approach. In fact, a new generation of service architectures has emerged. In the banking industry, we observed that a number of firms realized the importance of modular and flexible platforms that will still be performing reliably in 20 years. According to Forester Research, service-oriented architectures are already being used by some 40% of European financial services firms in 2006, and a recent European survey has revealed that by the end of 2008 about 80% will use it.[17]

## *Service Implementation*

Service-oriented architectures make it easier for firms to create applications on top of existing solutions. In addition, the value of current business processes and applications can be increased while reducing costs. Firms are also able to meet the business challenges that arise from the trends discussed earlier in this book. Giving just a few of the obvious merits explains why some institutes recently launched huge strategic programs with the aim to renew their infrastructures toward more flexible service architecture. We saw three main categories of projects. These include the renovation of the core banking capabilities to reduce operational risk, shorten time to market, improving client-facing services along business processes, real-time online processing, and access through various channels 7 days and 24h. Second, there are huge efforts around implementing new business functionalities to meet future business demands, integrating clients, and adding value through better services and advice. Increasing flexibility and improving financial and management reporting are more internal initiatives but not less important. In general, firms can meet compliance requirements more cohesively and cost effectively through service-oriented architectures. Last, there are complex technological issues such as replacing the core banking systems to reduce maintenance costs or take better advantage of open technology and industry standards. Research evidenced that especially for transforming core banking platforms, small ad hoc changes are not keeping pace. Accordingly, radical initiatives reduced operating expenses by as much as US $250 million annually (see survey by Accenture and SAP, 2005). Although such efforts usually improve productivity and financial performance in a first step, they should not be viewed as merely cost reduction initiatives. What is more the next generation of high-performing banks needs to learn how to master operational efficiency while simultaneously increasing their innovation capabilities. The transition from highly customized systems to less complex and flexible standard business applications in return facilitates consistent customer experience across distribution channels and product flexibility through open architecture.

A number of banks run strategic programs with the aim of radically renewing their banking capabilities and replacing the diverse mix of legacy systems with a flexible service-oriented banking architecture. The decision to replace core banking systems is a clear reaction to global need for flexibility and desire for integration, as flexible systems will help banks to remain competitive. In view of that, banks design its information and communication technology needs for business, strive for operational efficiency, and simultaneously reinvent banking technology to explore new opportunities. Technology supports, for example, the client–advisor relationship but never supplanting it. We presume that the large sums that many firms have recently invested in technology to improve efficiency in producing and delivering products and services to clients will also enable a number of business innovations.

## *Winning Through Competitive Service Architectures*

An organization with flexible service architecture is able to respond rapidly and easily to changing business conditions. Therefore, it allows the firm to introduce new business practices and processes more rapidly and at lower cost. Such a structured framework is very valuable for expansion strategies where acquisitions are part of the strategy. Explicit and well-structured service architecture might be used as a metacommunication platform to gain a comprehensive overview on the organization during due diligence activities. The easy integration of acquired firms and efficient integration of products and services from third-party providers are other benefits. Integrating IT systems has been a crucial part of bid battles for banks, as the takeover of Abbey National through Santander in 2004 confirms. Santander's intention has been on cost cutting at Abbey that missed to tackle the issue of its old legacy systems. Therefore, much of the cost, estimated over £307 million per year, in addition to generating extra revenues of an estimated £100 million per year, have been saved by replacing Abbey's IT platform, and integrating its services to Santander's modern and flexible architecture. Meanwhile, Santander has built up a reputation as a busy buyer that has the capacity to efficiently integrate its acquisitions. The bank's confidence was anew demonstrated when it acquired Alliance & Leicester in July 2008, its second big mortgage lender buy after Abbey National and Bradford & Bingley in autumn 2008. The acquisitions of these established English firms confirm the quest for buying assets cheaply from troubled mortgage lenders.

Besides cost reduction, firms with service-oriented architectures may generate new sources of revenue. Encompassing flexibility is evident in the growing number of banks, which pay to use other institutes' IT capacity. Our opinion is that small- and medium-sized banks will focus on their core competency and further reduce their production depth by outsourcing supporting functions (e.g., such as transaction processing) to larger banks. In addition, modern service architecture fosters efficiency in implementing change. This is important for keeping up to date and complying with all the regulations, revolutionizing distribution channels to meet the changing nature of demand, or the creation of new business opportunities. Look at Basleel II, one of the most significant changes to bank regulatory standards in 20 years. This framework had to be adapted into many countries and regulations worldwide. The complexity of such implementation for a global bank is unquestionable, as new infrastructures and processes must be designed, developed, and embedded within the entire firm. A flexible service architecture will definitely embrace such projects.

## Learning from the Strategic Transition

### *Organizational Learning Through Collaboration*

The process of change has been understood as the transition from a starting point – old paradigm and the end point – new paradigm. This transition process leads to organizational transformation and renewal. This is what we would like to point out with the evolution of a new paradigm. Such transition is always of strategic significance as it has the power to change the very nature of the organization. But it is also a complicated long-term process and means for some a radical new beginning. How to get there and understanding what happens between the starting point and the end point is actually the learning process.

Learning is essential for the development of individuals. We are learning throughout our whole life – with every situation and every experience, our knowledge increases and our range of potential behavior changes. Learning in an organization is learning at a collective level where the knowledge generated by individuals, known as *human capital,* is incorporated into the organization, which is then known as *structural capital.* A number of renowned researchers emphasized that individuals perform knowledge rather than the organization itself.[18] Knowledge, therefore, has to be shared with others and amplified from employee to group to organizational level. Organizational learning is a process of several learning processes from which organizations can develop new knowledge, namely congenital learning, experiential learning, vicarious learning, searching, and grafting. Hence, organizations learn through the experiences and actions of individuals, while they interact recurrently in the context of established routines and procedures. In any case, organizational learning is more than the sum of the parts of individual learning.

One important aspect of organizational leaning is how individual knowledge can be translated into a collective form. This is embedded in the concept of collaborative learning, which provides access to a partner's knowledge and therefore involves learning from a partner, or learning with a partner. Interorganizational knowledge creation might occur if customers, suppliers, distributors, and even competitors form alliances and share their experiences and knowledge. A company that does not share its knowledge can be seen as one with a closed approach. We discussed this previously in this book. Besides the accumulation of new knowledge, organizational learning is also about having the capacity for using and building such knowledge through interactions between the partners. Knowing how to learn from its partners is one of the most vital intangible assets of a company. The main rationale for collaborating is seeking resources and knowledge. Therefore, the creation of a social infrastructure that facilitates learning, where firms gain access to the knowledge of their partners, is a key success factor.

While intellectual capital is essential for the generation of new ideas and the raw material for any type of innovation, organizational learning might be seen as the principal process by which innovation occurs. We know that organizational knowledge is not a resource that can simply be transferred, nor is it embedded in organizational processes. We believe that the processes of knowledge creation and transfer are mutually dependent. Emphasis should be placed on disseminating information related to the *process* of generating.

We have seen that the transition to open innovation is based upon flexible service architectures. Although this is the basis for the discussed initiatives, a set of new resources and capabilities needs to be developed to leverage the full potential. This is crucial because major changes cannot only bring large rewards but also present challenges. Therefore, firms facing organizational transformation should have the capacity to renew knowledge, to achieve congruence with the changing environment. It is also important to embrace a *nontechnologically* view that includes cultural and social issues. Learning from the transitions strategies means, above all, to challenge strengths, weaknesses, opportunities, and threats continuously.

## *Meeting the Challenges*

The role of the top management is to provide the organization with conditions that facilitate radical change and the strategic transition. To gain a clear vision about the future business direction, trends and opportunities must always be considered. One important finding is that if banks want to become *industrialized*, they should learn from other sectors and industries. We discussed some concepts around the topic innovation in manufacturing. From leading automakers, banks could learn much about operational flexibility. However, the focus of the book is not how these capabilities can be adapted to the development of products and services at banks. But one thing is for sure, employees need freedom in which they can develop and adapt ideas that are unusual in the banking industry. Creating a work environment in which ideas flow is a leadership task that demands full commitment. It has to be directed top-down but concurrently a firm must initiate collateral bottom-up activity.

One of the first steps in changing and developing an innovation culture is to make sure that everybody understands the market drivers that have transformed banking businesses. If there is no justifiable, rationale for change, people will resist it and adaptation of new ways to work will fail. After the workforce has acknowledged these circumstances, we can go one step further and introducing innovative forms of thinking. The top management has to provide conditions that enable employees to see the world differently. This means establishing an intelligent disobedience that challenges business as usual. In some cases, such contingency approaches may motivate to think more openly and out of the box. At the same time, they have to trust their staff by empowering them and pushing decision-making authority down. We see that as indispensable for an innovative enterprise culture to prosper. It reflects that open minds can open markets and that is why global diversity of cultures such as multiple perspectives, skills, and experiences should be guiding principles for every firm.

Every manager knows that a future-oriented and strong leadership is key to survive strategic change, in particular in phases of uncertainty that occur typically between the old and new paradigm. The reason for this is that it takes time to create the organizational conduct required to deliver innovative results. In fact, there is a phase during organizational transformation where things might get worse for employees as well as for the organization as such, before it gets better. This phenomenon is known under the perils of the *J-Curve*.[19] With individual experience growing, an organization as a whole may increase its transformative capacity for managing the transition process as well as for generating business opportunities.

What is also challenging are the intervening conditions that either facilitate or constrain the discussed transition strategies. One main intervening condition that is bearing upon bank's actions to achieve the business priorities is the new way of doing business openly and in collaboration with external partners. One consequence is intraenterprise competition because of the fact that a proprietary product is only sold to clients as long as there is not a better similar product available from third-party providers. Some argue that such an intraenterprise competition might motivate employees to monitor market offerings more rigorously. On the one hand, this can lead to continuous improvements of the bank's own products, where opponents see reliance on different business partners as a threat. Open and flexible operating models tend to cannibalize own products. Being open is an individual trait. Some experienced bankers feel pressure on them. They are not used to pressure that comes from colleagues in addition to pressure from external competitors.

Since we are aware of the importance to view business conditions differently, rather with an open mindset, adapting open innovation comprises a cultural change. It is therefore normal that some employees have difficulties to cope with this change. Some might have felt more comfortable with the old traditional way bank business had been performed for decades. Not all employees are flexible enough to adopt new paradigms. Consequently, some may defend the old (closed) corporate culture and their peculiar interests. The challenge though is to build an innovation culture as fast as possible. Combining and synchronizing efforts that, although global, have a regional focus and are based on local cultures is crucial.

Many banks have adapted to open innovation. And, they understood that this new open approach requires operating models that embrace flexible service-oriented architectures that align business and technology. Complexity, cost, and risk have been increasing while at the same time client services deteriorated. As a result, innovation capabilities became severely limited. That is why a number of large banks launched extensive strategic programs with the aim of renovating the core banking capabilities to improve flexibility and increase efficiency.

## Notes

1. Information based on doctoral research, where about 50 semistructured interviews were held on senior executive level at a global bank. Fasnacht, D. (2005) *The transition to open innovation: A case study in the banking industry*. Ph.D. Thesis, University of Nottingham, UK.
2. Professor Noriaki Kano of Tokyo Rika University developed a method to analyze customer needs that became popular under the term Kano model. There are a number of articles on the Internet that discuss the Kano customer satisfaction model and how to do survey and analysis, e.g., 'Kano's methods for understanding customer-defined quality', *Center for Quality of Management Journal*, 2(4), Special Issue, Fall 1993.

3. For practical thoughts about customer profitability, customer segmentation, and customer centricity, see Selden, L. and Colvin, G. (2003) *Angel customers and demon customers*. Portfolio/Penguin Group, New York.
4. In 2006, the number of ultra-high-net-worth individuals (UHNWI) grew to 94,970, an 11.3% gain, up from a 10.2% gain in 2005. The total wealth accumulation of UHNW individuals grew last year by almost 17%, to US $13.1 trillion. For more information on global wealth, see Capgemini & Merrill Lynch (2007) *World wealth report*. Gapgemini and Merrill Lynch. America.
5. Among many other rankings and lists, since 1987 Forbes has scoured the globe tracking the fortunes of the world's wealthiest people. More than a catalog of individual wealth, the global rich list reflects the changing nature of the world economy. Since it began, old world power players like Japan and Germany – along with the billionaires who dominate their businesses – have given way to the latest global hotshots such as booming China, India, and Russia. New fortunes are also emerging in developing markets like Kazakhstan, Ukraine, and Romania. For the list, see http://www.forbes.com/2007/03/07/billionaires-worlds-richest_07billionaires_cz_lk_af_0308billie_land.html [January 3, 2008]
6. Table compiled from various sources but main information derived from the interviews conducted during the doctoral research by Fasnacht, D. (2005) *The transition to open innovation: A case study in the banking industry*. Ph.D. Thesis, University of Nottingham, UK.
7. Ibid 3.
8. Data for life expectancy and average widowhood of women are from the U.S. Social Security Administration (2006). *The 2006 Annual Report of the Board of Trustees of the Old Age and Survivors and Disability Insurance Trust Funds*. U.S. Government Printing Office, Washington, DC.
9. Data based on Datamonitor (2007) *Targeting women in private banking 2007*. Datamonitor, March 2007.
10. Ibid 9.
11. For the economics of complementarities and the adaptation of models that discuss collaboration and competition, "co-opetition", see Nalebuff, B.J. and Brandenburger, A.M. (1996) *Co-opetition*. HarperCollins Business, London.
12. For studies that researched customer–bank relationships, see Howcroft, B., Hewer, P. and Durkin, M. (2003) 'Banker–customer interactions in financial services', *Journal of Marketing Management*, 19(7–8), 1001–1020; Ennew, C.T. and Binks, M.R. (1996) 'Good and bad customers: The benefits of participating in the banking relationship', *International Journal of Bank Marketing*, 14(2), 5–13. For trust relevant research in banking, see Saparito, P.A., Chen, C.C. and Sapienza, H.J. (2004) 'The role of relational trust in bank', *Academy of Management Journal*, 47(3), 400–410; Bejou, D., Ennew, C.T. and Palmer, A. (1998) 'Trust, ethics and relationship satisfaction', *International Journal of Bank Marketing*, 16(4), 170–175.
13. Booz Allen Hamilton and Reuters (2003) *Defining excellence in private client servicing*. Booz Allen Hamilton and Reuters, London.
14. Booz Allen Hamilton (2005) *Renaissance des Retail Banking: Untersuchung der Kundenerwartungen und der Performance der Banken im Filialgeschäft*. Booz Allen Hamilton, Zurich.
15. For studies conducted in the United States, see Frei, F.X., Harker, P.T. and Hunter, L.W. (1998) *Innovation in retail banking*. University of Pennsylvania, PA, The Warton School, Financial Institutions Center, Working Paper No. 97-48-B, January. For the United Kingdom, see Bátiz-Lazo, B. and Wondelsebet, K. (2004) *The dynamics of product and process innovation in UK banking* [Online]. Industrial Organization, Economics Working Paper No. 0405001, http://econwpa.wustl.edu:80/eps/io/papers/0405/0405001.pdf [January 9, 2005]
16. Accenture and SAP (2005) *Redefining core banking: Banks need to update core banking systems*. Global survey by Accenture and SAP, September.
17. Service-oriented architecture concepts are gaining recognition as a key element of strategic business transformation. Forrester Research is a major contributor of research and reports. For further information, see the overview report by Heffner, R. and Fulton, L. (2007) *Service-*

*oriented architecture*. Forrester Research, June 8, 2007. This report was compiled from a number of publications including *Planned SOA usage grows faster than actual SOA usage*, February 28, 2007; *When to use which type of SOA specialty product*, January 29, 2007; *SOA investment strategies*, May 19, 2006; *A taxonomy of service types for SOA*, October 25, 2005. For more pertinent research on service-oriented architecture in financial services, see Hoppermann, J. (2006) *The state of SOA in financial services*. Forrester Research Report, January 9.

18. Knowledge generation in the context of organizational collaboration is best discussed in the seminal work of Nonaka, I. and Takeuchi, H. (1995) *The knowledge-creating company*. Oxford University Press, New York.
19. Pettigrew, A.M., Whittington, R., Leif, M., Sanchez-Runde, C., Van Den Bosch, F.A.J., Ruigrok, W. and Numagami, T. (2003) *Innovative forms of organizing*. Sage, London.

# Developing a Set of New Management Practices

- Winning firms must open up their boundaries and harnessing external knowledge, resources, and capabilities.
- Sustain organizational energy by repeatedly forming new competitive advantages based on various resource combinations.
- Create a new mindset and dynamic management practices based upon the development of ambidextrous thinking, intrapreneurial attitude, and a systemic and holistic view on the firm.

## Structural and Implementation Requirements

We grouped the requirements for open innovation into structural requirements and implementation requirements. The basic structural requirements are organizational in nature and consist of adaptive capabilities. They include the adaptation of an advisory-oriented and product-neutral consultative process. Firms need the capacity to create flexible financial solution platforms that integrate third-party products to meet client needs with customized solutions. This is required to develop the capability for systematically gathering insights from qualitative and quantitative customer and market research, which turn into value-added knowledge and services for customers. On the other hand, firms also need basic organizational innovations to build new core competencies. These core competencies must be embedded into management practices. They include establishing clear service-oriented management responsibilities, implementing a systematic product development process, and employing a comprehensive and consistent product and service-positioning framework. The rationale for that is that relationship managers for affluent and high-net-worth individuals need to identify and communicate offerings to clients in a quick and decisive manner. They must see each product within a common context and cannot spend laborious time, matching individual clients' detailed life-stage needs with individual products on a one-off basis. This service is reserved for the very rich client segment, up to US $30 million, exclusively. They must invest their time building and enhancing client relationships and gathering assets, not searching for

D. Fasnacht, *Open Innovation in the Financial Services*,

appropriate solutions. It is a challenge and opportunity at the same time. That is why many wealth managers seek to position all existing and new products in a solution framework that front personnel around the world can easily understand. So, they know how and when to apply it with any client with any financial need seamlessly. The main argument alongside the product-positioning framework is that it is an innovative concept that provides the context for product development and helps to prioritize products. Further, it promotes collaboration among product groups, internally as well as with third-party providers.

In addition to the structural and organizational requirements, there are critical functional issues for a successful implementation of open innovation. These implementation requirements include client relationship-related processes and functions such as structured product and service development processes, customer relationship management tools, and processes and consolidated account information. What must also be considered are structural components such as due diligence factories, processes, and systematic and structured training capabilities and not to forget aligned incentive schemes. Besides these requirements, there is another form of competency that is not necessarily related to banking, namely the ability to utilize relationship management capital. Some firms understand this as a kind of soft skill, which should be used to integrate relationship knowledge with tangible banking knowledge and the new functional competencies mentioned above. It has been said that interactions of a bank's workforce with external business partners are increasing due to open operating models. This much is certain; the new dynamic core competency of the banker of the future integrates much more qualifications than in the last century.

## Resources and Capabilities That Meet Open Innovation

### *Developing New Dynamic Management Practices*

Our business environment is dynamic and markets are recently characterized through high volatility. The shift to open innovation forces firms into transformation and organizational renewal. To run such changes effectively, we suggest adaptive management. Precisely, we must consider management practices that integrate many resources and capabilities, and that deliver sustainable value. What is more these management practices must adapt as conditions change and as new knowledge becomes available through customer and any other stakeholder input. That is what we mean by *dynamic* management practices. For instance, the alignment of business strategy and IT strategy and its translation into frameworks and strategies alone call for a set of new capabilities. Regardless of whether this issue is discussed in general or specifically for the banking industry, firms will need to adapt their transformation and learning resources and capabilities as well as their technical competencies. New capabilities are constantly required for integrating internal and external knowledge into new product and service development processes. We also discussed that the collaborative nature of open innovation calls for a set of new specific processes and capabilities to incorporate knowledge from business partners and customers. The arguments above are reflected in the theory of *dynamic capabilities*[1] and are seen as essential for innovative companies in a knowledge-based economy.

To clarify, dynamic capabilities include a subset of competencies or capabilities that allows the organization to create innovation while responding to changing market circumstances. For practical adaptation, we added issues regarding the *dynamism and complexity* of the current business environment. This book already addressed "best practices," a notion of whose most of us are familiar with as it is widely used across industries. The concept basically represents an organization's established processes – specifically the processes to integrate, reconfigure, gain, and release resources – that use resources to match and even create change. Those are the organizational and strategic routines by which firms achieve new resource configurations as markets emerge, collide, split, evolve, and perish.

New capabilities that focus on relationship management are particularly required because of the fact that many companies consider collaborating with their suppliers, the suppliers of their suppliers, customers, the customers of their customers, other financial service providers, principally with all their stakeholders in the supply chain – and even with their competitors. From the manufacturing sector, we know that collaboration with competitors is remarkable. According to reports, 50% of new alliances are between competitors.[2] Collaboration with competitors is like competition in a different form. Ray Noorda, founder of the networking software company Novell, coined the term *coopetition* while others used the expression for firms that simultaneously have a cooperative and competitive relationship. This change can also be seen if we look back in history. The pure cooperation culture dominated the economy during the agricultural epoch, where the other extreme – competition – changed the culture of people during the industrialization. The logical consequence of an open market and knowledge-based society is the combination of both. There is a strong belief today that a firm can become more effective and competitive by simultaneously balancing strategies of cooperation and competition. Sometimes, it might even be easier to collaborate with enemies than with friends. Accordingly, the best partner in a strategic alliance can be a strong competitor.

Collaboration concepts are based upon the development of the ability to manage the relationships among individuals, groups, and members to an industrial network. Besides nurturing relationships, firms need to focus on a set of resources and other conditions that influence capabilities. In the perspective of strategic management, the organization needs to possess this set of resources to be able to cope with a hypercompetitive environment in which change is rapid. Simplified, firms require additional capabilities for managing the strategic renewal. They must be capable of balancing exploration and exploitation or efficiency and flexibility.[3] As it seems to be a paradox, we argue that it is a tradeoff that can be managed by changing established routines and introduce new routines into the activities of individuals.

This may lead to a convergence of competitive positioning, as firms execute the same activities more efficiently.

A good example of the changing basis of competitive advantage through redesigning organizational capabilities was evidenced in the 1970s in the credit card industry. By that time, most banks that issued credit cards also processed their own transactions. With increasing computer-automated transaction processing, major issuers pooled their transaction processing while others outsourced it in favor of focusing on customer value-adding services. Later firms, one of it was American Express, developed new core capabilities in marketing, services and risk management and even spun-off its transaction-processing business in 1992. American Express was flexible enough to let go from what they considered at the beginning as strategic capability. Ensuring long-term cost effectiveness through outsourcing and at the same time taking the chance to explore new business opportunities is what counts. A new era of capability sourcing has recently emerged. The firm's ability to control and make the most of its resources and capabilities rather than owning these capabilities is one core message of open innovation.

## *Redeploy Support Functions in Favor of New Capability Development*

A series of geopolitical, macroeconomic, and technological trends drives the transformation of the labor force in high-cost economies to make it more adaptable, flexible, and knowledge-based. The outsourcing of noncore competences and moving of nonvalue-generating functions to low-cost locations will free the resources and money required for new business opportunities. Firms like Citigroup, Credit Suisse, Deutsche Bank, JP Morgan Chase, or UBS have recently created *centers of excellence*, with the aim to redeploy resources by taking advantage of the global workforce. We estimate that between 10 and 30% of support functions such as IT and operations could be deployed from the United Kingdom, the United States, or Central Europe to near and offshore locations. This means that development, testing, network monitoring, or database administration will in near future move to countries like India and operational functions such as customer call centers, trade confirmation, reconciliation, administrative account management, fee calculation, and the like to Eastern European countries. This makes sense if we consider average compensation cost of support functions, including salary, benefits, and bonus of about US $100,000–120,000 in the United Kingdom, the United States, or Central Europe compared with US $45,000 for India and Eastern Europe. The trend seems to be accelerating in recent months with several major offshore announcements – JP Morgan Chase is about to send 4,500 jobs to India across the end-to-end value chain; Citigroup is planning to move European private banking operations to Singapore; and UBS is to deploy 500 employees for business operations and 1,000 employees for IT in India.

Through centers of excellence, knowledge can be efficiently pooled, managed, and reused in low-cost locations. This knowledge is commonly transferred through repeatable procedures that have proven themselves over time. The problem though is that documenting and charting these procedures and practices is quite laborious. But utilizing capabilities effectively and institutionalizing them through iterative processes is crucial. Proactive actions, such as anticipating changes and even altering the environment, is often seen as a way where firms can actually benefit from changes – regardless of whether they come from the external environment or from within the organization. This can cause a dilemma of latent ambiguity. We are aware of the fact that our thoughts provoke a number of crucial questions:

- *How can some firms develop the ability to manage strategic change while focusing on their daily business activities?*
- *Why firms get to be good with this approach?*
- *Why and how can they sustain, improve, and leverage their capability for innovation?*
- *What new resources and capabilities are required for open innovation?*
- *How shall capabilities be combined to form a core set of dynamic management practices?*

In the next sections, we provide some answers that explain a firm's overall ability to nurture, enabling conditions to initiate, plan, and execute strategic change. We accentuate the alignment of such enabling conditions with a set of three interrelated dynamic capabilities. These are ambidextrous thinking, intrapreneurial attitude, and systemic more networked and interactive view of the firm. The identified capabilities are linked together through social capital to a system that is based on an open innovation culture. What we mean by this is explained in the last chapter of the book. We argue that this integrative framework asserts the creation of value, competitiveness, and sustainability upon the systematic development of a firm's leveraging capabilities. Based on this approach, we show how firms can master the transition to open innovation and leverage their capability for innovation.

## Ambidextrous Thinking: Investing into Multiple Strategic Directions

### *Exploitation vs. Exploration*

In an uncertain and rapidly changing business environment, it is a challenge to address contradicting phenomena such as developing radical innovations while protecting traditional businesses. If we talk about the ambidextrous organization, we attempt to encompass two types of business models – exploring new opportunities for growth and exploiting capabilities for profit. This is easier said than done, as the two strands require very different strategies, structures, processes, and cultures. First, let us compare exploitative and exploratory businesses as shown in Table 6.[4]

**Table 6** Scope of the ambidextrous organization

| Dimension | Exploitative business | Exploratory business |
|---|---|---|
| Strategic intent | • Cost<br>• Profit | • Innovation<br>• Growth |
| Customer view | • Customer value<br>• Economies of scale | • Customer satisfaction<br>• Needs-based segmentation |
| Critical tasks | • Operations, efficiency<br>• Efficiency<br>• Incremental innovation | • Adaptability<br>• New products and services<br>• Breakthrough innovation |
| Structure | • Formal<br>• Mechanistic | • Adaptive<br>• Loose |
| Competencies | • Operational | • Intrapreneurial<br>• Systemic-thinking |
| Control, rewards | • Margins<br>• Productivity<br>• Steady revenues | • Milestones<br>• Growth<br>• New customers, new inflows |
| Culture | • Efficiency<br>• Low risk<br>• Quality | • Risk taking<br>• Speed<br>• Flexibility<br>• Experimentation |
| Leadership role | • Authoritative<br>• Top-down | • Visionary<br>• Open-minded<br>• Involved |

The different alignments can be held together through leadership qualities that foster a common vision and values. Let us refer to the context of this book. We learned that it is vital to balance closed innovation and open innovation, product focus and client focus, efficiency and flexibility, and proprietary and central systems and flexible service-oriented architecture. For each dimension, a firm must analyze strategies, structures, processes, and cultures and consider all the little things that make finally the difference. A bank, for example, has to make specific considerations whether it strives for the *service bank* or the *product bank*. In the 1980s, we learned from Porter the importance of the explicit choice between differentiated positions and low cost and global growth and national responsiveness.[5] Regarding open architecture, this implies developing own products and in-sourcing third-party products, in addition to distributing own products through internal channels as well as through a network of distribution partners. Paradoxical demands like these are concurrently experienced. Another observation linked to Porter is that of the following two strategic directions – one for mature markets and a more aggressive one for exploring new markets.

## *Different Strategies for Different Markets*

We know that there are growth opportunities in established mature markets like North America or Central Europe, but we also know that the great potential lies in emerging markets and to a certain extent in frontier markets. Recapitulating the research made by Capgemini/Merrill Lynch or Boston Consulting Group, wealth markets in Brazil, Russia, India, and China (BRIC) are expected to grow in the next 4 years as twice as fast as the global average of about 6% per annum.[6] In contrast to North America and Europe, where growth will predominantly come from established people, in Asia, Eastern Europe, and Latin America, growth will come mainly from entrepreneurs, and in the Middle East growth is mainly expected to come from inherited wealth and from commodity businesses. New sources of profitable growth call for aggressive growth strategies that are different to moderate gain market share strategies in mature and saturated markets. Thus, an ambidextrous firm must be able to adapt to two different strategies, which cause a number of crucial implications.

One major issue and success factor for exploratory wealth management business is the hiring of relationship managers in the identified markets. It is obvious that new clients and new money can only be attracted if there are enough talented front personnel that understand the local culture and client needs. The problem though is that local institutes that prevent their territory and foreign new entrants that are striving for market shares drive the competition in emerging markets. The traditional hiring methods as it has been done in established markets for decades would not yield into success in emerging markets. This is because of fierce competition and war for talents with a higher demand than the supply. Therefore, some institutes launched *strategic hiring* initiatives. Strategic hiring is a method to rapidly grow businesses in emerging markets, whereby the recruiter acquires assets and resources and knowledge of the competition and markets. A strategic hire can be a relationship manager with a 2–3 year business case as it is believed that this length speeds up the time for the new business to kick-in. In fact, the new hire must bring new clients and business to the firm. Strategic hiring seems to work. We know from a large wealth manager that 60% of the new money in Asia Pacific in 2005 came from strategic hires and that revenue efficiency (revenue per hire) was more than four times higher with strategic hires compared with traditional hiring. Another benefit is that cost savings can be achieved by utilizing internal sources for potential candidates compared to expensive executive search fees. The downside of strategic hiring can be friction between the new hires and established relationship managers. The reason is obvious. Where employees who have been with the firm for years are compensated based on continuous revenues, the measures of strategic hires are primarily based on acquisitions of new clients and money. As they run after their figures, they are hardly collaborative and willing to integrate. What is more, if they achieve their business case objectives, they often earn more than their established colleagues do.

Another application of ambidextrous thinking can be seen in the work processes of relationship managers. Appropriate structures may empower them to use their own judgment as to how they focus on current customer accounts or nurture new opportunities. They have to decide whether they offer their clients proprietary products or third-party products. As banks strive for providing excellent client advisory experience, one attempt is often to standardize the process. This restrains actually flexibility in favor of efficiency. The art is to balance flexibility and efficiency. As reflected in the clients' perception, the client measures whether the relationship manager is able to provide the expected value added.

If we open our perspective and look at strategic initiatives of large banks, we see that comprehensive programs often support ambidexterity. For example, the firm is doing both exchanging and modernizing its IT infrastructure with the aim to increase efficiency, while implementing radical business and process innovation to explore new opportunities. Focusing on increasing assets under management, market share, and growth may lead to insufficient profitability. The explanation is that profitability is a matter of creating the right product and client mix, while managing efficient operations and tightly controlling cost and the margins that drive profitability. Managing cost and simultaneously maximizing revenue-generating capabilities definitely calls for an ambidextrous organizational design.

The examples discussed above show that for strategic hiring, one key success factor in emerging markets is to attract open-minded intrapreneurs with a corresponding compensation model. Further, relationship manager needs to focus on both – maintaining and servicing existing customer and seeking new money. The ambidextrous organization is also required for dual strategic initiatives – increase operational efficiency while seeking breakthrough innovations or exploring new sources of growth. The capacity to operate two very different strategies or business models with pertaining structurally independent units, each having its own processes, structures, and cultures is what maters. However, the firm must be committed to operate ambidextrously and the two streams must be integrated into the existing senior management hierarchy.

## *Building the Ambidextrous Organization*

There is a management debate whether tradeoffs between conflicting demands may be better managed by putting dual structures in place, so that certain business units, or groups within business units, focus on alignment, while others focus on adaptation. Although this thought was probably appropriate in a more stable environment, the logic of separated structures is unlikely to be successful in a dynamic and uncertain environment as we experience it in banking today. In particular, if a firm additionally to maintaining established markets attacks new growth markets. The problem of dual structures for different markets is due to the need of strong information and communication flow between the two streams. Communication across different structures would hamper the information flow. Permanent emphasis on integrating resources and capabilities yields into success. This would be difficult to achieve in managing separated or isolated organizational units. We argue that firms with multiple strategic intents should balance seemingly contradictory tensions not only simultaneously but also more flexibly at individual level. Consequently, one organization form or structure to address multiple needs appears to be inadequate.

Such organization calls for dynamic capabilities that are able to concurrently handle a number of conflicting demands. Firms need to develop the ability to move beyond the tradeoff and do two opposing things at the same time. A collective ability enables the organization to integrate knowledge, processes, and systems to enact forms of connectivity that create the capacity to respond to change. It is important to understand that by building ambidexterity into the organization, business practices of the old – in our case, the close innovation paradigm must not be replaced completely although focus in the new paradigm is on open innovation, customer integration, and flexibility.

Figure 6 explains the traits of the old and new paradigm on the discussed four dimensions, namely client and products, financials, operating model, and architecture. The bar indicates the shifting to the new dominant business practices of open innovation (dark gray).

Changing the form of organization and allowing ambidexterity to a certain extent is a big step for most firms, For some firms, it is more than a matter of competitive dominance – it is a matter of survival. We are convinced that the management of dualities and achieving both alignment and adaptability at the same time is possible without dividing organizational structure. Building ambidexterity into the organization, in which strategic and operational thinking across the organization is derived from exploration as well as exploitation, is a possible way of gaining competitive advantage. Therefore, the ability to simultaneously execute today's strategy while developing tomorrow's arises from the context within which the organization's employees operate. To avoid rigid and bureaucratic structures, we suggest developing a behavioral capacity that concurrently permeates all functions necessary

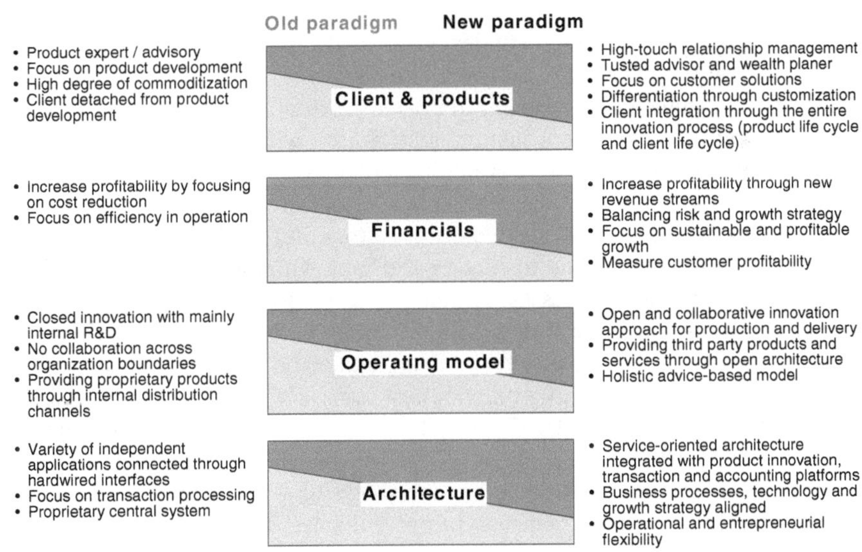


**Fig. 6** The balance of business practices between the old and new paradigm

for alignment and adaptability within the same organizational unit, rather than building up distinctive structures in which the two demands are kept separate.

There is evidence of multiple paths in the process of establishing systems that result in ambidexterity. We suggest the development of a carefully selected set of systems and processes that collectively define an organizational context, which allows alignment and adaptability to simultaneously flourish, and thereby sustain performance. This can be achieved through a number of formal and informal initiatives and actions across the organization. Providing a supportive organizational context derives from a strong leadership that put systems on all appropriate levels in place. A clear and compelling vision, relentlessly communicated by the firm's senior management, is vital in building ambidextrous designs. As a reaction, individual behavior emerges toward a more open innovation culture. Building such contextual ambidextrous capabilities into the organization is complex, causally ambiguous, widely dispersed, and quite time consuming to develop. Nevertheless, it should be viewed as a key source of strategic advantage for leaders in the twenty-first century. The discussed aspirations permit exploitation and exploration to coexist.

Now, let us turn to examples where ambidexterity was not considered. In the 1980s and 1990s, most banks were trying to optimize operation and reduce costs by pushing customers out of their branches in favor of ATMs and the Internet. After a while, the institutions realized that they had begun to lose touch with their customers. This shortfall of nurturing customers is actually one reason why banks are now focusing on reintegrating customers. The crux of the concept of ambidexterity goes beyond the alignment of current operations, while being adaptable to changes in the environment. What challenges this concept even more is that clients must never be neglected whatever initiatives drive through the firm. The development of the Midland Bank in the United Kingdom is another good example that shows that being too focused on efficiency and neglecting innovation opportunities might be dangerous. We know that technological innovation has the potential to transform an organization, including the way in which tasks are performed and work organized. However, it is just the platform on which success regarding the dichotomy of exploitation and exploration can be built. After the development of a new system based on eight large district service centers for check processing, the Midland Bank became one of the lowest operating cost retail banks in Europe in the early 1990s and, according to experts, the bank with the world's largest banking application of such processes. Although Midland's program was in its own terms a success story for technological innovation, the bank's innovative capacity regarding clients was very low. It failed to anticipate the developments in the market and industry and struggled with poor customer services. These circumstances finally led to the takeover by HSBC, which switched Midland's strategy from cost reduction to growth in market share. While the switch of the strategy might be considered as at the other extreme, the case shows how focusing on core banking systems exclusively might contribute to operational efficiency, but also hinder a bank's adaptive capability.

Similar cases of ignoring ambidextrous thinking can be seen in numerous organizational transformation initiatives across industries. As a thorough transformation of an organization affects every department and business of the firm, the transition strategies must be managed with each of them. Obviously, in some cases, decisions have to be taken to a disadvantage of other units or in favor of other businesses. Mastering dualities is a crucial task, which has to be systematically managed over all. We argue that the decisive factor is upon the development of management practices that facilitate ambiguous business priorities. In respect to the dedicated dynamic capabilities for balancing traits of the old and new business paradigm, additional capabilities for the transition process are required. We suggest a mindset that signifies balancing issues such as efficiency, flexibility, innovation, and at the same time negotiates the capabilities required for transition strategies. This is what truly ambidextrous thinking stands for – considering multilateral strategic directions with the aim to align top management continuity and organizational renewal.

One of the most important lessons is that ambidextrous organizations need ambidextrous thinking managers – executives that are sensitive to the needs of very different kinds of businesses. This ability incorporates attributes of rigorous cost cutters and free thinking *intrapreneurs* while maintaining the objectivity required to make difficult tradeoffs.

## Intrapreneurial Attitude: The Basis for Profitable Growth

### *What Is an Intrapreneur?*

*Intrapreneurship*, as we coined it for our purposes, is the act of innovation by the initiator of a new business idea within the organization. This is similar to definitions, where an *entrepreneur* is someone who builds up a new business in the form of a company. Thus, intrapreneurship encompasses the creation of new businesses within an organization, as well as the transformation of organizations through the renewal of the key ideas and assumptions on which they were built. This is a learning process in which the *intrapreneur* integrates the external environment and organizational context as well as individual processes into a business plan that produces value. The intrapreneur incorporates similar capabilities as the entrepreneur but considers the organization's domain, values, and existing business models. Main difference is that the intrapreneur acts in the firm and hence additionally exhibits synergizing and energizing capabilities to bring together ideas from specialists and managers throughout the organization. Individual creative and innovative thinking contributes to the organization's intellectual capital.

## *Creating Value Through an Intrapreneurial Attitude*

Staying alert and entrepreneurial is an ultimate ambition of every firm. Thus, success calls for entrepreneurial spirit and initiative from each individual. This is reflected in the individual intrapreneurial attitude of employees and an imperative ability of the employee of the future. But as growth continues, the complexity of global business increases geometrically. Hence, the organization requires structures and systems such as procedures, policies, budgets, standards, rules, and the like for managing growth. Therein we find another ambiguous paradox of bureaucracy and innovation. Within a structural separation model, coordination and communication problems would hamper creativity and innovation. The solution to this dilemma is that top managers include both streams without separating business units. From an innovation perspective, this means operationally intrapreneurial attitude and incorporating its processes so that they become part of the organizational culture.

Intrapreneurship of the firm's employees is not only about innovative thinking. What is more managers need to understand the business idea as a complete new venture creation including its implementation and value creation measures. In the banking industry, we found that some firms noticed that its managers were familiar with planning processes, but were lax on creating new businesses. Therefore, they launched a number of training programs, which showed managers how to design business plans. In addition, of setting up specific trainings, top executives must provide a set of structures, procedures, and incentive systems that facilitate intrapreneurship and at the same time, they must develop ambidextrous thinking. A firm's business units must feel free to a certain degree to adapt these guidelines to meet their requirements. With such initiatives, a less rigid organizational structure on business unit level and empowerment of employees within these bounds can be achieved. Referring to that, a business unit as a whole manifests itself in the specific actions of intrapreneurs throughout the organization. Likewise, the context of the system and structure at the organization that enables innovation must be flexible enough, so that employees are driven to act in an intrapreneurial manner. For example, every business unit should have a mandate in which it acts as a kind of autarky organization. The heads within such business units are free to a certain extent, to decide whether they collaborate with external companies or use internal resources, products, and services. To operate in this way, a number of jobs have to be enriched or enlarged. Job enrichment in this case adds new vertical tasks, while enlargement adds new horizontal tasks to jobs. Importantly, both modes have the aim to empower employees.

The culture of delegating authority and distributing decision making is considered as significant for organizational change and fundamental to a firm's agility. Through job enrichment, product managers are responsible for the product life cycle and client life cycle and are hence given more scope for decision making. Thus, product management may evolve as a new discipline, fitting between operations and delivery at the same time. As we discussed earlier, product managers have to understand the complete value chain where he or she acts along this chain as an intrapreneur. Remember that within an open architecture model, sales representatives only sell proprietary products to clients as long as there is no better similar product available from third-party providers. Also interesting, they can move freely between the flexibility given to offer special terms and tariffs to their clients. The rational for flexible pricing can be the changing market conditions or the attempt to increase client satisfaction and get additional assets. In all cases, the responsible person must understand how profitability is generated at the level of each product, since profitability may increase greatly in part because of pricing components that are not directly noticeable. This is especially valid for discretionary mandates where the bank charges fees and commissions for management, administration, or custody. The decision, however, is part of the relationship manager's or client advisor's intrapreneurial capability. What is more the relationship manager must know the profitability of the entire client relationship to become a genuine intrapreneur. If we look at business development, we find another ground where intrapreneurial attitude is strictly required.

## *Opportunity-Driven Business Development*

Business development encompasses a number of methodologies and techniques designed to grow a business. Business development involves evaluating a business and then exploiting it, using such tools as marketing, sales, information management, and customer service. Concisely, after having analyzed the entire business environment, key opportunities to better and more profitably meet client needs are identified. Lastly, an implementation plan for the proposed business model is developed. For a sound firm able to withstand competitors, business development never stops but is an ongoing process. The orientation of business development is toward creating and pursuing opportunities. It involves idea generation as well as opportunity investigation, and includes the permanent development of conceptual open business models. Opportunity-driven business development requires an intrapreneurial and multidisciplinary approach to management. Such assimilated attitudes foster creativity in meeting new and unforeseen challenges and are vital to keep a firm on a path of sustainable growth.

In today's hypercompetitive and dynamic environment, there are too many elements of uncertainty and situation both outside and inside an organization keeps changing. Strategic intent should thus convey a sense of directions that can be used to challenge current opportunities. With an opportunity-driven business development approach, focus is on increasing the effectiveness of a firm through the pursuit of new business. Within an ambidextrous organization, such approach is considered parallel to the traditional process of renewing business strategy. Later is known as *top-down* approach (vision, mission, strategy, actions). Regardless whether a firm is already both very efficient and very effective, external change is a constant factor. Besides, it is often easier to obtain resources for new opportunities when the firm is doing well. Pointing to the importance of an intrapreneurial attitude for business development managers, we suggest that they define a number of challenges each year and necessary steps toward realizing the strategic intent. In particular, during transformation, the challenges and strategic direction may well change along the way. We recommend splitting these challenges into a number of key initiatives. Opportunities, on the other hand, arise and crystallize on a continuous basis. Our experience tells us that every firm meets new opportunities as well as threats regularly – if not daily. For example, an employee discovers an opportunity to sell a current product in a new market segment or a competitor suddenly goes up for sale. Such opportunities do not wait for the next strategy meeting. Where some opportunities may shape new challenges or influence the strategic intent of the firm, other just require incremental changes with the aim to improve the performance of current businesses.

## *Developing Intrapreneurs*

As collaboration increases, the capability to collaborate leads finally to organizational learning as part of nonroutine work processes. Many firms not only empower managers but also enable employees to become more innovative and flexible even in the course of their daily activities and routine tasks. Through empowerment, employees become owners of their tasks. Described on a larger picture, we can talk about *identity building*. In other words, employees require opportunities to make informed choices. They must accept personal responsibility for their actions and its consequences as traditional entrepreneurs across markets would do. Within private banking, empowered relationship managers offer clients an optimal interface with the organization. To enable services that suit to each client's individual needs and personality, they must be able to act instantly, capably, effectively, efficiently, and proactively.

The observation saw empowerment to a certain extent as a state of mind that employees must enter on their own. The management, in that case, exploits the firm's distinctive resources by creating routines. Therefore, they seek to extract enhanced services from successful *reutilized* resources. This process creates and institutionalizes knowledge by linking content, process, and emerging context in a systematic way over time. Institutionalizing client relationships means to tie client loyalty to the bank instead to an individual person. A team-based coverage model must replace exclusive relationships between clients and their assigned relationship manager. Within such a model, the relationship manager is purely responsible for the relationship where the client has additional direct access to product specialists and other service advisors. Ultra-high-net-worth clients usually request such models. On the other hand, it helps the bank in terms of monopolized client relationships by individuals who are not willing to share their knowledge about client relationships. Therefore, sharing client relationships through team-based approaches can lead to resistance. In fact, relationship managers may reject modifying traditional client advisory with routines and processes that disclose implicit knowledge. It is understandable that especially older front personnel worry of losing their *status quo*. To avoid resistance to the use of routines and team-based client coverage models and to preserve the task autonomy and variety of individuals, we suggest various modes of empowerment as initial vehicles to promote intrapreneurship. Furthermore, the process has to be accompanied by change management activities as well as an incentive model that fosters team-based approaches.

There are really threats of empowerment strategies. For instance, once a firm has implemented such approaches, employees expect continuous enrichment and enlargement that is reflected in salary increase and career development. This system of working, if not controlled properly, may lead to a vicious circle. Particularly, in upstream financial markets where employees will only stay as long as the firm is able to meet their wishes. As they gain intrapreneurial skills, they are more in demand on the job market. This has both positive and negative effects where, on the one hand, the firm has to invest in its workforce's employability, yet, on the other hand, this investment can have an adverse affect on the entire organization. We therefore suggest a management approach regarding intrapreneurship that encourages ambidextrous behavior that is both aligned and adaptable. In other words, organizational processes should not only focus on how work is done effectively, but also ensure the empowerment, development, and commitment of all employees. Such approach would enable the workforce to become more risk averse, innovative, and flexible in their routine tasks. Further, individuals would become responsible for exploitation as well as creation-oriented activities. It is an adaptable approach, which is open to ideas from managers on different levels, and responsive to the changing environment.

For creating sustained value through building intrapreneurship into the organization, a strong management commitment is essential. The management of the firm is eventually responsible for providing the conditions that facilitate individual intrapreneurial attitude with the aim of opening the employee's minds. Framing the organizational context is anticipated as one enabling condition for developing the open innovation culture. As we discussed in *Chapter One*, a chief growth officer may be the cohesive power to align intrapreneurs within the organization. Embedded in the organizational structure, the growth officer takes the overall responsibility to drive operational linkages and sustain the energy and commitment of a number of intrapreneurs from various business units. Structuring and incorporating innovative thinking is the prerequisite to avoid chaos and key to turn new business opportunities into profit. EFG International, a global private banking group, headquartered in Switzerland with roughly 1,900 employees in 50 locations in 30 countries, runs a business model that is entirely based on empowering their relationship managers who are called *client relationship officers*. Since its formation in 1995, EFG International has grown during a period of unprecedented change and turmoil. Its net profit increased from CHF 48 million in 2004 to CHF 332 million in 2007, or in relation to assets under management from CHF 22.1 billion to CHF 98.3 billion. The root of the bank's success is believed to be in their openness. Not only do their client relationship officers have the autonomy to pick products from a world of investment options to design solutions best suited to the needs of their clients, but also there is no geographic or psychographic segmentation of clients. The management of the bank faiths in their experienced intrapreneurs to decide whether they want to acquire and manage clients in Latin America or Eastern Europe, depending on the expenses that occur. Further, they allow their client relationship officers the freedom and entrepreneurial flexibility to offer clients solutions that provide growth opportunities or protect capital. Each of them is an intrapreneur, to use the term explained in this book, who runs an own profit and loss entity based on the business they get from their client portfolio. They are remunerated in consequence and thus only succeed when their clients do. The bank's distinctive business model proved to be the right one – in good as well as in bad market environments.

The example reveals that ambidextrous thinking and an intrapreneurial attitude on individual level are sometimes not enough and for some firms not practicable. Where, for smaller banks or startup firms, radical empowerment and intrapreneurial business models may fit, large wealth managers are often unable to empower all employees and enable the discussed flexibility. A systemic view on the firms – one that is interactive, embraces collaboration, and fosters networks – would complete the set of practices required for being successful in the new open innovation paradigm.

## Systemic and Holistic View on the Firm: Do Not Think in Silos and Release Organizational Energy

Looking to the future, it becomes readily apparent that global business complexity, fierce competition, and scarce knowledge resources remain great challenges. Strategic management in the open innovation paradigm requires change in the management mindset. There has been a shift in our assumptions regarding the means of knowing from analytical thinking and mechanistic resource capability orientation to systemic and holistic thinking. Indisputably, to build up an agile, ambidextrous, and flexible organization that is globally connected, we need a better understanding on how to handle interdependent sets of variables. It does not surprise that the World Economic Forum Annual Meeting 2008 program was based on an interdisciplinary and systemic view of the major economic, political, societal, and technological forces currently at work in the world.[7] We are glad that this finally reached the top end of global leaders. What is discussed on a global large scale at the Forum underlies principally the same ideas as what we discuss on company level. As the people in developed economies are sophisticated and demand much from their political leaders, stakeholders of companies make great demands on managers today. It is expected that managers have the ability to see the organization as a multiminded system in addition to the understanding of chaos and complexity.

We need to combine the analytic approach with systemic thinking capabilities with a strong intuitive sense for capturing opportunity. The rational for that assumption is that organizations are *nonlinear*[8] and *complex adaptive systems*.[9] These *systems* have the capacity within them to respond to their *environment*. Applications of chaos theory to organization science are reflected in the increasing interest in the science of complexity. The science of complexity theory presents us with a completely different metaparadigm. Through this lens, the world of organization is seen as a *system* held far from equilibrium. In a business world characterized by dynamism and complexity, links between strategies and their long-term outcomes can sometimes get lost. What remain predictable are the system dynamics and the archetypal comportment it produces. The analysis concludes that predictability is possible at the general level but not at the specific. The opposite of the conclusion reached applies if firms would follow conventional closed, pure analytical, rigid, and unilateral management thinking.

If we view an organization through the lens of systemic thinking, we perceive it as a system with a high degree of ambiguity and complexity. Thus, organizations have two ways of adapting to the environment: complexity reduction and complexity absorption. For achieving this, we argue that systemic thinking as based on the emerging science of *systems dynamics*[10] is a vital capability, which is going beyond just managing complexity. The key message is to understand and transform the organization as a whole system, whereby the overall business context must not be lost – also commonly referred to as failing to see the big picture. In other words, missing the crucial connective elements of cause and effect within decision making and strategy implementation might be catastrophic.

Systemic thinking implies the integration of structures, processes, and patterns such as relationship and learning. In particular, addressing relationship and learning and view these elements as part of a whole system not only strongly affect a firm's renewal ability, what is more employees continually expand their capacity to learn to deal with interdependent set of variables. The form of learning, how to learn together within a network of relationships, is similar to what Peter Senge conceptualized in the 1990s as the *fifth discipline* – the art and practice of the *learning organization*.[11] That is, the organization facilitates collaborative learning processes at individual, group, and system level and hence transforms itself continuously in a direction that is increasingly satisfying to all its stakeholders. One possible way from systemic thinking to organizational learning can be achieved through empowerment of employees as the examples of the product manager, relationship manager or growth officers explained earlier in this book, evidenced. Their empowerment gives them the overview of the entire innovation process rather than just parts of it such as planning, development, or delivery. Their views were expanded as a matter of the fact that their activities automatically included more decision-making authority and interactions within the firm as well as across organizational boundaries. Therefore, it can be said that organizational learning is based on human communicative interaction. The more collaboration, the better for the firm's knowledge development. This is in stark contrast to analytical thinking where empowerment, collaboration, trust, care, nurturing, and personal fulfillment are not included. Leveraging effects can hardly be achieved within a closed innovation culture that is based upon routine activities, linear, mechanistic, and narrow thinking.

Another good example of systemic thinking is the bundling of a number of key initiatives and projects with the aim of improving efficiency as well as to exploring new opportunities. Such bundling into an overarching strategic program yields into a number of synergy effects. The top management, responsible for its compliance and alignment with the all-embracing strategy, monitors all initiatives with its interrelations holistically in the form of the strategic program. It is clear that viewing a program as a whole is more valuable than the implementation of its individual projects. Implementing only a few projects at a time would therefore not yield in all the benefits that are available through a fully coordinated program. Many firms attempt to do many projects in parallel, while they always keep the consequences of the entire program in mind. We assume that performance effects depend upon a management mindset that is based on systemic and holistic thinking capabilities. This notion is reflected in a vast longitudinal study that observed innovative forms of organizing, in particular transformation, in countries such as the United States, Japan, and Europe.[12] Accordingly, system-wide change, in which the firm considers strategic change, structural change, and process change, paid off best. This is what we understand under the integral design of total transformation and is in contrast to management thinking that rarely takes the risk to lead innovation with a *grand design* of total transformation. The implementation of partial combination of full system elements is commonly termed *piecemeal approach*. For mastering transformative change – that is managing a complex system of innovative organizational change – systemic and holistic thinking are required capabilities and the recommended approach.

The suggested ambidextrous thinking, intrapreneurial attitude, and the systemic and holistic view on strategic things are coherent. A successful manager must develop these capabilities and be able to handle the challenges of paradox. He or she must be prepared to manage ambiguity, complexity, uncertainty, and chaos by developing adaptive strategies. But these efforts can only show full advantage if we understand how to integrate single capabilities into a cohesive whole.

## Leveraging Dynamic Capabilities

As we have seen, the transition from existing strength to future potential, identified as the new paradigm, requires capabilities that make existing resources more valuable and sustainable. Besides the discussed set of dynamic management practices, it was observed that the availability of enabling conditions is crucial. Enabling conditions include a clear vision, strategic focus, strong leadership qualities, and sufficient financial resources. Therefore, every firm needs leveraging capabilities to capitalize enabling conditions, manage, and execute transformative change. Auxiliary to these leveraging capabilities, architectural capabilities are important for aligning business and IT and provide the firm with an appropriate flexible organizational and technological infrastructure. These infrastructures help the firm to manage and balance multiple strategic directions such as growth, innovation, and operational efficiency. Overall, the collective ability of nurturing enabling conditions and aligning them with architectural capabilities and current management practices is represented with leveraging capabilities. This ability is becoming increasingly important. In particular, in a world of Schumpeterian competition, where innovation is a recombination of existing resources and capabilities with the aim of increasing knowledge and intellectual capital, and where competitors can imitate products and services and reproduce capital, or technical and marketing capabilities rapidly and easily.

Based on the assumptions made, the potential for sustainable competitive advantage lies in anticipating trends sooner than competitors and systematically leveraging capabilities. In fact, to achieve new and innovative forms of competitive advantage, dynamic management capabilities and inimitable combinations of resources that cut across all functions are required. We see the above arguments as essential for doing business in the new open innovation paradigm.

As we learned, firms in the financial services industry operate in a dynamic, uncertain, complex, ambiguous, and hypercompetitive environment in which they do not just respond to the change, but instead, create them by their own actions. Therefore, it is crucial to find appropriate forms for addressing various resources and capabilities across the organization with the aim to enable them to make the right decisions about what to focus on, abandon, or maintain. Several discussion throughout the book made clear that intangible assets such as knowledge, relationships, and experiences are difficult to identify and hard to copy. Here again, a strong leadership is required to determine which skills are most promising and select them as priorities for development. The management has to provide the required organizational conditions to capture these emerging, potential, and hidden resources and build them into a set of management practices. Through this process, over time, firms may evolve a set of explicit organizational processes and designs that they can turn into capabilities, and leverage them across the appropriate market opportunities. This also points to the importance of leadership, vision, and strategic focus, represented in the enabling conditions, to install systems and policies that create appropriate values and cultures for the process of embedding and enhancing capabilities within the organization and shaping them to market opportunities. Leveraging capabilities means that managers need to find opportunities tailored to a set of capabilities; but at the same time, opportunities must also shape capabilities. Based on these arguments, it is suggested that innovative firms develop a set of sustainable and rare capabilities by leveraging their evolving unique experiences and relationships.

Although the thoughts discussed go sometimes beyond individual resources, the idea is consistent with the resource-based theory of the firm. It can be said that the leveraging capabilities are more fundamental than resources because they represent abilities to create resources and make them more valuable and sustainable. Leveraging capabilities are interwoven and amalgamated, and build a *knowledge system* that is characterized by tacit resources, causal and contextual ambiguity, and social complexity. The system, in this case, is more valuable than its constituent elements and outputs. It is further inimitable, immobile, nonsubstitutable, and hard to duplicate by competitors. This system can make a firm distinctively different from its competitors. Although complex, it is argued that the system is something that can be managed by focusing on it as a whole rather than on its individual elements. That is why techniques adopted from systemic thinking have been suggested.

We strongly believe that only executives that consider all the discussed practices coherently get the rewards of the strategic transition, and hence will lead their firms successfully in the new open innovation paradigm. The generation of a holistic model opens the door to the potential of organizational learning and is believed to be the key mechanism for stimulating and reinforcing the firm's innovation capability. With such visionary thoughts, we are moving closer to open innovation. Having reached this stage, we should embrace *social capital* upon the development of an *open innovation culture* as this includes mapping human, structural, and relational capital and incorporating it into strategy, processes, and organizational structures. Providing the organization with an open innovation culture completes our framework.

## Notes

1. For the theory of *dynamic capability*, see Eisenhardt, K.M. and Martin, J.A. (2000) 'Dynamic capabilities: What are they?' *Strategic Management Journal*, 21(10/11), 1105–1121; Teece, D.J. and Pisano, G. (1994) 'The dynamic capability of firms: An introduction', *Industrial and Corporate Change*, 3(3), 537–556; Teece, D.J., Pisano, G. and Shuen, A. (1997) 'Dynamic capabilities and strategic management', *Strategic Management Journal*, 18(7), 509–533.
2. Harbison, J.R. and Pekar, P. (1998) *Smart alliances: A practical guide to repeatable success.* Jossey-Bass, San Francisco.
3. The balance between exploration and exploitation is explained in March, J.G. (1991) 'Exploration and exploitation in organizational learning', *Organization Science*, 2(1), 71–87. For efficiency versus flexibility, see Adler, P.S., Goldoftas, B. and Levine, D.I. (1999) 'Flexibility versus efficiency? A case study of model changeover in the Toyota production system', *Organization Science*, 10(1), 43–67.
4. For one of the first articles about *ambidextrous organizations,* see Tushman, M.L. and O'Reilly, C.A. (1996) 'Ambidextrous organizations: Managing evolutionary and revolutionary change', *California Management Review*, 38(4), 8–30. Further articles brought together ambidexterity and innovation, see Tushman, M.L. and O'Reilly, C. (2002) *Winning through innovation: A practical guide to leading organizational change and renewal.* Harvard Business School Press, Boston, MA; O'Reilly, C. and Tushman, M.L. (2004) 'The ambidextrous organization', *Harvard Business Review*, 82(4), 74–81.
5. Porter, M.E. (1980) *Competitive strategy: Techniques for analyzing industries and competitors.* Free Press, New York.
6. Figures compiled from Boston Consulting Group (2007) *Tapping human assets to sustain growth.* BCG Global Wealth Report, September; Capgemini and Merrill Lynch (2007) *World Wealth Report 2007.* Report by Capgemini and Merrill Lynch.
7. The World Economic Forum is an independent international organization committed to improving the state of the world by engaging leaders in partnerships to shape global, regional, and industry agendas. Over the course of its 35-year history, the World Economic Forum has provided an unrivalled platform for leaders from all walks of life to shape the global agenda at the start of each year. At the core is its multistakeholder model that leverages the collective wisdom of leaders from business, government, the media, academia, the arts, and civil society by building a global platform for collaboration and action to address priorities on the global agenda. World Economic Forum Annual Meeting (2008) *The power of collaborative innovation.* January 23–27, Davos, Switzerland.

8. We are convinced that organizations are *nonlinear* systems. For further explanations, see Thietart, R. and Forgues, B. (1995) 'Chaos theory and organization', *Organization Science*, 6(1), 19–31.
9. Holland, J. (1975) *Adaptation in natural and artificial systems*. MIT Press, Cambridge, MA; Stacey, R. (1995) 'The science of complexity: An alternative perspective for strategic change processes', *Strategic Management Journal*, 16(6), 477–495.
10. For the seminal work of *system dynamics*, see Forrester, J.W. (1961) *Industrial dynamics*. Pegasus Communications, Waltham, MA.
11. Senge, P. (1990) *The fifth discipline: The art and practice of the learning organization*. Currency Doubleday, New York.
12. Pettigrew, A.M. and Fenton, E.M. (2000) *The innovating organization*. Sage, London; Pettigrew, A.M., Whittington, R., Leif, M., Sanchez-Runde, C., Van Den Bosch, F.A.J., Ruigrok, W. and Numagami, T. (2003) *Innovative forms of organizing*. Sage, London.

# Providing a Culture of Open Innovation

- Establish profits from integration but also remain flexibility and agility.
- Unlock the full potential of the firm's resources and capabilities through social capital.
- Translate and embed knowledge, shared values, and objectives and trust among people into the corporate culture.
- Become a leader in providing an open innovation culture.

## Gaining Maximum Strategic Flexibility

### *Integrate or Separate Core Business Divisions?*

Let us briefly discuss some critical issues of the integrated banking model. From time to time, experts postulate the separation of a bank's investment banking and private banking arms. The losses that the banking industry is facing from the recent credit market turmoil sparked a new interest in this debate. The writedowns have especially affected banks that combine wealth management and investment banking under one roof. Assuming investment bankers have lost a lot of money with their division consequently generated losses where the wealth management division has contributed with profitable growth. We now know that the financial crisis was largely the result of investment banks, making them more vulnerable to the sudden downturn in the credit market. One may argue that separating these divisions would reduce reputational risk and incidental effects to the wealth management franchise, and so create better shareholder returns. It would also solve the conflicts of interest between investment banking and private banking businesses. You might have heard from the concept of the so-called "Chinese walls." The Great Wall of China was constructed to protect the people of China from invaders. The concept of Chinese walls came into investing in the 1930s, when the securities industry regulators embodied the Glass–Steagall Act in the United States. This restriction on banking embraced the separation of investment banking from brokerage operations. In other words, it prevented banks from doing stock brokerage business, or stockbrokers from doing most forms of banking business. Whatsoever, the Act was dismantled in 1999 while president Bill Clinton was in office. The new Gramm–Leach–Bliley Financial Services Modernization Act allows commercial and investment banks to consolidate. The repeal enabled commercial lenders to underwrite and trade instruments like mortgage-backed securities. Clients were henceforth able to do savings and investment at the same bank. Much consolidation occurred in the financial services industry since. Interestingly, China has maintained a separation between commercial banking and the securities industries. Today, one of the major problems is that insider information, of for example investment banking-led merger, acquisitions, and initial public offerings must under no circumstances flow to private banking investments within the same legal entity.

Until the outbreak of the financial crisis, the integrated banking model appeared to be a dying breed. Either a business model focused either on investment banking or wealth management seems to have favorable effects on clients, shareholders, and employees. This was evidenced since dedicated wealth managers have been less negatively impacted by the current crisis than universal banks. Albeit some of these thoughts are valid, we state that banks usually do not fail because of the integrated banking model – they fail because of poor risk management. The negative implications of the trend to securitize subprime mortgages for the global financial industry can be clearly attributed to the underestimation of complexity and risks. More than ever because risks in an open market driven through collaboration is spread over a number of players across the globe. Without doubt, stronger government regulation is needed. What we see now is that regulators and banks around the world attempt to fix the broken financial system. The US Federal Reserve and the United Kingdom Treasury are pushing for greater supervision. The European finance ministers and central bankers agreed on a closer collaboration between national regulators in the 27-member states of the European Union. In April 2008, finance ministers and central bank heads from the world's seven leading industrial nations further agreed to a series of new measures to combat the crisis in the financial sector and to more closely monitor the practices of investment banks. They even proposed an "international college of supervisors" that keeps an eye on each of the world's largest financial institutions. Overall, they promised to boost cooperation among central banks and government agencies to catch threats earlier in the future. These initiatives among others shall bring stability and trust back to the markets, and prevent a slowdown of the global economy. The good thing though is that we once more realized how central financial markets work. Integration increases complexity and complicates a bank's internal workflow. In a world of change and periodic economic turbulences, bank executives must learn to quickly adapt to difficult situations and adopt creative strategies.

## *Integration Means Collaboration and Learning*

As discussed several times, clients require sophisticated, integrated solutions and access to a broad spectrum of products and services in response to their increasingly complex needs and global orientation. In addition, individual businesses are facing growing competitive pressure and are undergoing consolidation. Considering these conditions, firms are forced to increase scale and greater added value as a service provider in their core business to remain competitive. One answer is a strategy that offers cross-selling opportunities by integrating various businesses. Many large banks have put in place radical business integration strategies at the beginning of the year 2000. What they labeled "one firm" or "one bank" strategies included a brand repositioning with a new logo, to build real brand value behind the name. The new integrated organization usually consists of three divisions focusing on client coverage and best product delivery, namely Private Banking, Investment Banking, and Asset Management. Other so-called shared services functions such as finance, legal, risk management, information technology, corporate development, human resources, or communications provide high-quality, cost-effective services to support the divisions.

We found that it is the top management's vision and early coping with the trends and challenges that pushes one firm ahead of the other. Openness, flexibility, and customer integration capabilities are all assets that make up a learning organization. To keep pace with changing trends, learning faster than the environment changes is crucial. Indication that one firm leads the way in some fields is that competitors adapt the leader's strategies and initiatives. This can be evidenced at many market participants. Regarding to learning and innovation, we see firms launching corporate universities, business schools, or leadership institutes. Those schools attempt to enhance shared understanding and the initiation of actions associated with the firm's strategy. A closely aligned training strategy to business strategy is essential for success. The overall goal of corporate schools is to support the systematic transfer of experiences and best practices, and to promote innovation, shared values, beliefs, and culture at all levels.

## *Benefits and Challenges from Integration*

We would like to discuss two interesting cases of integration: UBS and Credit Suisse. Both banks integrated their business divisions, UBS in 2003 and Credit Suisse in 2006. From a customer perspective, we think that separation of banking businesses is against what clients want – solutions that best fit their needs. These solutions include products and services from investment banking as well as asset management and private banking. Especially, entrepreneurs and executives benefit from alternative investments, lending, trusts, private equity, hedge funds, tax and succession planning, and many other solutions, provided from different business units. Credit Suisse's ongoing efforts to intensify collaboration in the integrated bank delivered total CHF 5.9 billion revenues for the year 2007. It announced that the integrated banking model is to deliver more than CHF 10 billion collaboration revenues by 2010. By continuously increasing collaboration between the different areas of the organization, Credit Suisse is seeing tremendous progress and potential on the amount of business that has been done and will be done between their divisions. The majority of the money flows are between the divisions Private Banking and Asset Management. Key initiatives run on the product development side as well as on the distribution side with collaborative product innovations and private equity and hedge fund distribution. Between private banking and investment banking, we usually see asset referrals, structured investment products, and special client solutions for ultra-high-net worth clients. Integration opportunity between asset management and investment banking could be pension and insurance solutions or alternative investments distribution via securities business. At Credit Suisse, 40% of their initial public offerings in 2007 ended up with a private bank account being opened; in addition to roughly 10% of their net new assets in private banking that came from cross-divisional referrals. Another good example for crossdivisional collaboration is that the private banking and investment banking divisions together recently brought to market a hugely successful IPO for a leading company in the United Kingdom. This was recognized as a landmark and award-winning transaction by the industry trade press. A long-standing relationship of the bank, the combined Credit Suisse, raised £673 million of capital through a highly innovative combination of hard underwriting and book building. Not only did Credit Suisse lead manage the equity capital markets transaction, but also they underwrote a new syndicated bank loan for their client, executed foreign exchange transactions for the selling shareholder, and provided private banking services for certain key personnel in the company.

Where Credit Suisse still adheres to its integrated bank strategy, UBS, on the other hand, announced on August 2008 that it will separate its investment banking and wealth management divisions to allow maximum strategic flexibility in its future development. Abandoning its one firm strategy was driven after huge losses caused by subprime-related writedowns that led to increasing pressure from investors. From a financial point of view, separating the lucrative wealth management business that contributes to more than 70% to the Group's revenue makes sense. Operating with more autonomous business divisions can help to salvage reputation and manage crises. Especially in times of uncertain outlooks for global financial markets and potential changes in regulatory capital requirements, effectiveness of organization, processes, as well as agility may improve. Further, layers of complexity can be reduced as there will be focus on core competencies within wealth management and within investment banking. This effects compensation plans balancing risk and reward but also client-driven growth as the dissimilar divisions have clients with varying needs. The challenge of this repositioning is, once more, the transformation in terms of structural, legal, financial, and cultural aspects.

## *What Is the Right Strategic Direction?*

Organizational research gives essentially reasons for the integrated firm. We learned that organizational structures should be developed to maximize the company's effectiveness and optimal resource allocation. Therefore, resources should mainly be allocated to divisions with excellent risk-adjusted returns and promising growth opportunities. Although the value creation levers of integration are divers; at the current economic situation, this would most likely be the private banking division. High-growth opportunities in wealth management-targeted markets can be better exploited through an integrated approach.

There are also huge benefits from integration and collaboration if we look at integration from an efficiency perspective. Synergy opportunities can be achieved through optimized use of information processing, supervision, task assignment, and the coordination of interactions across activities. Shared services and other central items contribute to a more effective and efficient infrastructure by bundling core skills, leveraging international expertise, and reaching critical mass. Thus, banks can benefit significantly on the expense side from their integrated business model. Operating on an integrated platform gives firms an advantage in terms of procurement, especially for purchasing of technology. Just think of a single investment operations system and human resources platform. However, firms should not dedicate themselves to an absolute cost-cutting culture; rather its managers must attempt to provide the organization with a culture of efficiency and productivity. Continuous cost management where the firm assesses what to process internally and what to outsource to business partners is what yields into sustainable operational excellence.

Approaches that integrate, on the one hand, and disintegrate, on the other hand, entail ambidextrous organizational design as discussed earlier in this book. There are good examples of outsourcing and offshoring initiatives. We observed that some banks created centers of excellences in India, Singapore, Eastern Europe, or even rural areas in the United States to tap local expertise in areas where the firm can access lower-cost talent. Besides increased efficiency, firms are so able to restructure processes as they moved into these centers. Such integration benefits are required for growth and at the same time have a positive effect on scale economies. From a client perspective, strategic objectives of integration are to improve and broaden client relationships by delivering combined skills and expertise. In particular, a one face to the client and single point of contact increase service level and hence customer satisfaction. Global product expertise through the centers of excellence and collaborative innovativeness across all divisions optimizes access to products. This is essential to banks to be able to implement client centricity as it provides clients with valuable solutions from a full range of assets classes and investment styles. Ultimately, optimizing costs translates into profitable growth.

Having discussed the benefits, we must also consider a clear framework on how to measure the integrated firm. Although we already touched the most indicators, we would like to recapitulate. Note that the indicators vary strongly between investment banking, wealth management, corporate and retail banking, and asset management. We need to define one measure for every business, but for measuring the integration an overall target for the firm must be set likewise. Efficiency is commonly measured with the cost–income ratio. Performance indicators can be return on equity, total shareholder return, and the price-earning multiples compared to a defined peer group. As measures, we propose to use the discussed collaboration revenues, in addition to the annual net new asset growth and the annual earnings per share growth.

Despite the financials, integration is always associated with organizational transformation. Transformation, on the other hand, is not only about changing things – it is much about people. It is obvious that this process must be supported by change management activities to ensure that all involved people agree on how they will change themselves. There is a lot of literature about change management and we do not want to elaborate on this here. What is more interesting is that the development of an open innovation culture is eminent to integrate general resources and single capabilities into a cohesive whole. What we would like to point out is the need to understand how things work in between teams and individual people within the organization. We presume that people are an undervalued asset – not only for the transformation but also to any business. The ultimate question though is *how can we all bring together and make it work?* One answer is given in the next section.

## It Is All About Social Capital

### *Understanding Social Capital*

Social capital is a set of resources embedded into relationships into which other resources can be invested with the expectation of future albeit uncertain returns.[1] It is indispensable for letting knowledge flow and facilitates learning from the experiences of others. Otherwise, knowledge will be blocked and rejected. Social capital is about collaboration and combining information and experience to create value for clients and the firm. Where the relational dimension of social capital refers to direct relationships of the intrapreneur within the organization to others and the assets rooted in these relationships such as trust and trustworthiness, the structural dimension of social capital is about social interactions, in fact, the sum of relationships within a social structure. The cognitive dimension provides a set of norms of acceptable behavior such as shared values and beliefs that allow a common understanding of appropriate ways of acting. Social capital is an asset and considered a vital contribution factor to effective management. It is relevant for the strategic transition process as well as for driving innovation and growth of businesses in the new paradigm. We anticipate that social capital, and in particular its management, will become an equally essential part of a firm's intellectual capital along with human, structural or organizational capital, and customer or relationship capital.[2]

Since relying on existing resources and capabilities alone is not enough, social capital provides a firm with the ability to leverage its existing knowledge assets. Thus, all resources and capabilities are conjoined through social capital to enhance its synergy. Social capital is imperative for knowledge integration as it turns existing knowledge into new intellectual capital. Social capital is a pervasive element of human collaboration that grows with use. It moves knowledge fast and influences learning. As we have discussed previously, understanding an organization as a social and complex system requires multiple views at once. Social capital is just one of many lenses through which to view an organization. The more we utilize social capital, the more we are able to understand how a firm works as a living, evolving social system. The concept of social capital offers a wide view on the firm including internal and external relationships that help managers to get a sense of what to do and what structures, processes, and cultures need to be in place to do it. Therefore, it needs to become more central to strategic management thinking.

## *Why Social Capital Matters*

We know that business in services is always characterized by dealing with people. The explanation of that social capital is the product of working together, is that services act on customer's information, and always involve customer interaction. This means that customers are the primary suppliers of inputs to the service process. The source for developing, distributing, and rendering services is, on the other hand, knowledge. In effect, services are bidirectional with information flows in both directions. Projecting these assumptions to a firm and its environment means that all people in that context can be stakeholders, e.g., customers, suppliers, business partners, and even competitors. Our point we would like to make is that with an open collaborative innovation approach, widespread knowledge from all stakeholders can be incorporated. Remember the logic of open innovation and link it with social capital. Thus, open innovation embraces external ideas and knowledge, and combines it through social capital with internal resources and capabilities.

If we believe that the empowerment of employee's collaboration is increasing, this included many aspects of the social context. Consequently, social interaction, social ties, trusting relationships, and value systems would facilitate the actions of the firm's employees. As we just stated, social capital is embedded among employees, as well as in the relationships the firm has with its customers and business partners. In particular, social capital with business partners is paramount for the firm to develop and maintain collaboration with its third-party product suppliers and distribution partners. In this case, social capital serves not only as a basis for collaboration, but also as the seed for accumulating stronger relationships. It is said to be both the origin and the expression of successful network interactions. To simplify, empowerment plays an important role in facilitating interaction; hence, it is vital for the firm's intrapreneurs to utilize and develop. What applies to every firm is that a good relationship among the workforce and with clients engenders involvement, respect, contribution, and mutual support.

It is the business model of the modern firm – in our case the open innovation model – that defines which portions of the value chain are provided internally and which externally. The value of the surrounding network, in terms of social capital, will link those portions to customers. Where the individual knowledge resides in the firm's human capital, social capital resides in the relationships among individuals and is considered as the glue that holds them together. As knowledge increases when shared, it can be said that one vital role of social capital is in the creation of human capital through a network of formal and informal ties with others. Where personal development and learning are put into action through various activities, informal ties are spun based on an open innovation culture with free intrapreneurial thinking.

The value of social capital becomes apparent as we see more and more firms in the banking industry hiring teams instead of individuals. Hiring a star wealth manager or investment banker, for example, would suppose that individuals could do what they do alone. Reality is that teams of people with their ways of working, shared norms, values, and beliefs really contribute to performance. Hiring just individual talents would mean that they have to be integrated into the existing organizational culture, but what is more they had to create social capital from scratch. In contrast, a team is a kind of social and complex system and hence automatically includes social capital. Such thoughts become even more popular as banks are to adopt key account management concepts from the manufacturing industry. This means that the teams are led by a single point of contact – the key account manager – who is then supported by a relationship manager, portfolio manager, credit specialist and insurance specialist and financial, estate, and tax planners. The justification for this model is that in past many key clients of banks were served by several relationship managers, often even without knowing from each other. This led to duplications in client coverage, problems in developing comprehensive client plans, and no holistic view on client needs. The benefits of a stringent key account management result into a coordinated client approach that increases client satisfaction and account transparency. For the bank, this concept opens up opportunities in terms of hiring entire client coverage teams and rewarding team collaboration on client sales. In the wealth management market, we can see similar approaches. Through strategic hiring initiatives, some banks attempt to acquire a package consisting of a client relationship manager with existing clients and pertaining assets under management and a business plan.

## *Social Capital: The Clue and Lubricant for Boosting Innovation and Growth*

Our three dynamic management practices – ambidextrous thinking, intrapreneurial attitude, and systemic and holistic view – only release their full learning and innovation potential if there is social capital. The reason is that knowledge usually does not really flow – it tends to be sticky and resides in individual's heads. This means that social capital inheres in the structure of relations between and among individuals. Therefore, it signifies the *glue* that holds relationships together and acts as the *lubricant* that eases interaction between those individuals. For example, the empowerment of employees on various levels implies that employees act as intrapreneurs and develop a more holistic view on their activities as well as on the organization as such. Intrapreneurship cannot flourish if linear and analytical thinking dominates businesses, or if there is no open and collaborative climate, in which information can flow between individuals. In this case, social capital occurs in the form of trust and trustworthiness that the management has in its workforce. This approach of interacting with other resources leverages the ability of anticipating trends and translates ideas into actions. In many ways, the social glue is manifested in a number of patterns in the transition mechanisms of adaptive firms.

For accelerating growth in terms of new money for wealth managers, we can think of a lubricant in the form of client referrals. It is common practice that wealth managers can gain roughly 70% of their new clients through referrals. The best sources of referrals are exceedingly satisfied existing clients or secondary external asset managers or lawyers. As simple as it is, the better the client relationships between the relationship manager and his/her contacts, the more new business can be generated. This works similar to what we discussed previously with the collaboration between different divisions and organizational units. These so-called external referrals can sometimes even be easier as some colleagues within the firm are reluctant to provide internal referrals. This may be because of high administration for client transfers, the lack of global incentive systems or just because they do not know or trust their colleagues. Another problem is the combination of the aging and the success of senior relationship managers. There are often weak procedures for career and human resources planning. If a relationship manager or account manager has been very successful, reached a certain threshold of assets under management or revenues generated, he or she is promoted and moves into a management position. This causes a dramatic shortfall of talented junior relationship managers that could take over large client portfolios. In an industry strongly characterized by individuals, succession is a serious challenge in the coming years for many firms. We assume that this problem will accumulate in wealth management and investment banking and mirror that of professional service firms more closely than that of, for instance, retail and commercial banking. Therefore, we advise early solutions that include new recruiting pools and integrate junior hires quickly while building knowledge in a systematic and institutionalized way. Clear and transparent career paths must be put into practice and integrated into the corporate culture.

These challenges should not prevent top management from integrate their businesses and foster collaboration and referrals within the firm. Rather, they are asked to think about ways on how to provide the organization with global and transparent incentive systems and compensation models that reward referrals. We strongly believe that social capital leverages the interactions between the firm's resources and capabilities, and facilitates relationship management. It provides the conditions for the management of the strategic change in an ambiguous and complex environment. For successfully navigating in the open innovation paradigm, we need to integrate enabling conditions, architectural capabilities, and the three suggested management practices. To gain an overall understanding of the *system* that underlies open innovation and to be able to reveal where and how collaboration is created and what it relies upon, we suggest that you look through a social capital lens. The challenge is that social capital is incorporated in the social structure of the organization in the form of learning, knowledge exchange, shared norms, values, and beliefs, in which individuals operate. Social capital can only be created in an open corporate culture.

## Open Innovation Culture

### *The Shift in Culture*

According to a McKinsey global survey, 94% of senior executives across industries stated that people and corporate culture are the most important drivers of innovation.[3] Without question, this reflects our opinion. We interpret organizational culture as unconscious, adopted beliefs, perceptions, thoughts, and feelings that form and shape the behavior of the employees in the firm. Based on these principles, organizational culture is nothing else than a set of shared values and beliefs that characterize an organization. Many firms have put much effort in establishing new values, norms, beliefs, meanings, and behaviors that are shared by the organization's employees and can be conveyed to new hires. Where organizational culture provides identity and strength, *open* business values are the individual degree to which company representatives share, perform, and communicate. Firms on the way to open innovation are in transition from being organized around geographies, functions, and products to being organized around customers and services. Such firms are giving up existing structures and routines to search for new structures, processes, and collaboration forms. To people, this is always stirring uncertainty.

The transformed organization, with its reduced hierarchies and empowered employees, embraces an open innovation culture in which customers matter most. Such customer-centered structure and practice mean that managers and employees think naturally and in a sophisticated way about creating profitable growth by delivering superior customer value propositions. Earlier in this book, we told you from experience that the relationship between the bank and a client is characterized by trust, whereby one party has confidence in its partner's reliability and integrity. Trust between the bank and clients is due to increasing product complexity – particularly in wealth management where the bank has implicit responsibility for the management of its clients' assets – an important factor for the generation of customer benefits. Consequently, sustainable success is based upon a good long-term relationship with customers and excellent collaboration with business partners. In other words, a personal trusting relationship between the client and the relationship manager has been built over the course of years, or for so-called old wealth, across generations. The foundation of trust is vital in identifying the client's specific needs and risk profile that takes into account the unique personal situation. Once trust is established, the general parameters of the client's relationship with the bank can easily be adapted to actual facts and needs. We explained how this works with the holistic advisory model. An appropriate open innovation culture that provides the necessary condition for creating trust is therefore favorable – if not imperative. For the bank, this thought includes the incorporation of individual knowledge and ideas to serve new customer segments, to produce new products and services, and to create new business opportunities. It helps to serve clients with products and services ranging from comprehensive mandates to needs-based tailored solutions.

Under open innovation culture, we additionally understand that a firm needs the organizational capability to think openly and not narrow-minded and biased. This means approaching unfamiliar customer segments such as that of the previously, in the book, discussed wealthy women cautiously but openly. A good example is the growing Islamic banking market that traditional Western banks can only develop if they are adaptable, flexible, and accessible. There is widespread support across industries that organizational culture is something that can be manipulated through transformational leadership. One leadership priority is therefore to postulate open innovation culture as basis for organizing in the new business paradigm.

## *The Challenges*

In the first chapter, we explained innovation as a very important driver for growth. We also found that innovation has to be integrated into the strategic management agenda to turn into sustainable growth. Remember Fig. 2 of *Chapter One* that shows the differences in shareholder returns between innovative firms and the S&P Global. Although the equation seems to be clear, in the practice there are still many banking executives that lead and manage innovation on an ad hoc basis. We should not focus on budgeting and forecasting instead of integrating innovation and growth into their strategic planning process. Problems often occur because of the cultural attributes such as bureaucracy, hierarchical, and fearful environment. It starves innovation of resources and uses incentives intended to promote short-term performance and intolerance of failure.[4] Such cultures clearly inhibit employees from innovating. Creating an appropriate organizational culture is indispensable. Operating with a common set of values and a unified open innovation culture is something that is more easily said than done. Strong leadership and having excellent managers in the right place are often not enough. It is required that leaders take explicit steps to foster a culture based on trust among employees. All employees must understand and be able to work together in a way that makes the most of their potential.

Establishing transparency is a prerequisite. Before one can understand, knowledge must be made explicitly available across the organization. The process of transforming tacit knowledge into general available knowledge and routines is acknowledged as one vital mechanism. Embedded in most organizations' architectures, supporting concepts can be recapitulated with best practices or knowledge sharing. Every firm should identify and study practices from successes, failures, and even from its competitors and make the knowledge explicitly available and adapt the best approaches to other organizational units. This results in practice-based knowledge, which refers to the way individuals do their tasks and includes the intricacies of thinking and acting in everyday work. The collective practice is a significant contribution to organizational knowledge, learning, and innovation if accumulated and reformulated systematically.

Today, firms combine knowledge sharing tools such as Internet, Intranets, besides personnel regular meetings, and conferences, with the aim of allowing the free flow of information, experiences, and opinions. Collaborative technologies are a means to enable new organizational forms in a bid to overcome the twin tyrannies of spatial and temporal dislocation that impede global reach. GlobeSmart[5] for instance, a modern Web-based tool, provides business personnel with quick and easy access to extensive knowledge on how to conduct business effectively with people from countries around the world. The tool embraces all the activities of a globally active workforce. This includes working on global project teams with employees from diverse cultural backgrounds as well as just communicating across time zones via telephone and email. Subscribers have access to a collaboration forum that discusses global diversity, strategy, and best practices on a regular basis. Other features are the global advice section where members can increase their skills on, for example, how to offshoring to India or China. By using modern tools, firms are able to expand the reach of global business training throughout their organization, reduce the risk of costly mistakes doing business abroad, accelerate the acquisition of global business skills organization-wide, or increase support for investment in global knowledge. It can increase interactions with other people through greater understanding of differences and similarities. This kind of knowledge sharing tools can certainly help to communicate, build relationships, and collaborate with new and existing colleagues, customers, and suppliers worldwide. On the other hand, such tools, however, may become *electronic fences* if organizational boundaries are dismantled without control.[6] So can knowledge sharing across countries and departments through Intranets or Web-based tools decrease collaboration rather than increase it. This may exacerbate the problem of global knowledge fragmentation. Therefore, we have to consider carefully to what extent technology is used. One is for sure – tools should never exchange reasonable face-to-face meetings. What is reasonable is simply based on each client's valuation. Some may favour Web-based video meetings as provided by banks like Nykredit where others clearly don't want technology support.

Open innovation culture creates a work environment in which ideas flow. To be more precise, an open culture encourages the free exchange of ideas. There is no question that openness influences organizational learning. On the other hand, there are skeptical voices, mainly from employees who have been with a firm for many years. They see too much openness and transparency as a threat that decreases their level of safety and value within the organization. For instance, they are addicted to the ways in which the traditional client relationship used to be done and are hardly willing to contemplate change. These rigid values and beliefs of the closed innovation paradigm are mirrored as *organizational maturity culture* and a hindrance for change and transformation.[7] Nevertheless, the fear of those opponents is, to a certain extent, acceptable and is heightened by the anxiety of *routinization* as analyzed earlier. The more individual expertise the firm is able to incorporate and transform into structural capital, the more employees become exchangeable. It may be the ultimate goal of the firm to capture all client relationship procedures and experiences made into customer relationship systems and make it easily retrievable for others. This is obviously not the absolute goal for many employees. But also think from a client perspective – some wealthy individuals are not eager to see their confidential conversations stored in customer relationship management systems of the bank. The tradition of confidentiality and banking secrecy in the wealth management industry is still considered by many potential clients as a determining factor when making their investment decision.

## *The Benefits*

The business outcomes of open innovation culture are that they provide predictability and reliability in the organization, through shared values and shared beliefs. A culture driven by openness and intrapreneurial attitude reduces the need for formal controls as it fosters collaboration by minimizing time spent on negotiation, formal guarantees, and enforcement. These mechanisms clearly enhance the levels of trust. If employees understand that their ideas are valued and that they can trust in their managers that it is safe and welcome to express ideas, they will be more likely to share their knowledge. Further, such open culture creates a shared context and common view, which helps employees to align them with corporate goals and enables them to combine various types of dynamic capabilities, businesses, and customer knowledge. This is crucial in a time of consolidation, convergence, and change, in particular, if a firm needs to move from selling pure products to providing customer value provisions with focus on premium services.

The findings suggest that strategic advantage of the integrated firm can only be achieved if openness is considered as a source that is accepted by all employees as the organizational reality and truth. We recapitulate that a customer relationship manager's expertise is and will be built on experience, innovation, and learning. Cultural openness and an intimate understanding of clients' needs will be an important lever for every relationship manager's development of experience. Creating and maintaining an open innovation culture that enhances the work environment makes learning part of the transition process. Such culture is a vital basis for developing capabilities required for open innovation. Building a firm's resources of knowledge and capabilities based upon the development of an open innovation culture should be every leader's concern – regardless whether it is for the strategic transition management in migrating from a closed to an open innovation paradigm or to shape the values and beliefs as, for instance, required for better client integration.

## Notes

1. As a member of the Academy of Management, I would like to refer to some articles about *social capital*. For the initial concept, see Nahapiet, J. and Ghoshal, S. (1998) 'Social capital, intellectual capital, and the organizational advantage', *Academy of Management Review*, 23(2),

242–266; Tsai, W. and Ghoshal, S. (1998) 'Social capital and value creation: The role of intrafirm networks', *Academy of Management Journal,* 41(4), 464–477. For further applications, see Adler, P.S. and Kwon, S. (2002) 'Social capital: Prospects for a new concept', *Academy of Management Review,* 27(1), 17–40.
2. The link from the notion of *human capital* to *social capital* was made by adapting thoughts made by Coleman, J. (1988) 'Social capital in the creation of human capital', *American Journal of Sociology,* 94, 95–120. On *relationship capital*, see Stewart, T.A. (1997) *Intellectual capital: The new wealth of organizations.* Nicholas Brealey Publishing, London.
3. In September 2007, McKinsey conducted a global survey with 722 senior vice president-level executives and 736 lower-level executives on leadership and innovation. In August 2007, 600 global business leaders were surveyed about innovative business cultures. See McKinsey (2007) *How companies approach innovation.* McKinsey Global Survey, The McKinsey Quarterly, October.
4. McKinsey (2008) 'Leadership and innovation', *McKinsey Quarterly*, January.
5. *GlobeSmart* was originally created for ten countries in 1999 by Aperian Global and continues to evolve and grow through an extensive and ongoing process of research, interviews, updates, and reviews. Over the years, countless people from over 40 countries have enhanced the GlobeSmart content with their insights and advice. http://www.globesmart.com/ [January 17, 2008]
6. Newell, S., Scarbrough, H. and Swan, J. (2001) 'From global knowledge management to internal electronic fences: Contradictory outcomes of intranet development', *British Journal of Management,* 12(2), 97–111.
7. Schein, E.H. (1997) *Organizational culture and leadership*, 2nd ed. Jossey-Bass, San Francisco, CA.

# Conclusion

As you have read through our practical examples and latest theories, we hope that by this point of the book, you may be persuaded that open innovation can translate capital into capabilities to provide clients with experiences that, in a closed innovation paradigm, were infeasible. To sum up, we started by describing the strategic value of growth and innovation. With examples – from Banco di San Giorgio or Wells Fargo – we attempted to show that profitable growth and continuous innovation is a perpetual endeavor to survive. Remember that rapid growth is easier to achieve as profitable growth; thus, it requires good management. The underlying influences from global markets, economics, finance, demographics, customers, technology and policy, and regulations are always evolving. It has ever been a challenge for banks to effectively set their growth strategies with the environment, create value for their customers, and manage to generate returns for their shareholders. This is true not only during periods of growth but also during turbulent times. This challenge remains, but even so, we hope there are many lessons that you learned from this book. After having analyzed the trends in the financial services, we found that the industry is in transformation. To react to long-term trends as well as to short-term events such as the current financial crisis, firms must develop the ability to adapt and rapidly implement the right transition strategies. This is crucial, as most global firms in the financial services will come face to face with the need for fundamental change. Even though the financial crisis has caused tremendous value destruction, we believe that global wealth continues to rise in the long run. Private banks are operating in a growing market. To fully grasp this opportunity and work profitably, wealth managers must have a clear strategy. The transition to the discussed new business paradigm includes open and flexible business models that integrate the clients better. Similar to what firms in manufacturing started two decades ago, financial service firms must open up their innovation models and integrate new ideas hatched outside their company boundaries. Our research into open innovation in the financial services clearly showed that this is the final call for leaders to examine the opportunities arising out of open innovation and to plan the transition to the new business paradigm. We suggest that firms innovate their business model before it is compelled to act by financial stresses. Such business model transformation clearly requires visionary leadership.

D. Fasnacht, *Open Innovation in the Financial Services*,

To master the transition from a closed model to an open model of innovation as well as for managing through economic turmoil, a set of new and dynamic management capabilities need to be developed. We suggested an integrated approach for the transformation from a traditional organization focused on products, hierarchical, and bureaucratic structures, and functions to a firm that follows the principles of openness, flexibility, and customer focus. Knowing that this is a challenging journey, we strongly believe that competitive advantage can be achieved if business leaders understand what enabling conditions they must provide and how resources and capabilities can be leveraged as an integrated system. It is paramount that growth and innovation strategies are flexible enough to respond to changing circumstances. Most importantly, we delivered some ideas on how to build and strengthen trust within the organization as well as with clients and business partners. This is essential, as trust becomes increasingly important in an open, dynamic, and interconnected world where closed approaches to innovation are rapidly becoming obsolete. Establishing closer relationships with a broader set of participants with trust, as the system's lubricant, is therefore just one promising approach we proposed.

Providing the organization with conditions where newly learned management practices can flourish is a clear leadership task that goes beyond the readiness to change and a good transformation story. Surely, many bright senior executives realized the need to change their business models and organizational structures and capabilities. Regarding organizational capability, we would like to stress once again that it is of utmost significance that every employee contributes with his/her intellectual capital to unleash energy to transform the organization as a whole. Soft facts such as the ability to develop social capital and embedding it into a culture that is open to innovation and change correspond perfectly to the open innovation idea. This is vital, as unsupportive culture and climate inside the organization are the biggest obstacles to innovation and profitable growth. You may appreciate that employees as well as customers are two greatly undervalued assets to your businesses, and that by creating open innovation culture the resultant performance may be far higher than through a traditional, closed command and control system. In conclusion, as you may have noticed, we promote rather intangible measures for addressing open innovation, though these final efforts can mean the difference between managing the transition successfully and frustration.

We hope that we were able to close the gap between theory and rhetoric of open innovation and the reality and that you can use much of the material from this book for your business. Given the open innovation imperative and our assumptions, in terms of practical guidance for the daily business, we suggest considering whether you have contributed to bridge the open innovation gap between your intent and the actual realization of collaboration. Before you set about starting the transition to open innovation and designing an open innovation culture that will enable profitable growth in your firm, you need to ask some hard questions about the current organizational setup. Continuously question is to what extent your innovation efforts go beyond the traditional innovation areas or to what degree collaboration is supported in your firm. Also, assess the level of intrapreneurship within your organization by experiencing your daily freedom of actions and failure tolerance. Reflect on whether open thinking is an organizational capability part of everything you and your colleagues do. Following, you find a selection of specific questions that you should be able to answer with yes. If not, it probably reveals the gaps that must be closed in the quest to open innovation in the financial services.

1. *Do you have a thorough understanding of local market dynamics and client needs?*
2. *Does your management proactively approach trends in the markets?*
3. *Is your firm flexible and adaptable in terms of innovation opportunities and crises?*
4. *Is innovation on the regular agenda of senior management?*
5. *Is innovation related to your growth strategies?*
6. *Do you differentiate from your competitors to solutions (i.e., services, products, and processes)?*
7. *Is your brand and reputation built on a superior customer experience?*
8. *Do services contribute to the majority of your revenues?*
9. *Do you understand the intricacies of service innovations?*
10. *Do you systematically develop services?*
11. *Do you have a measurement system in place for service innovations?*
12. *Do you understand the advantages of the open model of innovation?*
13. *Could you explain open innovation in services?*
14. *Are there structures and processes defined for collaborative innovation?*
15. *Does your organization have the capacity to offer service models based on geography and client needs (i.e., holistic advice, brokerage services)?*
16. *Is your firm organized around clients?*
17. *Do you know the profitability of your clients?*
18. *Do you know your client's dreams?*
19. *Do you co-create services and solutions with your clients?*
20. *Is your firm delivering a sound client value proposition?*
21. *Do you know how to become an intrapreneur?*
22. *Are you contributing to the firm's open innovation initiatives?*
23. *Do you understand the solution provided or are you just focused on a specific part of a product or service?*
24. *Are there flexible and service-oriented architectures in place?*
25. *Do you understand your firm's risk-related interdependencies (e.g., between private banking and investment banking or retail banking)?*
26. *Is there a climate of open communication and idea sharing?*
27. *Is knowledge exchange and transfer institutionalized?*
28. *Do you understand social capital?*
29. *Do you know the levers to increase social capital?*
30. *Does the management provide a culture that encourages open innovation?*

31. *Does your firm attract the best people in the industry because of its open and flexible approach to work?*
32. *Could you identify the gaps in your organization in terms of openness, flexibility, and customer integration?*
33. *Are you capable to suggest improvements toward open innovation?*

Definitely, 33 questions raised are not exhaustive. Many other questions would unveil whether your firm openly finds and develops new business ideas or not and whether it is truly engaged in open innovation. We understand the questions as food for though that gives you an idea about the level of your innovativeness. Some questions may indicate on how advanced your organizational structure and culture in terms of open innovation. One thing can be said for sure – the more the firm focuses on the opportunities of open innovation the better. Some explanations of this book may help you to transform your organization to new levels of growth where others can be adapted for navigating through economic turbulences and challenging business situations. During writing this book, about a third of the global banking market capitalization disappeared. Although many banks have been strong enough to deal with the consequences of the recent turmoil in the credit markets, only well-positioned banks will find clear opportunities. We are aware of the fact that some banks may be struggling to take advantage of the opportunities because their organization is not yet designed to adapt to radical changes, including possible consolidation but also not for the transition to open innovation.

Further, we argue that industry and universities must improve their partnerships. Consistent knowledge exchange and collaboration between universities and practice would be much appreciated. Both must find ways to better incorporate business research in the services. We advise academia to increase research in service science drawn upon our opinion that science is the root of everything that effects key developments. This notion applies to the financial services too; service science must not only intensify the adaptation of open innovation but also include real life customers and situations. Until now, sciences attempted to understand what banking was doing. That is no longer enough. To reduce the risks of an institute or to limit the play instinct of some bankers in trading, universities must learn to provide precautions and solutions. On the other hand, the industry must respect the demands of the university system. As we learned, to be successful in the global market, you have to collaborate. Through collaboration, we can increase knowledge, seeing that no professional in banking can possibly know everything there is to know.

After having analyzed the financial services, we can say that many job profiles have changed radically. The changes in the environment – regulatory requirements, increasingly sophisticated customers, innovations in technology, and so forth – constantly call for new skill sets. Just look at the output of all the new and complex products that have to be bundled to solutions and customized for specific markets or even for new emerging financial centers. The entire industry is more and more becoming specialized in terms of everything we do. That leads to a relentless growth of knowledge, which is necessary to do our jobs in the new paradigm. Businesses and individuals must be able to move at the same rate as the environment, by adapting, innovating, and growing. A new brand of collaborative and innovative leadership in banks and universities is urgently required to address these challenges. We must be able to identify the right people in the organization to drive the strategic change. The chief financial officer needs to be involved as he or she is responsible for the way the business generates revenues from its products and services and for communicating the results of a new business model to investors. The chief legal officer must be involved likewise. He/she is particularly important in negotiating collaborating models where intellectual property is an important contributor to the ability to capture value from open innovation. It is crucial to target new global growth initiatives and to deliver profitable growth by creating substantial platforms for businesses on that the organization can grow. In essence, this responsibility can be given to a chief growth officer position with dual roles as both the leader for developing new growth opportunities and platforms, and as the head of sales and marketing focusing on brand development and distribution channels. Finally, only the chief executive officer has the ability and overall responsibility to drive the entire business. The other involved leaders must ensure that the chief executive has direct hands-on involvement and takes an active part in enabling and framing of the issues surrounding open innovation. That is why we wanted to get the strategic thoughts regarding certain topics of the book from a chief executive officer. In our case, he may complete the views of renowned academics and consultants.

At this point, we would like to introduce the interview. We are glad for the views of Walter Berchtold. In the role of the chief executive officer of Credit Suisse Private Banking, he successfully leads a truly global and innovative bank. You will ascertain that there are many practical examples that correspond to the assumptions made in the book. We further embrace the insights of Professor Henry Chesbrough, who set off the open innovation discussion and whose initial ideas served as basis for our research in the financial services.

As a final remark, although we do not want to comment on the responses of our interviewees, our strategic thoughts made throughout the book are confirmed. This strengthens our belief that open innovation in the context of the financial services must always be part of strategic thinking – at every managerial level. It is our wish that the concluding interview of the top leaders motivates you for innovative moves toward openness, flexibility, and customer integration and inspires you to get started to this auspicious journey.

*What are the overall trends across industries?*

**Henry Chesbrough.** One important trend is that traditional corporate research laboratories are giving way to more distributed models of research and development. Innovation is shifting from a marathon to a long distance relay race, with multiple parties involved along the path to market.

*Services are today responsible for the main part of employment in the Western countries, yet academia has not yet developed a robust research agenda for understanding innovation in services. Why is that?*

**Henry Chesbrough.** This is a deep question. Part of the answer is that the modern university arose during the rise of manufacturing. The academic disciplines that exist in most universities today reflect the partitioning of knowledge that served a manufacturing economy and society well. It is clear today, though, that we are moving into a postmanufacturing society. And, those academic partitions no longer reflect the urgent needs of our society. But universities are built to last, not to change quickly. And the leaders of most universities have their own roots in those arguably obsolete partitions. So, it will take some time still for this to change.

*Banking has become a very dominant service industry. Which trends – other than global economic developments – are shaping, e.g., today's wealth management industry?*

**Walter Berchtold.** We have identified four key trends that are having a significant impact on the industry. First, there is an increasing tendency among wealth managers to focus on a client's total wealth rather than just his/her investable assets. This holistic approach also takes account of current and future liabilities, as well as illiquid assets such as real estate or company shareholdings. Based on this new perspective, wealth managers are developing broader and more sophisticated advisory solutions to meet client needs.

The second key trend is that clients – especially very wealthy ones – are no longer satisfied with traditional private banking services. They expect their bank to combine its entire private banking and investment banking expertise to create customized, state-of-the-art financial solutions. As a result, ultra-high-net-worth individuals are increasingly seeking integrated financial services providers who can provide the type of comprehensive service they desire.

The third significant development is the emergence of a new form of client segmentation. Leading players in the banking industry are now moving beyond pure asset-based segmentation and are developing value propositions that are geared toward the specific needs of strategically attractive target groups. This shift toward needs-based segmentation will ensure that financial institutions are well placed to satisfy increasingly complex client demands in the future.

The fourth major trend is the advancing globalization of the wealth management industry, as leading providers look beyond their home markets and traditional industry hubs. As a result, top wealth mangers are today building up both their onshore and offshore capabilities in all major regions.

In short, wealthy private clients now expect their banks to combine their entire private banking and investment banking expertise to create innovative, specially tailored financial solutions.

*How can a firm in the financial service industry react to these trends?*

**Walter Berchtold.** As an integrated bank, Credit Suisse is committed to using its entire expertise and resources to create added value for both clients and shareholders, while capturing opportunities for growth. Its global capabilities, progressive approach to client segmentation, and comprehensive solutions are key elements of its strategy in Private Banking. Our ultimate aim is to establish Credit Suisse as the premier private bank in both Switzerland and worldwide.

We have defined five priorities to ensure that Credit Suisse is well positioned to respond to new challenges in the wealth management industry, and to capitalize on the four key trends I have already mentioned. First, we will drive the expansion of our onshore capabilities in private banking in markets that offer strong growth potential. Second, we will continue and further explore offshore capabilities in all major regions. In Switzerland, our home market, the goal is to increase our market share by leveraging private, corporate, and retail banking and to realize cost synergies in particular. Third, we want to create innovative value propositions for clients and to further build our industry-leading position in client solutions by fully leveraging the capabilities of our integrated bank. Fourth, we will focus intensively on enhancing our productivity and financial performance. And finally, we want to recruit and retain the best talent in our industry to help us realize these goals.

*One early adaptor of open concepts was the financial service industry. A decade ago, visionary firms launched open product architectures, where they made third-party products available to its clients in addition to its own offerings. This was the beginning of a transition from a product-based approach to a focus on client needs. What are your views on this development?*

**Henry Chesbrough.** I have learned a great deal about this from reading Daniel Fasnacht's book, *Open Innovation in the Financial Services*. It reflects a larger trend in society from a producer-focused economy (think of the Soviet 5-year plans that were dominated by producer needs) toward a consumer-focused economy. Consumers do not all want the same thing in the same way. So, this invites greater differentiation, and indeed demands it.

**Walter Berchtold.** Product innovation is certainly an essential part of the Credit Suisse brand. In 2006, for example, we launched several innovative new theme-based products such as the Credit Suisse Healthy Living Index or the Credit Suisse Global Alternative Energy Index. In total, we created more than 1,000 investment products last year, including many tailor-made solutions for individuals or small groups of clients. Cooperation within the integrated bank, where we leverage our strengths and expertise across all our businesses, has proved to be of key importance in enabling us to produce compelling value propositions for clients. We always assess which product is best suited to each client's needs. If it happens to be a third-party product, we integrate it into our offering as part of our open product architecture.

The most important aspect of our strategy in Private Banking is our client-centric approach. This implies that we want to gain an even better understanding of our clients and want our clients to understand us. Credit Suisse has, therefore, designed a comprehensive structured advisory process, which is currently being rolled out globally. This process enables us to systematically assess each client's assets and liabilities, so that we gain a comprehensive picture of his/her needs and expectations and can tailor our financial solutions accordingly. Importantly, this uniform approach also helps to ensure that we provide the same quality of advice throughout the bank.

*Can a bank offer leading products and be a premium service bank at the same time?*

**Walter Berchtold.** Yes, I think it goes hand in hand. In a client-centric model, client value and financial performance are aligned. Look at assets under management, for example. We use this term to refer to discretionary mandates, funds, structured derivatives, and investment products managed professionally by internal and external specialists. These products give us additional potential to implement our clients' investment strategies as part of the structured advisory process. Moreover, our innovative solutions allow for broad risk diversification and offer our clients performance advantages by improving their risk/return profile. At the same time, they have a positive impact on our own revenue generation as we increase our service depth. Product pricing is another good example. A differentiated approach to clients means a differentiated approach to our pricing models. By looking at a client's overall needs and potential, we can price our products and services in an attractive way across our product range.

*Leveraging a firm's client relationships to create superior shareholder value is imperative. But what needs to be changed and what approach do you suggest to customer focus?*

**Walter Berchtold.** We have made fundamental changes to the way we see and serve our clients. "Client Centricity" – which defines our new approach to our clients – is one of the most important initiatives in our integrated business strategy.

This new approach means that we no longer segment our clients solely on the basis of their assets. Instead, we look at them from three different angles: the source of their wealth, their investment behavior, and their life cycle phase. This three-dimensional approach gives us a better understanding of their needs and enables us to better define our advisory services, products, and value propositions – significantly increasing client satisfaction. "Client Centricity" also has a direct impact on the profitability of our client relationships.

*Can you elaborate further on the "Client Centricity" initiative at Credit Suisse?*

**Walter Berchtold.** "Client Centricity" is a long-term initiative which aims to place clients at the center of all that we do and thus enhance the way we serve them. It has three main objectives: to improve our understanding of client needs, to increase client profitability, and to drive client-based innovation.

In the past, our approach to our clients was governed primarily by their volume of assets under management and the revenues we expected each client relationship to generate. We now look at client relationships according to qualitative or psychographic criteria. One important insight that we have gained is that clients in the same asset-based segment do not necessarily need the same services. To ensure that we can provide truly customized solutions, we now perform a precise and comprehensive analysis of client needs, investment behavior, asset volumes, and the potential future development of their wealth. We have also conducted detailed interviews with clients in all our business areas to gain additional information for the purpose of needs-based segmentation. Since not all client groups are alike, each region has developed dedicated segment initiatives and value propositions. Hence, we are redefining our entire approach to our clients.

We are also looking at the overall economic profitability of client relationships as one means of determining the amount of time relationship managers devote to each client. This allows us to increase our efficiency and productivity when dealing with clients and to allocate resources more effectively. In this way, we will be able to influence both our top and bottom line.

Our new segmentation model – combined with our analysis of economic profitability by client type – will ultimately reveal where we are profitable and which main target groups we should address in which way. As a result, we will be able to take specific client needs more effectively into account and thus enhance the profitability of this business. We are convinced that this approach will help us to achieve growth – even in a saturated market – and will thus help drive the realization of our overall strategy. This, in turn, will satisfy investor expectations regarding the growth potential of Credit Suisse.

*Can you give us examples of specific value propositions for key client segments that have resulted from the "Client Centricity" process?*

**Walter Berchtold.** Entrepreneurs represent a key client segment. For example, we have developed comprehensive advisory services for this client group in Germany and have launched a dedicated European midcap initiative. We provide comprehensive solutions and advice to meet their personal needs and the needs of their businesses, drawing on the expertise and capabilities of the integrated bank.

Other similar initiatives have been launched in Asia, where the majority of our clients are entrepreneurs whose wealth is linked to their business and real estate holdings. Meanwhile, in Switzerland, we have developed a dedicated strategy for ultra-high-net-worth individuals and entrepreneurs.

*Serving specific client segments calls for open innovation. How can open innovation help?*

**Henry Chesbrough.** Not all the smart people work for any single company or organization. Open Innovation can help serve client needs by accessing the best-of-breed offerings, no matter where they originated.

*Let's turn to the role of the integrated bank. Which initiatives promote cooperation within the bank and thus help to increase revenue growth?*

**Walter Berchtold.** With the launch of the integrated bank at the beginning of 2006, we substantially strengthened cooperation between our three divisions: Investment Banking, Private Banking, and Asset Management. This has helped to improve the quality of our advice and has enhanced client satisfaction and increased revenue growth.

Previously, investment bankers had few opportunities to refer private individuals to Private Banking, and likewise, we rarely passed clients onto Investment Banking. For years, both businesses acted as if they were essentially two separate institutions. We have since implemented incentive systems within the integrated bank that encourage the active referral of clients between divisions.

*To what extent has Credit Suisse so far succeeded in exploiting the opportunities provided by the integrated bank?*

**Walter Berchtold.** One measure of the success of the integrated bank is the level of crossdivisional referral activity which has been achieved to date – resulting in the creation of exceptional and truly innovative solutions that would not have been possible under the old structure. Private Banking has played a leading role when it comes to generating additional revenues for Investment Banking and Asset Management – particularly in the areas of trading, structured products, discretionary mandates, investment funds, and pension products. We also have very ambitious goals to further intensify crossdivisional referral activity going forward.

*Can you give us an example?*

**Walter Berchtold.** Some of the largest and most complex referrals have taken place in the field of real estate. Here, I am thinking specifically of the referral of ultra-high-net-worth clients from Private Banking to Investment Banking's Real Estate Group. However, there are also daily examples of small-scale referrals, which collectively generate significant benefits for the business. In the United States, we have seen numerous examples where investment bankers covering corporate clients have simply called their interface contact in Asset Management and directly referred their clients to that division. Asset Management has then taken the lead, made several follow-up calls to the US corporate client, and subsequently secured a significant cash mandate. Of course, given the restrictive legal environment regarding the sharing of client information in many of the jurisdictions in which we operate, that may not always be possible.

*Which mechanisms and incentives can be used to promote open collaboration?*

**Henry Chesbrough.** Some mechanisms are cultural, some are organizational, and some are monetary. Cultural mechanisms must include the recognition and celebration of the role that externally accessed ideas and technologies play in the success of a firm. Many firms have had one or more experiences with external technologies, and some of these have worked well. But this is downplayed or ignored today. Organizationally, you cannot delegate the search for valuable external technologies to your purchasing organization. Instead, your own smart people must actively engage with the many other smart people out there, to identify and then access potentially valuable stuff. And monetarily, some reward should accompany the successful incorporation of external technologies when those help to solve a real problem for a real customer.

**Walter Berchtold.** We recognized that an overall reward concept is essential to ensure that our people systematically deliver the capabilities of the integrated bank to our clients, and we therefore introduced an incentive system that we refer to as the Single Global Currency. This reward model forms part of our regular year-end performance review and discretionary remuneration process, and benefits the sales people or relationship managers who make crossdivisional referrals. Information about the transactions and referrals that meet the criteria of the incentive system is collected and verified in a central log to ensure that the awards are distributed fairly.

We feature examples of top referrals – including details of the benefits that the integrated bank has created for our clients – on an internal "One Bank Wins" Web site on a monthly basis to encourage people to take home new ideas and apply them to their own area of responsibility.

*Can you explain how this works?*

**Walter Berchtold.** I will give you an example of how crossdivisional activity is rewarded using the Single Global Currency model if a specific transaction is not already covered by an existing Revenue Sharing Agreement.

Investment Banking sells a structured product to an ultra-high-net-worth client referred to it by a relationship manager in Private Banking. The product structurer or marketer in Investment Banking records the relevant revenue credit and the relationship manager in Private Banking who referred the deal records the Single Global Currency amount that is equal to the revenue credit recorded by the product structurer or marketer. This is then taken into account in the year-end review process, as mentioned previously.

# Index

SPRINGER NATURE

# GPSR Compliance

*The European Union's (EU) General Product Safety Regulation (GPSR) is a set of rules that requires consumer products to be safe and our obligations to ensure this.*

*If you have any concerns about our products, you can contact us on ProductSafety@springernature.com*

In case Publisher is established outside the EU, the EU authorized representative is:

Springer Nature Customer Service Center GmbH
Europaplatz 3
69115 Heidelberg, Germany